**CALIFORNIA STATE UNIVERSITY, S**

This book is due on the last date sta
Failure to return books on the date du
sessment of overdue fees.

D0498475

①◇OSP

3 0600 00276 5965

# Advice and Planning

# Advice and Planning

## Martin H. Krieger

Temple University Press  Philadelphia

Temple University Press, Philadelphia 19122

© 1981 by Temple University. All rights reserved

Published 1981

Printed in the United States of America


Library of Congress Cataloging in Publication Data

Krieger, Martin H.
  Advice and planning.

  Bibliography: p.
  Includes index.
    1. City planning—Methodology.  I. Title.
HT166.K74       711'.4       81-4461
ISBN 0-87722-217-7            AACR2

*To my parents*

# ◦§ Contents

# ঙ্গ Preface

Although I was trained as a natural scientist, soon after I finished my doctorate I found myself working on problems of planning, design, and public policy. Having some idea about how science and scientists worked, I was somewhat surprised at my colleagues' use of the notion of science. What they called science did not capture the everyday reality of my experience. Could I give a more adequate account of what we do when we design, plan, and give advice, one that is more in accord with what we actually do, yet that keeps in mind the way scientists do their work?

I believe that planning, policymaking, design, science, and advice-giving are more like than different from most of our other everyday human activities. Even if some of these are our greatest and most noble endeavors, they are done by us, and we cannot avoid being the fallible and richly endowed persons we are when we do them. I also believe that we might well borrow from the traditions of religion, literature, and history, their theories and methodologies, when we try to understand what we do in these activities.

These are essays in demonstration and description. Most of them demonstrate a way of thinking about what we do, a way that is analytical and descriptive, that depends both on theoretical and philosophical concepts and on poetic and rhetorical words. At the same time they are descriptions of how we plan, how we make big decisions, and how we give advice. Just what is it like to have a problem, and how does it go away? How does the ecstasy we sometimes feel when we are in the middle of figuring out what to do relate logically to the decision we are developing?

I want to capture what everybody knows about their everyday lives and what they seem to have forgotten. It would be nice to hand it back to our selves in a more respectable form, so we do not sacrifice our common sense to such idols as science or rigor or economic efficiency—perfectly sensible goals until they become abstracted from their concrete meaning and their historical sources. Since most of us plan, and make decisions, and give advice, I wrote this book in such a way that it would describe what we do every day, and not be only for professional planners, designers, or policymakers.

My examples and metaphors are not meant to be esoteric evidence for the argument so much as reminders of what we already know. I hope the descriptions feel familiar enough so that examples, and counter-examples, will come readily to the reader's mind. So even if the discussion is sometimes theoretical and abstract and conceptual, it should be rather close to what we do every day and so be comprehensible. I am writing for persons.

One of my major claims is that rhetoric and writing and form matter in planning and public affairs, that plans are works of art and artifice and experimentation, and that they share the literary and analytic virtues. These essays should exemplify what they claim, in their various forms and as experiments. So the essays cover similar material from different angles, elaborating on one aspect in somewhat greater detail, unfolding what is only mentioned someplace else.

"Advice" describes how we use what we know to make a more satisfactory world together. The fundamental picture is that of persons giving advice to each other in a community, telling each other stories that describe their problems and so making claims on each other about what to do. My basic claim is that we can learn a good deal about how we apply our knowledge in professional and bureaucratic settings by thinking about what we do in more intimate ones. I am especially interested in describing when advice becomes un-personal and formal and alien to us. I give a more detailed summary in the Introduction to "Advice."

"Criticism, Conversion, and Confession" describes what we do when we evaluate policies, make plans, and make decisions—using notions from criticism of literature and art, from utopian designs and religious conversion, and from transcendent experience. These latter pictures are central to humanistic thought. I believe these pictures are also useful for describing what we do in science, just as I argue in "Advice" that science is a form of everyday advice-giving.

"Planning in Time" examines the cultural strategies we use to create time—the motivating notion in planning—so as to understand how we make plans and arguments that seem logically universal and absolute, how we make big conversionary decisions, and how we give an account of what we do that will pass the test of rationality. It reviews many of the arguments of the previous essay from a somewhat different point of view.

"What We Are Up To" describes how we differ from each other in politics, and how that difference makes for what we call rhetoric. Many of the arguments we now make about the necessity for a certain way of life, or for acting in order that we survive, or for how we are to work on particular social problems, are standard rhetorical tropes. In other words, many of our political arguments about the dilemmas of liberal reform and the conservative response to them may be seen as arguments concerning the forms we use to describe our lives.

"What Planners Do" is a schematic description that sets planning among activities such as magic and soothsaying, yet allows it to be rational and scientific too. I want to emphasize the inaugural and scene-setting aspects of planning, the fact that planners make a world for us. It is, as well, an epitome of the book.

I hope that my use of a few recurrent notions—such as that of a person with capacities and skills for managing everyday life in a community, my claim being that we must be a person to plan, design, and make policy—suggests that it is fruitful to think about what we do in these terms. The problem is not that our idols are always wrong, but that we do not question them when they are patent nonsense. If science is a truly critical endeavor, and art and religion are about transcendence, most of the time science is not so self-critical, and art and religion are performed in this mundane world. We need a variety of ways of thinking about what we do if we are to challenge the idols yet not be without alternatives in times of need.

# ✌§ Acknowledgments

My teachers at Columbia University are in many ways still my models for how to live and work and think. Over the subsequent years students, friends, and colleagues have contributed to my work. As I reread the text I recall the phrases I have lifted verbatim from them, and the books they have led me to. Adequate acknowledgment would require a glossed text. Susan Krieger and Peter Marris come first.

Melvin Webber invited me to the Institute for Urban and Regional Development at the University of California, Berkeley, where I began this book. I encountered many of these problems in the context of a Social Policies Planning program, funded by the National Institute of Mental Health, housed at the University. At the Center for Advanced Study in the Behavioral Sciences, with a fellowship from the American Council of Learned Societies, Meredith Wilson, Preston Cutler, Jane Kielsmeier, and James March made me feel at home. My students at the University of Minnesota encouraged a critical discourse that made the second half of the book possible. And Charles Frankel and William Bennett provided a sunlit space at the National Humanities Center to put it all together. Janet Douglas, Jeanne Antonini, Barbara Waggoner, Susan Stwora, and Marie Long, as well as other members of these institutions, tended to the manuscript, and to me.

Harvey Sarles and Jay Caplan have taught me a great deal in our conversations. I benefited from the lectures of Hanna Pitkin, Hubert Dreyfus, and John Freccero. Dudley Burton, Bayard Catron, John Forester, Jan Dekema, John Vranicar, and Barbara Noble represent the many students who kept asking me questions and bringing me stuff to read. I wrote this book at various times in the past ten years, at five institutions. My debts to others are extensive and numerous. Among those who have helped me along the way are: Patricia Bourne, Stephen Blum, Leonard Duhl, Richard Meier, Lawrence Hirschhorn, John Seeley, Michael Teitz, William Alonso, John Friedmann, Clare Cooper, Beryl Radin, Todd LaPorte, Guy Benveniste, Arnold Meltsner, Anthony Dubovsky, and Russell Ellis; Ulric Neisser, Chie Nakane, Keith Lehrer, Walter Ong, Yehuda Elkana, David Premack, Arpad Szabo, Robert Merton, and Terence Turner; Britton Harris, Tracy Strong, and Grant Barnes; Tom Dewar, John Brandl, Donald Geesaman, and Nancy Anderson; and Martin Rein, Donald Schon, and Langdon Winner.

Susan Krieger, Stephen Cool and Bruce Payne were home. Patricia Bourne, Judith Tendler, Nell Painter, Ann Douglas, Trudi and Peter Riesenberg, and Tom Glanzman cheered me on. William Soskin and Paul Meehl have made me more aware of what I am trying to do.

"What Planners Do" originally appeared in a somewhat different form in the September 1975 issue of the *Journal of the American Institute of Planners*.

Kenneth Arnold and the staff of the Temple University Press have appreciated my intentions. I am grateful for their support.

Cambridge, Massachusetts                                          M. K.
October 1980

I

# ✑ Advice

## Introduction

In "Advice" I use a picture of ordinary everyday advice-giving to understand and justify what people do when they apply their knowledge in ways that are rational, purposeful, effective, and good—and when they fail to do so. More generally, it is a study of the relationship between some everyday practices and their more abstract and formally proper theoretical cousins. It is about how science makes its presence felt in the world. Finally, it is an essay in conceptual synthesis, drawing many of our ordinary concepts and observations about the practical use of our knowledge into a more coherent and consistent whole.

### THE ARGUMENT

Persons in a community figure out what to do in their lives by using what they know and understand about the world, including their scientific knowledge and their own experience. They consult with and advise others, and conduct a political life too. These activities permit persons to make justifiable claims and counterclaims on each other about what to do and why, allowing them to come to a reasonable way of living together in a community.

We can understand this process if we think of the actors in it as ordinary people going about their lives together. We'll have to have some picture of how we act ordinarily and how human idiosyncracies are part of our sensible lives. It turns out that it is just the fact that we are persons in a community that lets us avoid most monstrous ways of being, and also permits us to identify those monstrous ways when they do occur.

The basic picture or model will be that of persons advising each other about what to do. When we are unsure of what to do we can ask for advice, and then, having resolved our unsureness we can go on in our lives. The model is close to the kinds of situations that it is meant to illuminate. For example, we shall be concerned with how social science, which is a way of understanding persons in a community, is applied in public policy. The context for applying our knowledge and understanding is an advice-giving situation.

In the first ten sections, I explore the nature of *advice*, the roles that *advisors* (and their opposites) take, and the *problems* they deal with. Advice is an ordinary everyday activity.* The formal roles that accommodate it in society, such as those of professional, or planner, or expert, are adaptations of everyday personal advice-giving to the inevitable breakdowns, in larger organizational contexts, of trust, self-evidence, or understanding.

The basic scheme of analysis is to note how our pictures of advice leave out the ordinary capacities of persons, and how they then generate a variety of monstrous dilemmas, many of which are products of our "leaving out" error, rather than genuine dilemmas. For example, in advice we tell stories to each other about what to do. If we forget or leave out the fact that these stories are told in the context of our ongoing lives and that they derive much of their meaning from that context, then we might treat those stories as universal and abstract. And then they often make no sense or seem irrational. Or we might see our advice-giving activity as a matter of problem solving. Sometimes that is a good picture of what we are up to, but often the problem is never solved nor is it supposed to be. This may not be a sign of the failure of advice, for advice may not be a matter of problem solving in the first place. As we shall see, various kinds of forgetting or leaving out—a breakdown of the context of everyday advice—lead to our usual conceptions of roles, problems, and scientific understanding in advice.

The next two sections describe how persons giving advice tell *stories* that reflect their particular interests, their understanding, and the technologies they command. We may distinguish the scientific basis for this advice, and then sketch how in organizational arenas we tend to forget that we are persons giving advice to each other.

The life of inquiry pursued by scholars and scientists is an organizational one, too. Scientists and scholars and artists live in communities, they advise each other about what to do in their work, and they try to control deception and dishonesty among their members. Inquiry is not particularly dangerous, inhuman, wrong, or evil, at least no more so than most of the other things we do. But we may forget the organizational and human structure of inquiry and think instead in terms of an abstract model of inquiry, and that will surely mislead us. Inquiry is a civic activity, and we can understand how we use inquiry to improve our lives if we think in terms of advice.

Sections thirteen through twenty-one describe the kind of *understanding* of the world that we must have for advice to be possible. We

---

* I use *advice* and *advice-giving* interchangeably. Both refer to asking for and receiving advice.

must be able to tell rich and relevant stories that we can feel our way around in. Persons tell stories to other persons in particular situations. This accounts for how our knowledge is useful for advice. As I have mentioned, when we forget this we find ourselves with seeming dilemmas, which I detail here.

*Conflicts* in our understanding of the world are natural in advice. We may work on the conflicts by give-and-take and bargaining, and by telling alternative stories to each other. Advice may then be seen as dramatic and interactive. If we forget that it is persons who tell stories, we may be tempted to resolve conflicts in mechanical ways that lack the power to involve us and ensure our understanding and commitment to our advice.

Human beings are fully embodied, decently conducted persons. Persons have *feelings* and affect each other; they care for and aid each other, too. If we let those feelings play an actual role in our lives, we will get reasonable and sensible advice. The last sections argue that persons without affect, the potential for feeling, would be inadequate persons for advice. Empathy, eros, and education make advice possible, necessary, and viable.

## Advice

*After setting up the fundamental notions of a person and a community, notions that mutually define each other—the basic conceptual apparatus for the rest of this essay—I then define advice. Advice has three constitutive qualities or requirements: a relationship of persons of trust and truth; a basis in the world through knowledge and experience, expressed in reasonable and justifiable stories; and a public understanding of who we are as a community. These three requirements seem to be necessary; leaving one out makes for inadequate advice. In actual life, however, the qualities are not readily fulfilled, in part because we human persons are limited, and in part because society's scale makes it hard to be intimate, reasonable, and public. We adapt to these limitations by taking on the roles of professional, planner, and expert, which provide formal compensations for the limits. Yet because we demand that the roles reflect the ideal of advice, built-in contradictions haunt them.*

Persons in a community advise each other about what to do, how to feel, and what to believe. Giving and receiving advice is an everyday experience in most people's lives, whether the advice occurs in intimate, public, or bureaucratic situations. When we give advice we claim that we know what to do. It is a way to show our understanding of the world. At the same time, in asking for or receiving advice we reveal the problems and situations in our world that require special attention.

## I PERSONS

Human beings are persons, members of a community. A person may be characterized in two ways. In one characterization, a person incorporates body and mind. A person is something to which corporeal attributes and states of consciousness and experience apply. Persons have bodies and feelings and experiences. Persons are both material objects and thinking subjects. This naturally leads to a concept of others who are objects for me, and who are also speakers reporting their feelings, thoughts, and experiences. And I, of course, can report my own to others and to myself.

A person is also someone "like me," a member of my community whom I recognize. Each member of the community thinks of himself as a member; the community is the scope of the "we." The corporeal and experiential aspects of being a person are less important in this conception, but being like me usually requires having a body and having had some experiences similar to my own. It is conceivable that a plant or a non-human animal could be a person, although it may be hard to make a convincing argument for that. More generally, persons not only recognize members; they can distinguish nonmembers, members, and marginal cases. Persons know how to treat persons as persons, and how to conduct themselves in the community.*

These conceptions of personhood usually imply an enduring identity for a person, allowing us to speak of personality and character. Persons know how to play a role in the ongoing drama that is community life. They know when people are out of role, and when situations seem to have gone awry and become monstrous.† They know what a person would not ordinarily do. At monstrous times what is "not possible" appears. It is a sign of what is most fearful for us.

---

* I use *community* to emphasize the homogeneity and belongingness of a collectivity, *society* to emphasize its interdependence and differentiatedness, and *polity* to emphasize its collective direction and purpose. Note that persons and their community are mutually defined.
† Persons and situations become *monstrous* when they are outside the range of what we understand as what persons in a community do. Boundary setting and

None of what I have said about persons should be surprising. It is what we usually understand by the notion of a person. As we shall see, if advice is to make sense, it must depend on the capacities of persons.

## 2 ADVICE

Asking for, giving, and receiving advice—in short, advice—is an ordinary activity about extraordinary situations. Advice need not occur if things are going smoothly, as in ordinary taken-for-granted everyday activities. Yet one of the ordinary situations in life is that there is a difficulty about what to do: the policy, the regular response to unsure situations, does not automatically apply or kick in and let the activity go on as usual. We're stuck. At that point we need and seek a worthwhile recommendation regarding our decision or course of conduct. The ordinary way of dealing with the difficulty is to seek advice. Not only do you not know what to do, not only are you stuck or lost, but you show it by what you do next.

Asking for and giving advice comes between a difficult situation and what we eventually do about it. Advice is what we ordinarily do at those times. Advice converts that extraordinary situation into a problem we may work on. When advice becomes necessary, two roles appear, advisor and advisee, when there were none before. Those roles may be shared by one person who figures out what to do, or by more than two. The roles are co-ordinate. It will not make sense to give advice if it cannot be received, although one may risk offering it when it is not desired, or asking for it when none can or will be given.

Advice requires a *relationship of persons* who have a *basis* for advice in their sense or knowledge about the world, and who *understand* one another and that world. We fulfill particular social roles in each problematic situation when we give and receive advice, and I discuss them further on. Now I want to look at the fundamental requirements for or constituents of advice. These constituents are necessary for even the most ordinary everyday advice involving intimates or acquaintances, as well as in larger bureaucratic and political settings. Advice is a quite general activity that combines processes of understanding and acting in situations. It bridges the often-made dichotomies between thinking and acting, between planning and implemen-

---

monstrosity are related to each other, for monstrosity is determined in part by how we distinguish ourselves as persons from other creatures. Monsters may be humorous or sad, and in the extremes repulsive and horrible. Our notions of personhood and our feelings about others who might be persons are intimately connected.

tation, between the mind and the environment. So we might hope
that this analysis will be widely applicable.

## 2.1 A RELATIONSHIP OF PERSONS

Advice occurs in a relationship of persons. They are actors—persons
who act thoughtfully, willfully, and freely—who, as members of the
community, are capable of speaking to and understanding each other,
aware of what may and may not be appropriately said. In advice a person can demonstrate, develop, and confirm that he is a person by what
he says and how he acts. Persons are, for example, sensitive to moral
and political appeals and will be affected by them. And advice requires that a person recognize ordinary situations, distinguish the
problematic ones, and appreciate when situations have become monstrous. In order to know when advice is appropriate, a person must be
able to recognize when someone is lost.

Your being a person does not ensure that your advice will be good.
Persons can be bad listeners, or good at forgetting advice and ignoring
others. They may be inarticulate or, because of the situation, incapable of asking for or giving advice just when it is needed. Many of our
institutions, such as professional practice, were developed to make up
for part of the gap between what an idealized person would do and
what an actual ordinary person does when human beings give advice.

If advice did not involve a relationship of persons, where advisor
and advisee acknowledged and treated each other and themselves as
persons, what might happen? If the corporeal and consciousness aspects were separated, then we might rely on oracles, dice, or chance,
or perhaps automatically interpreted rules or tests. Nothing need be
wrong with these ways of figuring out what to do. We might comfortably call them appropriate sources of advice—until we applied them
in incorrect situations and they gave monstrous results. Then it
would be hard to know how we might point out to these inanimate
advisors that their advice was monstrous. Persons, on the other hand,
would understand that, even if they eventually disagreed with our
judgment about monstrosity.

Actually, the problem as I have presented it could not arise. These
un-personal sources of advice require interpretation of their outcomes
by persons.* If the signs they give us are to have anything to do with

---

* I use *un-personal* when we have a situation in which persons would naturally
be involved, but we (choose to) ignore the distinctive qualities of persons. Similarly, I shall later use *un-dramatic* to describe situations in which persons
ought to act as if they are in a drama together, but we (choose to) ignore that
personal and dramatic context.

us, we shall have to have an understanding of their meaning. Since we interpret their meaning, it is possible for us to cast doubt on absurd or overly ambiguous signs, and to avoid simplistic interpretations that would be monstrous. Oracles and tests were never meant to be understood in other than human terms. Originally, I suspect, they were provisional abstractions from the complexities of our lives. They did not come out of nowhere.

Outside the context set by persons, situations can easily become monstrous. Extrapolating a statistical decision theory or the *I Ching* into areas in which we have no reason to believe they apply, we may well end up with advice that makes no sense. When persons exceed their authority we can call them to account; when impersonal sources of advice exceed their authority we must call their users to account.

If we forget that advice involves persons "like me" in a community, then advice easily becomes orders or directives or, conversely, pleas in the dark of confusion and lostness. But when we act as if others are like us, we are more likely to be empathetic than pathetic. A person who is like me will also be, as I am, constituted by the interests, orientations, and values he exhibits and harbors. A community is made up of such prejudiced members, and advice always comes from someone with a particular set of prejudices. Prejudices are not simply a set of abstract interests, orientations, or values, ready made to fit each situation. The meaning of the prejudices depends on the situation. We could not ask for or give advice without the prejudices, yet their concrete expression depends on the advice that will be offered.

Advice is constituted not only by empathy and prejudice, but by error as well. Since an advisor is a person like me, his advice could be wrong or error-filled, just as mine could be. That does not imply that the advisor is a bad advisor or not a person. I can gracefully recover when I err and then give good advice. I am still a person and not a monster.

Persons must trust each other in advice-giving. While that trust cannot be absolute, they need to be able to acknowledge that the other is a person, a person who can have their interests in mind and who can understand them. Yet they ought not be so trusting that deception, unintentional misunderstanding, or error is not questioned. Nor can trust be so absolute that we are not legitimately able to use saving ambiguities, to be silent or not hear, or even to willingly prevaricate at times.

How others have your interests in mind may not be the way you want them had. There is room for play, as well.

Trust is not a childlike belief in another. That gives too much to the other person. The saving ambiguities we use in advice are warranted because the person who uses them and the other person who appropriately understands them take the risk that their use may be wrong. But these unstated agreements and understood ambiguities are different from mutual self-deception, for, while acknowledging the complexities of human relationships, they do not deny the importance of truth.

Advice requires that we have a commitment to truth, so that we may get around in the world and maintain a coherent picture of what we are up to. Otherwise, advice would not be grounded in the world, and it would be of little practical value. If we systematically deceived ourselves about others and the world, our community could not ultimately make sense. But say that we, all of us, participated in a sufficiently rich systematic deception. It is possible that the deception would no longer be a deception. It might work. There seem to be few sufficiently rich ways of organizing our ongoing life together, so that even if there are alternative ways of organizing things, we need not worry about rampant relativism. Surely our advice would be different under different organizations of the world. But it would be as appropriate under one organization to that organization's purposes and needs, as advice-giving under another organization would be to its purposes and needs.

Advice needs trust and truth. Trust and truth set the ground rules and the foundation for the relationship of persons in advice. But after the rules are set, trust and truth do not determine the game or exclude entirely different games from the usual ones, dialectical games that make advice much more complex than a matter of finding the right answer.

In advice, the advisee wants to know what to do. He makes a claim that the situation is problematic. The advisor claims to know what to do, and in giving advice confirms the authority of his claim. Treating each other as persons and trusting each other, advisor and advisee express the needs associated with their roles. Yet it is in the problematic situation where both needs are tested. Are they genuine and how do they work out?

Advice seems to have some natural, if provisional, inequalities. Advice may be in the form of a dialogue that is intimate, face-to-face, and private, or it may be more public or directed to a community. In either case, the roles of advisor and advisee feel different and seem unequal in power. In practical terms, the roles coordinate and stabilize interactions when we are giving and receiving advice. They formally resolve whose problem is at hand at the moment, and they specify how the advice is to be checked. The roles control instabilities that are inherent in them. For example, an advisor is often supposed to be respected and knowing, yet advisors depend on the respect of advisees and their capacities to probe his knowledge. Advisors logically and psychologically (as in counter-transference) depend on advisees. The advisor role helps to stabilize this circle of mutual dependency. It gives us a place to start.

Of course, it might be best that advisors doubt the respect they receive and realize the limitations of their knowledge and advice. And advisees should appreciate how they set agendas and control knowledge, not to speak of their own capacities to advise themselves. But the division of labor in the inquiry of figuring out what to do, implied by the two roles, seems to be very important for us, even if we sometimes reverse roles and then reverse them again and again.

## 2.2 A BASIS IN THE WORLD

Advice depends on our sense about how the world works. To some extent that will be a matter of detailed technical knowledge. But in many situations, advice involves no direct technical knowledge of the world. We are likely to seek advice just when such knowledge is not or could not be available, as for hypothetical future situations or when we are making big decisions with seemingly unpredictable outcomes. Then we may depend on our past experience to guide us. But that experience may be inadequate for understanding new situations, and we sometimes supplement it with technical knowledge. To assess where we are, we combine what we know about ourselves and our world, with back-of-the-envelope calculations and scientific pictures, and what we've read in novels and legal precedents.

It is possible for us to understand strange situations because different situations are similar to each other. Our technical knowledge is not intrinsically abstract. It comes from and is abstracted out of concrete situations we have been in, and so it makes sense that we can apply it to other, what we suspect are similar, situations. And past experience can be extrapolated from and speculated about. So the basis for advice is not just that we have knowledge and experience, although we do, but also that we can reasonably and justifiably use them. A basis for these reasonable uses is our being persons in a community, persons who have a sense about what is appropriate and relevant. Yet a person whom we consult for advice because he has special access to certain areas of knowledge or to particular situations, may still not appreciate when that knowledge or those situations are relevant to our concerns. We must judge whether we are being given a bum steer.

Advice does fail. Some situations are quite out of the ordinary, and the applicability of the best available experience and knowledge may seem farfetched. Persons sometimes cannot assess their own capabilities, nor need they always do so. And issues other than ones we are most adept at understanding may be at stake. Politics and moral values may be more important than expertise about atoms or the price system.

What do we do when we give advice? In asking for, giving, receiving, and responding to advice, each person must figure out what to say about a difficult situation. In a reasonable and justifiable way, he must describe it as a problem and develop some sense about what we might do about it. The policy problem, for which the advice given becomes an appropriate response, must be set into a context in which we do know something about it, where our experience is relevant, and where we can bring to bear what evidence we have. The basis for advice is our ability to make sense out of a situation and tell a story that makes it meaningful for us.

To make sense out of a situation is to reformulate it in such a way that we understand it better: we recognize it as one we have seen before, we know better what to do, and we see our dilemmas more sharply and with less confusion. To be sure, the situation was not without sense before, but in advice we try to improve that sense. The story we tell puts the situation in perspective, so it becomes a situation we recognize more fully, and we are more comfortable with it.

The stories we develop in giving advice are like the stories of literature and history. Aristotelian novels and histories have beginnings, middles, and ends, and so do stories in advice. They must make coherent sense out of a situation for us. Stories depend on their readers or spectators, and the play between the author and his audience. And the stories we tell in advice depend on the play of advisees and advisors. And all of these stories have lessons, and moral and political import.

When persons give advice they make claims as to the reasonableness and appropriateness of a story and the situation and problem it describes. That is their response to the difficulty we face. Advice requires a set of protocols for making these claims, offering evidence for them, and assenting to or challenging them. Our basis in the world lets us make a claim to having provided a sensible description of what we're up to now. The story is for the situation at hand, not for all times or places. And persons involved in advice make that description and judge its quality.

To summarize, the basis for advice is that persons can reasonably and justifiably use what they know and experience, to tell a story of sufficient power, so that it makes a claim on other persons in a particular situation. What persons know, which abstract problems they can solve, or what they say only to themselves, are only incidentally the basis for advice.

## 2.3 AN UNDERSTANDING OF WHO WE ARE

Persons try to tell each other effective stories when they give and receive advice. In order to do so, they must have a well-grounded understanding of their situation. They know how to get around in their world, and they exhibit that knowledge by what they do. They have purposes that we can discern, and we feel that they know how to go on with them and they know what's up. A person who understands a situation has some sense about, is able to figure out, what others would do, feel, act, or think. But ultimately what we need is a public and rationally justifiable understanding of who we are, rather than a private and secluded one. The persons who give and receive advice constitute a public community. Even intimate advice between friends depends on an appreciation of what people ordinarily do in the world we inhabit together.

The understanding we claim to have about our situation is not passively held. Others may confirm or deny it, or may not comprehend or understand what you are trying to say, or may assume various completions to your unstated claims. The space or play offered by affirmation and misconception, acts of partial completion, gives us room enough to pose problems and offer responses in advice-giving.

Our understanding of a situation is measured not only by how effective our advice is—for coercion or blindness might give one a sense of effectiveness—but also by our ability to admit and deal with failures and breakdowns if things do not go smoothly. We need to be able to appreciate that it is possible to have misunderstandings, and that there is irony and humor in our stories.

If advice is to be successful, we have to care that our understanding works well. Misunderstandings have to matter to us; they have to tell us about how we fail in what we try to do; and we must care about the consequences of those failures. They are failures not only of advice, but of ourselves as persons. If we do not care about them as personal failures, then we deny some of the ways we do matter to each other, especially that we can care for each other. The failures are not simply a matter of what is commonly labeled distortion and misperception in communication, for the goal of understanding is not clear communication as such. Understanding constitutes us as a public community, and it makes it possible for advice as a public community activity to mediate between other activities. Understanding is a way we live with others. Others understand us even when they misunderstand us. They are able to somehow construe our conduct and then go on with us in our lives. We are able to convince them, eventually, that they did misunderstand us. The most profound failure in advice occurs when we stop acting as persons, forgetting our capacities to understand each other.

## 2.4 THE NECESSITY OF THESE REQUIREMENTS

The requirements of (1) a relationship of persons who (2) have a basis for advice in their sense about the world and who (3) understand each other are not sharply separable, and no one of them is sufficient to characterize advice. A relationship of persons can be the basis for responsible advice-giving, using the guarantees each person offers. But that does not guarantee practical effectiveness, for the relationship itself does not depend directly on having good sense about the world. Nor does it directly deal with others who are part of the community. But, of course, persons show themselves as persons by how they manage in the world and how they understand others in the community. So the relationship of persons does depend on these factors.

The basis for advice will lead to its being useful and reasonable. But a story is not enough. It is written by an author whose person we are curious about, and our knowing who he is can change our attitude toward that story. And a story has an audience; it must be for those who hear it, and it reflects an understanding of their lives as individuals and community members, and how they would understand that story. Understanding guarantees this, and is the foundation for a public stance, but good stories require more than understanding. Their rhetoric and evidence must follow good form. And understanding must come from trusted persons, for there is much that is beyond such evidence and we need to have some confidence in our sources.

Each of the constituting requirements for advice depends on the others, supports them and is supported by them in turn. When one of them is absent or dominant, the others compensate. But this defective form of advice seems to break down nonetheless.

## 3 BREAKDOWNS OF ADVICE

To summarize the previous section, advice requires that persons be in a relationship with each other, that the advice-giving have a firm basis in how the world works, and that the persons understand each other. When actual advice does not fulfill these requirements, then advice may be said to break down. I will argue that these breakdowns characterize some of the formal societal institutions of advice-giving, such as professionalism, planning, and expertise.

In my analysis, I shall make several presuppositions about how we live in the world. They correspond to the three requirements I used to describe advice. (1) Our experiences with each other and the claims we make to each other about those experiences play a primary role in advice. For persons in an advice-giving relationship, notions of experience and claims, rather than, say, laws of nature or statistical tests, are the proper level of analysis. (2) Our understanding of ordinary life is reliable; it makes sense; it will not usually deceive us. Hence the stories we tell, although they are stories, really are about the world we live in. It may be true that we often deceive ourselves, and science and philosophy can be seen to have developed in that skeptical vein, but mostly we can go along following our good sense. If things go wrong, advice given in this sensible vein is very helpful. (3) What we do, our agreements, are genuine and meaningful. Our understanding is not a fantasy; our public lives are not psychoses. Our understanding is public and shareable, although we may fail to be public and share or we may systematically blind ourselves for a while.

These presuppositions characterize how most of us act in everyday life. They gain a contrapuntal meaning when we compare them with another set: We quote from past experience, rather than from general laws (even scientists do); we tell stories that make common sense, rather than hide their true meanings; we have a good grasp on the world, and need not worry about that grasp. We live a benign rather than a diabolical life.

Of course, the presuppositions sometimes do not hold. We have a variety of ways of managing when we are lost. For example, formal abstract ways of thinking such as science or law may be helpful. But they tend to be reductionist about the nature of persons, they distrust the reliability of ordinary life, and they see our public agreements as too imprecise and incoherent. These theories are derivative abstractions from our ongoing lives; they are not fundamental. They are helpful diagnostic tools, and they cause us over time to reformulate our understanding of our ordinary lives and broaden our pool of experience. But they are often neither constructive nor therapeutic, since they are designed to sniff out error and illusion.

Let us now return to the breakdowns of advice. For the purposes of our analysis, the breakdowns are logical breakdowns, breaks in the net of interconnections in our concept of advice. But these breakdowns also represent perhaps necessary inadequacies in advice-giving due to the disjunctions characteristic of large-scale society. In actual advice-giving there are formal institutional structures such as professions that correspond to these logical breaks, structures that are attempts to patch up the social net. But the reweaving is always quite visible, as we shall see.

If we believe that it is only in intimate advice situations that it is possible to avoid the breakdowns, if at all, then the patch-ups characteristic of large social structures must contribute to the destruction of the cohesiveness of society, and the resulting inauthenticity of our relationships in it. Hence the logical and social structural breakdowns coincide.

But if society is more sturdy, more a series of wonderful adaptations to constraints that appear at various levels of organization and size, as my presuppositions might suggest, then the breakdowns may be seen as the way in which advice in larger social contexts is articulated into viable social roles that suit what persons can more or less do. Inadequacy yields not to failure but to tragic complexity.

When advice breaks down, we forget that it is persons—who have relationships with each other, who have a sense about the world, and who understand each other—who make advice possible. As we shall see, advice comes to seem beyond persons, formal, outside of human life, monstrous. This reductionist move leads us either to view human technique as out of our control, or to have nihilistic visions of infinitely regressing justifications for what we do. For no persons are present to take control, or to justify by their commitment and agreement what is needed in the community. Often we emerge with what look like technical solutions, ones that deny the intrinsic value of our ordinary lives and that ignore a person's communal and political constitution.

There are three interrelated kinds of breakdown. First, an actual advice-giving situation may not fulfill one of the requirements, and so not work. That may result in the development of more complex, but viable, social roles. Second, a society can break down, losing its gemeinschaft quality. Third, the conceptual net of requirements we use to describe advice may break, overly stressed by the breakdown of a particular constitutive quality, leading to conceptual elaborations and new models of advice. Our analytical problem will be to see if the breakdowns in the conceptual model parallel the breakdowns in the requirements and in the society.

### 3.1 ROLES AND CONTRADICTIONS

The breakdown of each of the requirements produces specific social roles. Advice becomes technical, based on formal techniques that may be religious, scientific, or scholarly, and distant from our everyday lives. Each breakdown also highlights how the roles have built-in contradictory impulses that are likely to make for the difficulties we experience in fulfilling an actual role.

When the relationship of persons in advice becomes problematic, so that trust has no foundation in ordinary experience, and problems of role coordination make it difficult to give or request advice, then *professionalism* develops. Systematic professional certification reassures us about the technical basis for advice, and the profession's public claim to an exclusive understanding of us re-establishes a form of authority. But professional certification and authority do not reinstate trust and the relationship as it was formerly conceived, actually and logically. Professionalization provides a functional substitute that, in aiming for formal legitimacy, will often deny that its special authority comes from human experience and from the claims it makes about that experience. The profession will, nowadays, speak of its objective and scientific foundations, inheriting a host of problems that we will explore a bit later.

When persons can no longer make coherent sense of each other's stories, when stories are viewed as being independent of the persons who tell and hear them, when the criteria for appreciation are no longer common, then *planning* appears. Planners offer stories that are explicit, reasonable, and rational, founded upon their knowledge of society's best stories and how these represent the public. Rationality (as universal truth) surrogates for community and for a public understanding. But planners' stories tend to be technical and deliberately distanced from our common ones. Common ordinary stories are then treated as if they can no longer be relied on to play themselves out in our lives. Our patterns of life seem to have lost their patterning, and an explicit concern with time, characteristic of planning, becomes important. Planners could tell their technical stories more in accord with the common ordinary ones in the society. But under the temptation of simple and neat technique they often do not. And if we take the technical stories to reflect the way things really are, rather than as technical, we again inherit a host of problems.

In both of these cases, and in the next one, the breakdown of a requirement yields a formal role that functionally fulfills the demands of all three requirements. Professionalism surrogates for trust, and provides for its own kind of stories and claims to public understanding. But at the same time, the role has built-in contradictions that are its ultimate undoing. The source of contradictions lies, I shall argue, in our exceeding the limitations of the formal role.

Finally, our understanding of who we are, how we should be and disagree together, the nature of our "we," may no longer hold up. Politics, this collective understanding, may be said to have broken down. *Expertise* becomes important. Experts are supposed to understand the world, to be willing to define it in a way such that we can be more effective. They replace political relationships with technical ones, and replace political disagreements with disagreements housed and argued in a more narrow vocabulary. But experts' understanding is not derived from persons' lives, as in politics, but from a particular person's understanding that is then claimed to be definitive of others'. That may be the case, and the experience that experts have and claim may be representative or inspirational. But it may not be. Experts may not deserve our trust and their stories may not represent our world.

Contradictions abound in these roles derived from the breakdown of the requirements. When trust becomes a product of a formalized relationship of persons in professionalism, then the caring nature of that relationship may conflict with the usual professional interdictions concerning the involvement of advisor with advisee. And the potential for moral leadership is limited by the professional personality, which is supposed to claim no strength or authority except within its sphere of professional competence. When reasonableness and storytelling become planning, then the formal character of technical thinking may prevent us from talking about nontechnical but important issues. A sanitized version of reasonableness, as rationality, removes from our consideration significant but perhaps non-rational forces in advice. When understanding in public becomes expertise, then genius, which might be a touch of the poet, can become monstrous and out of touch with us, and understanding become narrow.

In actual everyday advice, these contradictions are genuine tensions definitive of advice-giving. Formal interdictions concerning the involvement of advisor with advisee may prevent a professional's taking advantage of a client when the client is weak. The interdiction can be valuable. But sometimes we ought to act in a way that will violate the interdiction. The contradictions may destroy the potential for good action in a formal role if they cannot be acknowledged and honored flexibly. For example, confused with protectiveness, our caring for another person may prevent us from giving him the best advice. We must be able to examine our motives when we help our friends. Our need for caring, or desire to give our friends a chance to be helpful, will make us ask for advice when we really do not need any. But professionals can isolate situations when their affections may make them less effective, and they must be aware (under labels such as counter-transference) of their own need to be helpers.

Similarly, experts may know what to do better than anyone else. They can try to convince others of this, yet be sensitive to their own needs for hegemony. Nothing will totally prevent megalomania, but persons who are experts can be aware of the dangers of their role.

Our formal characterization of advice in terms of the three requirements has led conceptually to particular forms of advice: the professional, the planner, and the expert. These forms are products of breakdowns of the original properties of a relationship of persons, based in a sense about the world, and an understanding of others. The terms used to characterize these forms are identical to those that name particular and actual social roles. But this identity may not be a real one, and to that we now want to turn. In general, an ideal model must be close enough to what we ordinarily do so that in it we recognize what we do even if we fail in fulfilling the ideal. Using the analysis we have developed so far, we shall describe what the roles ought to be and see if the description is close enough to what these roles actually are, so that the prescriptive and diagnostic import of the analysis may be of some use.

## Roles and Advisors

*We, as persons, engage in advice by means of an interplay of claims we make on each other. We express our wills and our doubts—about what we believe, about what another person claims, and about his authority to make that claim. We look for adequate ways to get about in the world, ways that will be subject to our doubt. Claims are a way of speaking of adequate knowledge, rather than of absolute and universal truth.*

*After describing the nature of claims, I then discuss how they function in the roles of the professional, the planner, and the expert. In each case, when the give-and-take of claims is left out we get a less adequate form of advice. Advice breaks down. Professionals objectify their clients, planners treat their own stories as universal, experts become unrepresentative and prevent counterclaims. I describe the roles that advisors actually take, and how they justify their treating others with less than full respect. But these attempts to control the advisor's environment do not work well enough, and the advisor must face the limitations of his un-personal form of advice.*

There are times when advice breaks down. Trust, reasonableness, or our public understanding of our situation become inadequate to maintain an ideal or nearly ideal form of advice. We persist. In a complex society, there are formal roles that systematically incorporate these inadequacies, acknowledging and obviating them as best they can. Depending on the context, different aspects of advice's constitutive qualities will appear most inadequate and problematic, and corresponding formal roles will come into prominence. But all three roles of professional, planner, and expert, comprise and are present in advice, and we may not ignore any of them. For example, when the public-understanding character of advice is emphasized, experts become important, but we cannot forget the other constitutive roles, for example, how experts create an alternative form of trust and a special kind of rationality. For these are what make expertise work in the end.

## 4 CLAIMS

When a community has an explicit understanding of itself, what might be called a political theory, then what is said in public about it and its members is of consequence. For that political theory is supported or challenged by what we say. Hence, if we say that particular roles and the persons who enact them fail, and if we say how that failure has happened, we affect the effectiveness and authority of those roles. Because the roles in advice we shall be talking about do not have coercive force behind them, the only way they can be effective is if they do have authority.

Authority, as such, is always problematic. It is up for grabs. It depends on maintaining a complex order of social interactions that if disrupted may destroy the possibility of authority. Authority, like advice, is coordinate, that is, dependent on claims to authority, our assent to them, and the authority we give to others. In a complex society, such exhibitions of claims and assent require larger and more explicit doubts and affirmations. Authority becomes more subject to rationality and investigation, especially for the roles I discuss. Hence I want to emphasize the claims we make in advice as I analyze its roles.

If authority is problematic, then we might view advice as being composed of the claims and counterclaims that advisees and advisors make on each other. Claims logically demand responses that accept, reject, or modify them, since a claim is putatively preemptive of what has gone before. Claims are claims on others, and what they as persons have claimed. Claims are not made on "what there is." What there is cannot respond to a claim. Only persons can. For example, when we make a claim on a piece of land, we are claiming the rights to that land, rights that determine how other persons can make claims about it, and how they may explicitly and implicitly act and rationally maintain beliefs with respect to that piece of land. We are not claiming, by means of picking it up and carrying it away, a piece of the surface (to some depth) of the Earth, except in very special cases. These rights to pieces of land are only meaningful in a community of persons, who have roles in a political economy. The claims are about what is reasonable within the complex of rules that constitute the community. In making a claim in a situation, we offer reasons and evidence for it, all of which must be accessible to other persons. If they are not, we would not be effectively claiming. A claim to being reasonable, to rationality in the community, is a pointing out of what is or what must be apparent to others, what can be accounted for in a lifelike story that is appealing to them.

We might ask for more in our claims, for a universal certainty or for a revelatory self-evident certainty. Our story, our claim and its evidence and reasons, could be certainly true, tested out in some way, a cartoon of scientific research or of formal logic. It could also be exhaustive of alternatives, a true best of possible worlds, conceding for the moment the difficulty of describing the set of possible alternatives. Then advice would transcend all particular persons; it would be for an absolute person. It could supposedly be about "what there is." We might also require that the claim transcend itself, so that our evidence is self-evident. Were we to look more closely, and that is all we need do, we would see that what is claimed is so. The epistemic and communicative experiences would become identical. This need not be a matter of supernatural revelation. For example, mathematical theories can develop sufficiently complex yet familiar structures so that what was once thought to be the most difficult of proofs becomes straightforward and obvious once you learn to think in a certain way about the world.

We cast doubt on others' claims by making claims of our own. Doubt plays a different role in each view of how claims ought to work in advice. When we ask for certainty, exhaustiveness, or self-evidence, doubt and skepticism will assure us that we do not get off on the wrong track while going along in advice. Doubt in these cases is not cast on persons, just as claims are no longer claims on persons. Advice becomes an un-personal process. It often becomes a process of finding "the true answer." Historically, models of claims that can be certain and exhaustive, whether in theology or in science, have been highly abstract. They have had great difficulty in retaining their connection to our ordinary lives.

From the more modest point of view that claims are made on persons, the doubt we express in making claims is necessary to the personal relationship. Without doubting the other person, you have been signed on to advice without recognizing your own interests and claims, your own personhood in the community. You have been shanghaied. Claims are made in a context, considering what has been held to be the case, and in a community, considering what can be reasonably said. The doubt expressed in claims is a way of systematically and properly reasserting or proofing our own personhood and that of others. Claims are the manner in which we engage in advice, and in validating claims we figure out what to do. Advice is about practical, moral, and political questions in the world in which our knowledge exhibits itself, not only about the knowledge itself.

The social roles we shall discuss are ways in which claims are prevalidated over society. Pre-validation or warranting may be good for certain kinds of situations, and the roles may then be effective. But such roles deny advice. Claims must always be up for grabs, and for these roles that may not be the case. The presumptive claims become implicit and constitutive of the roles. Such pre-validations are claims about claims and they are to be doubted. We must question those claims when advice fails.

The claims that are being made in this essay, which is advice about advice, are these. That the characteristics of the social roles parallel those of breakdowns of the notion of advice; that in complex society such roles have natural failings related to that parallelism; and that if we view advice in terms of persons in a community, our responses to those failings can make sense. These are claims on how one should view actual roles and how one ought to tell stories about them.

### 5 PROFESSIONALS

A profession is a way to fulfill the societal commitments of a relationship of persons who ask for, give, and receive advice. The institution of a profession offers public guarantees, through its reputation and its warranted claims, of its capacity to retain and assure trust in an area. Certification is the formal method of regulating entry into the profession and maintaining its status.

Certification or licensure vouches for past performance. It implies that those past performances are valid in supporting claims about the future effectiveness of the service provided by a professional. Professions characteristically, and perhaps constitutively, demand that they control and administer certification. That demand is addressed to the government, which may then license professionals, or, more informally, to the community. The profession in return guarantees to regulate performance and agrees to punish malpractice as it sees it. The definition of malpractice, and the corresponding and often residual definition of proper professional behavior, become the surrogate for a relationship of persons and the trust it incorporates.

What is the past performance that is certified? Traditionally, it has been successful apprenticeship as well as study of the systematic knowledge fundamental to the profession. The growth of systematic knowledge, especially in the form of science, the university's hegemony in determining what knowledge is, and the size of modern society have made schooling, examinations, and systematic knowledge comparatively more important than apprenticeship. Although traditional scholarly training for the church is a precursor of many of these patterns, professions have also drawn from guild traditions. Hence the tension between knowledge and apprenticeship.

Systematic knowledge may increase our ability to perform effectively. It seems to be especially useful in the rare and esoteric cases where we have to think our way through to an understanding of what is going on. In ordinary cases, past experience proves to be enough. Our trust in others is based in part on their ability to distinguish the ordinary from the difficult cases and to perform effectively and appropriately in each. But trust is based on more than performance. Trust becomes crucial and seems to be needed just when the advice we give may fail, when it is difficult to guarantee performance. Then commitment to others, and its expression in the ideals of the profession, becomes important. That commitment can be authentic. But if we were to believe that professional trust is based solely on effective performance, then that commitment cannot have any meaning. Better put, the meaning it would have, about the likelihood of a profession succeeding when we are on the margins of its capacities, does not adequately characterize professional trust in difficult areas. There, we seem to be not betting persons but trusting or committed ones, sharing the consequences and together making sense of what happens.

The process of training professionals may prevent them from viewing trust in a sufficiently broad way. Long years of schooling or apprenticeship require and socialize commitment to the professional's work, and this is true even for those with more venial motives. Professionals need to have the systematic knowledge and training that can prevent quackery and improve their technical performance. But the formal processes of professionalization, as they have come to emphasize systematic knowledge, separate commitment from a relationship of persons. Commitment and trust become based on the sources of certification: school, knowledge, and professional peers. The claims professionals make on persons become transformed into assertions of technical competence. As professionals become more technically competent, they seem to become less personally competent. They are less capable of dealing with cases where their technical knowledge fails them.

As professionalization comes to emphasize systematic knowledge, the disjunctions that must develop between the professional and the person he advises are not seen as the breakdown of advice or its ideal. Rather it is argued that ordinary experience is deceptive, that a person's claim that his experience is significant for the professional is correct in only a very limited sense. It reflects the partial and regrettably incomplete view of the victimized client, victimized not by the professional but by his own bias and limited view. The failure of advice in this case is blamed on the limits of knowledge, rather than on the advice's lack of a relationship between persons in which such limits may be acknowledged in an authentic way.

Without denying its many benefits in complex society, as a view of persons professionalization has been a disaster, and not only for the so-called clients. From the perspective of advice, professions have no life. They are blank markers that hide what we do in advice. For example, credentials deny the person of the professional, whose qualifications then depend on rather limited criteria. Systematic knowledge treated as objective, as independent of a relationship of persons, will make the advice inadequate just when it is most needed, when it does depend on the relationship. Also, the professional comes with certain political values and perspectives as attributes. It is not clear that they are necessary or functional to a professional performance. When we try to challenge a professional performance, to doubt its claims, we find we are doubting, not claims made by persons, but the profession's institutional assertions of its competence. The client or the professional no longer engage in genuine advice. The client is reduced to an object molded by professional performance. And the profession can guarantee only the weakest and narrowest of its assertions if its performance is independent of personhood, especially if we cannot rely on the common sense of persons to interpret the guarantee so as to avoid the monstrous. Yet the profession and its clients must be creative and responsive to complex, demanding situations. As a result, they find themselves with greatly reduced guarantees and more limited areas of competence, just when they are called upon to be more overarching.

Were the professional and the client to rely more on the relationship of persons and on the capacities of a person to interpret and understand extraordinary situations, guarantees could be more generous and competence be enhanced. But correspondingly, the authority of a professional would become more subject to the claims of other persons who are not professionals. Hence the expansion of the dominion of professional authority would be balanced and supported by corresponding acknowledgments of the authority of ordinary persons, some of whom are clients.

## 6 PLANNERS

Advice is reasonable. The advice we seek and offer about the world and what we might do should be justifiably connected with what we know about how the world works and what is desirable. Still, the stories we tell to do this reasonable justification may become disconnected from the persons who participate in advice, and from the problems they work on in advice-giving. The stories are not motivated by advice, but by some other endeavor, whether it be the legal system, political ideology, or science. And we, as advisees or advisors, can claim that a story is irrelevant to us. In planning, one attempts to formally control these tendencies toward disconnectedness and irrelevance. But planning can become a role independent of advice. Then these tendencies can take over planning. The claims of irrelevance are forgotten, and planning comes to lack any relationship to advice. How does this occur?

Planners use what they know about what has happened already, about our current situation, and about the consequences of action, in order to influence present actions through the stories they tell. In this sense, we are always planning. Insofar as it is possible to distinguish an idea from an action related to it, then the planner may be seen as intervening between impulse and action. So we need explicitly plan only when our impulsive actions are not desirable, when the stories we would ordinarily tell are no longer satisfactory. Planning, like advice, is an ordinary activity for extraordinary times.

So far, the description of planning I have offered makes planning seem rather undistinguished. We all think about what we do. Why should such thought be especially interesting once it is phrased in terms of the technical role and language of planners and planning? While we may imagine cultures for which the idea of planning need not exist—ones that have no notion of consequences—ours is not one of them. What we shall justifiably do is a central question for us, and we demand a high degree of skill and quality in those justifications. Those who do that work have a special role to play in our lives.

How does a planner use what he knows to decide what should be justifiably done? I think it is fair to say that he does not decide. Rather he develops a way of thinking about what we might do. His descriptions and stories of how we should think about what we might do are too articulated to be called decisions. Planning is more an intervening between the worlds possible for us and the one that we experience every day.

A planner's knowledge of the world is about the differences between where we are now, where we might want to be, and what would be good. However, planning is not just abstract knowledge or technique apart from the community. It is not a universal science of all times and places. Abstracted and universal, it would be unlikely that planning could offer stories for advice. The claims that can be made in stories cannot be made in these absolute terms, for such stories speak to no one and to no problems. Actually, in fact, this is too strong a position. Some stories can be remarkably universal and abstract, yet still be powerful. For example, if our problems are viewed as ones involved in organizing a limited amount of goods, then the models provided by the notion of an economy can be helpful. But to make sense and be convincing, these abstract and universal models must be filled in with details of an actual situation. They gain their effectiveness from the concrete and the particular. And we sometimes may not want to use economic models because the notion of a limited good may set improper boundaries on our sphere of action.

Since planners tend to have more politically defined roles than professionals (most planners work in government), they should be quite sensitive to the dangers of abstraction and universalization. The stories they tell are oriented toward a community, a specific audience. The purpose of the stories is to make sense for the community of what there is to be done. In order to do so, the stories must be complete and in context. In general they cannot have vital parts left out because the narrator does not know what happened or will happen. He must make reasonable suggestions, identified as such, about those parts. And there are shared but often unstated aspects, what the planner is not expected to know uniquely, but what everybody can be expected to make reasonable guesses about. So a good story depends in part on creativity, judgment, and experience. An ability to synthesize a reasonable story for us is the special skill that a planner offers. Systematic knowledge of what there is in the world is sometimes a foundation for this ability, but planners are needed just when systematic knowledge is insufficient for advice. Planners may stand atop a tall ladder provided by such knowledge, thereby becoming capable of telling a better story about a problem in advice. But no one ladder, not even a scientific one, will be tall enough.

Unfortunately, and perhaps necessarily, planners easily lose their

ability to tell effective stories in advice-giving. Under a romantic at-
tachment to the technical, and in their bureaucratic roles, they may
lose their true audience, and end up addressing no one.

By looking at two models of how planners are supposed to operate,
we can get a feel for how planning can go awry. One model centers on
the knowledge planners have, while the other describes how planners
mediate diverse positions.

The model of planning that concentrates on knowledge describes
how we modify what we do by what we learn and know. Usually it is
cybernetic in orientation, and it assumes that we can trace the consequences of our actions over a period of time so that we may learn,
and so improve our plans. But there are other kinds of knowledge-
oriented models. A political model describes how a particular way of
organizing what we know and specifying what is important, let us call
it a theory, comes to dominate other such theories in the thinking of
planners. A cultural study describes the complex interconnections of
concepts that make up a theory and how they change. But until re-
cently the cybernetic model has been a dominant one and it retains
much of its appeal.

The cybernetic model tends not to pay sufficient attention to
knowledge's context, its political and cultural net. (Bateson's work is
exceptional here, and, notably, it does not lend itself to mathematical
calculation.) Nor do a planner's moral and political orientations in a
community easily fit into the model. Problems that come up in advice
are treated as matters of knowledge utilization, as if the knowledge
itself had a bare or abstract existence outside of the community. The
cybernetic picture of filling in and improving our story as we go along
does not say much about how we apply what we know. For that depends on the concrete context we are in.

In a cybernetic model we use our knowledge to create tentative images of what may happen that we can then compare to images we have
of the present. We then may tell better stories and thereby influence
what we do. But how do we compare two images? If they are reducible
to electrical voltages, then a comparison is straightforward. But if the
images are too different (for example, in cognitive style or semantic
content), then the comparisons are much more difficult to specify.
The cybernetic model would have little content without a detailed
notion of comparison. It is in those situations when comparisons are
particularly problematic, at those times when advice is needed, that a
planner is called for. Planners invent modes of comparison that are
reasonable for the community. They give content to the cybernetic
model, just as the experienced oarsman knows the seas and his ship,

and so steers her well. A story tells us how to make comparisons and we would find it inadequate if it did not do so. It is not only a narrative; it is critical study as well. Planners create in their stories the context needed at those times when knowledge is least likely to be able to stand on its own, to retain a meaning outside of context.

The cybernetic model uses not knowledge, but the concept of information as relevant and interpreted knowledge and signals. And so the problems I have sketched can be avoided logically. But substantively they still remain. The model's usual mechanisms for creating and processing information and its modes of comparison, almost always leaving out persons, are generally much too simple to be satisfying ways of understanding advice in our actual lives.

The knowledge-oriented cybernetic model is most useful when we can maintain narrow, well-specified prescriptions for what we need to know about our environment. Then the meaning and implication of what we learn is most clear, and it is easily articulated formally. Since certain kinds of data fit this model most straightforwardly, it seems reasonable to conclude that planning should be modeled on one of the natural sciences, whether it be one of the so-called quantitatively oriented ones, such as physics or chemistry, or the structural ones, such as biology. But even structural models, with their levels of order, do not say much about the comparisons we need to make in a society. The levels and organizational characteristics in biological systems may or may not do for actual planning stories. And as I have suggested, these natural science models often eliminate the person of the planner and the community of interest in advice, when describing the comparisons.

Scientific activity is an attractive model of advice. Science, like advice, depends on doubt expressed in a community where we are not sure or completely knowing. But advice must be given even when a natural scientist would demur for lack of good evidence and knowledge. A planner may tell a story that is speculative, unsure, and even ambiguous, although it is important that he distinguish the degrees of speculation he engages in. The scientist's usual tests for validity are not likely to be good guides for the planner. The rules for judging a story must come from too many other sources—such as the political arena, or the retrospectively judged effectiveness of the story as a convincing story—for the scientist's tests to be decisive. A cybernetic model suggests that the appropriate criterion is how well the story guides us in doing what we want to do. But the stories planners compose are also about what we want to do, as well as about how to do it and what will happen.

As I shall argue later, advice-giving is a model for science, not the reverse. Science is a special form of advice that functions by restrict-ing its domain of inquiry so that the limited roles persons may play in science are sufficient for that domain.

A second model describes how planners mediate diversity. This model explicitly denies the possibility of defining end states, of pre-dicting the likely consequences of action over the long run, or of ex-plicitly analyzing what we are doing and systematically combining that with our other knowledge. Like the cyberneticists, it suggests that decisions be made along the way. But rather than combining what we know, we should act in terms of the resolution and management of conflict as contrasted to the resolution of conflicting facts. This model is concretely and explicitly about political and social forces and realities. They are the powerful constraints on and the points of op-portunity for planners' actions and stories. This model may seem po-tentially more political and democratic than the knowledge-oriented model, since the planner's claim to legitimate involvement does not deny his partisan role.

This model does not say much about the linkage among the incre-mental decisions we make along the way that eventually permits us to see our history as coherent, or why our conflicts get resolved after all. It does not describe the stories we tell to make sense of what we are up to. We see our lives as continuous for the most part, we do go on, and changes must be part of the continuities.

The diversity model is closer to ordinary advice-giving than is the cybernetic model. But it too fails just when the planner is most needed: when we require an articulated and coherent synoptic vision realized in a story about us. For if we emphasize decisions made along the way, then a coherent story would at first seem to be precluded, unless we also believed in an invisible hand or providence.

Still, the stories planners tell, even if they are synoptic, need not be inconsistent with a diversity model. A story need not be exhaustive of all possibilities and absolutely comprehensive, but just needs to incor-porate one believable, reasonable possibility (such as our everyday world) that is inhabitable by us. Stories that claim to be absolute and complete should be distinguished from stories that claim to be ade-quate and sufficient for what we are up to, complex enough so that we recognize ourselves in them. Planners are persons in a community who can speak about the community, without having to claim they know all about it. They tell stories around the problems they de-scribe. They are not simply problem solvers.

Each of these two models denies in its own way that it is persons who give and receive advice. The knowledge-oriented model, in its de-sire to control bias and be objective, reduces meaning and significance to formal and abstract notions. In practice context becomes static and simple rather than rich and familiar. The diversity model, in its desire to attend to the limitations of our knowledge, makes the world seem more fragmentary and disjointed than it actually is. But planners enact their role in many contexts and are required to see the world whole, just as persons know how to conduct themselves in their community. When models of advice do not take advantage of these capacities, they become poor models of the planning role in advice-giving.

Planners must maintain their claims about their having a sense of the world, yet they must acknowledge the counterclaims of others. Advice is about a world inhabited by persons like them. Otherwise the foundation of advice and of their role disappears. They would no longer be telling us reasonable stories reflecting their knowledge of the world, stories that we can respond to. The stories would have no significance for us.

## 7 EXPERTS

Experts claim to embody more widely than do other persons the community's agreements and understanding. An expert claims that his experience is representative of the community's and is appropriate for guiding him and the community in the advice he gives. Acting in an advice-giving role the expert is a political figure, rather than just a specialist who knows a great deal about a small area. For he claims, and we may agree, that his specialized knowledge and competence has implications over a much wider area than his training and experience might lead one to believe at first. Hence, a physician whose special competences lie in the understanding of heart disease often is concerned with much more general problems about how a person ought live his life, and a physicist who knows about samarium tells a senator why we ought to have fewer nuclear weapons.

In an advice-giving situation, claims may be challenged. Yet even if expert claims seem to exceed the expert's manifest capacities, we may accept them. And after a while, experts and those whom they advise may view these claims as being independent of the give-and-take of advice-giving. Challenges then are not counterclaims but challenges to the role of the expert. They become too momentous for everyday use. The expert's representativeness and understanding come to be treated as independent of the community in which they originally made sense. The expert's understanding of who we are, his context for using his more narrow specialized competence, is no longer subject to the challenges in advice. It is entrenched, outside of our reach. This cannot be good, even if an expert may be a valid representative and his understanding is genuine. How are we to test his claims (actually non-claims) outside of the advice situation?

A community could just ignore inappropriate experts. It could also consider a person an expert who does not think of himself as being in such a role. And experts become entrenched in bureaucratic and political positions, and they will stay long after we would wish them to go. If their claims to expertise were always subject to contest, then we might more directly challenge them and explore their claims.

The problem is more subtle. The "we" that experts define may be in the interest of the community, yet the community may have lost or forgotten its own interest. The expert may then become an overtly political figure who demands that the persons in the community recover their capacity to doubt and to make counterclaims. In the give-and-take of advice, that recovery can take place and the expert's leadership can be legitimated. For the legitimacy of an expert's claim to represent us is never settled once and for all time. Challenges to the claim that an expert understands us do not destroy expertise (or advice), they affirm its possibility.

The expert is not just a specialist, he represents us. And that representation may be false or foisted on us by the expert or others in our community. Say that a person comes to be seen as a representative of part of the public. He has an understanding of us from a particular point of view. It is not unusual for elites to designate that person expert for all of us, and then proceed to innocently ask the expert for counsel. But the expertise has not been confirmed by us.

What happens when there are counterclaims that deny a putative expert's legitimacy? Other persons may challenge the expert, claiming that he was improperly selected. They may not respect his claims, or the claims made by others for him. But they do not seem to be able to make any claim of the sort that would be grounded in their being experts on experts. But in advice situations they need not be experts on experts. Their counterclaims, as such, demand responses from the putative expert and his supporters. Now, anyone can challenge another's expertise and then designate yet another person as an expert. But expertise is related to the superior performance and understanding in public. So the designation cannot be arbitrary. The politics of expertise and claims has a rational foundation.

The problems that people consider important, relevant, and worthy of attention depend on their milieu and who they are. A person may challenge another's expertise, and the group that designated the expert, by denying the worthiness of the problems about which the other person is expert. The rational foundation is balanced by our notions about what is important in the world, and those notions may be rationally founded too. Each group will have its problems and set of experts. And candidate experts will hunt for their own supporting groups. The groups need not confront and deal with each other. Their experts will.

But experts do not deal with disjoint problems; the problems impinge on each other. The disagreements are not merely a matter of what is most worthy for me. There are connections between the reasons we give for the worthiness of one goal with those we give for a conflicting goal. We live in one community in which there are disagreements, rather than in disjoint and harmonious sub-communities. Our claims affect others.

Advice makes little sense if problems exist independently of us. Experts cannot just work, all alone, on the problems they have defined for us. No one would seek advice in this case, or if it has been sought, the advisee is now forgotten. Experts go on as they will. Their legitimacy is grounded at best in their effective performance of duties, but the duties have become subject to the expert's definition and control. The public understanding character of the expert is no longer logically tied to what he does. We no longer designate, challenge, and control the expert. So the role of expert loses its connection with persons. It comes to be articulated in terms of criteria of technical performance, defined by experts. We may no longer call on or recall the expert. He comes to us unbidden.

## 8 THE REALIZATION OF THESE ROLES IN ADVICE-GIVING

The roles I have sketched appear because they are needed when advice breaks down. They reflect a logical breakdown in advice's conceptual structure, and are a societal response to the breakdown. A formal role can help to mend the break, but the role can then become independent of and irrelevant to its original purposes. The role need not diverge from the picture of persons giving advice to each other. But there are pressures to do so, and to become universal and to seem objective. And then the role denies that advice involves persons in a community. But we cannot ignore these alien roles. Their institutionally supported embodiments in actual positions, such as a professional city planner who is an expert on housing, can become powerful, even if they are inauthentic and defective forms of advice. In fact, we may be confronted with a justifying ideology that denies that these roles and positions should be based on our dealing with each other as persons. Rather, the argument goes, we need be dubious of such a per-

sonal basis, and we ought be scientific and impersonal in our foundations, and be aware of the subtle corruptions in the use of understanding and publicity in advice. Claims on persons are transformed into
assertions about things.

Professionals become credential holders, rather than bearers of personal trust; planners become scientists who manage complex interconnections and evaluate the success of what we do, rather than
claimants to the verisimilitude and reasonableness of their stories;
and experts become specialists, rather than developers of a legitimate
public political understanding of who we are. The legitimate significant stories remain untold. We make do, in these roles, as best we can.
What saves the community, what reveals the problems, is that this
making do is not adequate. As we have seen, contradictions in the
logic of un-personal advice reveal the inadequacies.

Persons fulfill a role by acting out socially prescribed patterns of behavior in their everyday lives. Roles, in my analysis, are abstractions
from advice's constitutive requirements. The roles should be distinguished from the requirements (for which I use identical terms) and
from a particular person's way of living or a particular social position.
A physician acts out a professional role. He makes claims as to the
proper relationship of persons in health care. But he also acts out a
planner's role in that the therapeutics offered are supposed to work
and be appropriate. And he also acts out an expert role in that he
makes claims about how health ought to be understood. A "professional educator" will act differently than an "expert in education," although both may be teachers. And there is a substantive difference between a health planner and a war planner, although they both tell
stories about us.

The role a person takes in advice is also defined by his stance with
respect to current societal policies. Often the man of knowledge legitimates what we do. But a person may define himself instead as a critical dissenter from those policies. The dissenter may or may not be
part of the social establishment, respectively a wise man or an intellectual. In either of these roles a person explicitly distances himself
from others in the society, especially from experts pursuing the currently acceptable societal goals. So intellectuals may claim that experts are only technicians or specialists who lack a larger understanding of the society.

The technician is the antithesis of the wise man or the intellectual.
He rarely questions goals and the context of problem statements. He
is dexterous at figuring out what to do within a small area. Now we
can be surer of the competence of a technician than that of an intellec-

tual or even an ordinary expert in advice, since technicians have explicit and prescribed areas of knowledge, and prescribed good behaviors and good performances. If there were no technicians, ordinary complex societal life could not take place. Yet many decry the technical in our lives. They fear the extension of technical competence, so that technique, conceived of as an attitude toward how we ought live, would control our lives. The issue is, I believe, what are the appropriate areas for technical approaches? Those who see a danger of technicians being everywhere and taking over and those who see technicians as the necessary basis for society do disagree fundamentally, but it is at the large and fuzzy border between them rather than at the extremes. The disagreement is whether the extension of the technical can get out of control, and just what it means to be out of control.

Some roles are intermediate between critical dissent and technical competence, and advisors fulfill these roles. Planners and experts, as scientific professionals, frequently advise government. Nowadays most are trained in universities. They include lawyers, economists, and natural scientists. Lawyers are familiar with the specific political and administrative processes of government, and they are flexible generalists. Economists have technical capabilities, especially insofar as government has become the management of the economy, reduced to a problem in resource allocation. Scientists can understand the high technologies that are now the engine of war and development. Each of these groups tries to get others in government to think and talk in its terms.

Most actual advisors do not operate in an ideal advice situation. They fulfill a role that denies that they make claims or that others make claims on them. They are high technicians. Their environment and community are objectified, and they do not deal with others like them, subjects with whom they might argue. Rather, others are challengers to their turf against whom they must defend themselves.

Professionals try to objectify the environment that is their clients. Better that clients be ignorant and meek than that they command and control the professional, or so it is tacitly believed. At the same time trust is objectified in actual practice, so that the environment is managed and made tame. For example, professional societies offer malpractice insurance and develop professional ethics. These provide a haven from demands that an advisor be godlike or completely subservient. The tenuous claims to trust characteristic of a formal professional relationship become even less potentially disastrous. Yet objectification is not inevitable. Persons may acknowledge the contingent character of integrity and develop modes of forgiveness to deal with failure. But we do not.

As a planner, the advisor has supportive peers who will check out the reasonableness and proper form of his stories, and debunkers who will create alternative stories. This tension in the planner's environment often leads him to deny that he does create stories, and to emphasize the seemingly factual nature of what he does. But persons can handle alternative stories. They need not deny that there are stories other than the one they tell. Rather than just defending their turf, they can compare stories, noting how one story is more adequate in certain aspects than another. They will argue why some aspects are important. And other persons will recognize when your rational story fails or is un-human. On the other hand, even if a story's claims violate the canons of a proper story, it may still be judged a good story. Persons can handle exceptions. And they know as well that good form and proper method do not automatically guarantee a story that requires our assent.

As in the previous two cases, an expert advisor's attempt to control his environment and to prevent the claiming and counterclaiming characteristic of advice can objectify and oversimplify his situation. Rather than engaging in the give-and-take of advice, the expert treats others as if they believe his formulations are just about right and only need technical adjustments (about which he is expert), or as if they believe his understanding is irrelevant to them and, unscientifically, they try to ignore him. But this polarization of the expert's environment undermines the legitimacy of his role. Experts claim not only to be narrow technicians but to understand all of us. As hired hands they no longer can maintain an enlarged representative role.

In each of these situations, the advisor engages in a defensive tactic to control his environment. The objectification of others is alienating and does limit his role. But he also may create a new, almost adequate, environment and model for action (often mediated by a professional society). The advisor may change how all of us think about what we are up to and how we ought to act. Insofar as the new environment and model of the world are effective, they are self-confirming and support the advisor. He delivers what he says he will deliver, and it "works." The re-created environment affirms the professional ideology.

So advisors find they are influential. As the communicators and travelers, they serve important conceptualizing and intelligence functions. Yet they feel subject to many external pressures, and it is more seemly to be less prominent. Advisors will then deny in good faith that they are influential.

I have been describing the various ways that advisors try to control their environment. They deny that the others they deal with are actually persons like them. They create ideologies that justify the effectiveness of their practical efforts. And after conforming the world to their own needs, they deny having done so, so that they are less subject to the counterclaims of others. But the world is not a closed system. The effort to create an objectified environment where the advisor sees a high congruence between his world and his capabilities does not quite work. Professional practice often fails. Other persons desire the advisor's power. The even more powerful will try to use and control him, or worse, ignore him. Other advisors will steal his thunder. The development of a form of objectified advice, without claims and persons, is an attempt to respond to these pressures. But advice-giving then becomes a brittle, unstable activity, for persons cannot rely on each other.

Plato and Machiavelli were actual advisors, and their counsel, developed out of their own experience, is interesting. Plato addressed the problem as follows:

> One who advises a sick man, living in a way to injure his health, must first effect a reform in his way of living, must he not? And if the patient consents to such reform, then he may admonish him on other points? If, however, the patient refuses, in my opinion it would be the act of a real man and a good physician to keep clear of advising such a man—the act of a poltroon and a quack on the other hand to advise him further on those terms. The same thing holds in the case of a city, whether it have one master or many. If a government that proceeds in orderly fashion along the right course, seeks advice about its advantage in some matter, it would be the act of an intelligent man to give advice to such a community. In the case, however, of those who are altogether astray from the path of right government, and will by no other means consent to go on the track of it, who on the other hand give notice to their adviser to keep his hands off the constitution under penalty of death if he disobeys, and order him to cater to their wishes and desires by pointing out the easiest and quickest method of attaining them permanently, in that case I should think the adviser who consented to such conditions a poltroon—the one who refused, a real man.

Our discretion may be quite limited and a principled person may need to be responsive to unprincipled forces, although he need not be a parrot. Machiavelli advises:

The advisors of a republic . . . are undoubtedly in a difficult position; for, unless they recommend the course which in their honest opinion will prove advantageous to that republic . . . regardless of consequences, they fail to fulfill the duties of their office, while, if they recommend it, they are risking their lives and endangering their position, since all men in such matters are blind and judge advice to be good or bad according to its result. Nor do I see any way of avoiding either the infamy or the danger other than by putting the case with moderation instead of trying to force its adoption, and by stating one's views dispassionately and defending them alike dispassionately and modestly; so that, if the republic accepts your advice, it does so of its own accord, and will not seem to have been driven to it by your importunity. When you act thus, it is unreasonable for a people to wish you ill on account of your advice, since it has not been adopted against the will of the majority. Danger is incurred only when many have opposed you, and the result being unfortunate, they combine to bring about your downfall. And, though, in the case we have taken, there is lacking the glory which comes to the man who in opposition to the many, alone advocates a certain course which turns out well, it has two advantages. First, it does not entail danger. Secondly, if you tender your advice with modesty, and the opposition prevents its adoption, and owing to someone else's advice being adopted, disaster follows, you will acquire very great glory. And, though you cannot rejoice in the glory that comes from disasters which befall your country, it at any rate counts for something.

Both Plato and Machiavelli try to define the kinds of claims we can make on each other. When survival is at issue we act the best we can, yet a community can still become monstrous. But if there is any discretion, and there almost always is, claims must be genuine for advice to work. One's relationship must preserve and ensure the personhood of others, one's stories must be true, and it must be possible to make claims to an understanding that is representative of us. If not, there is no advice. There is quackery, prevarication and ineffectiveness, and tyranny.

The analysis we have performed for advisors could also be made for advisees, with almost parallel observations and categories. The claims we make in advice engender counterclaims and counter-roles. We would speak of clients, peers, and citizens, instead of professionals, planners, and experts. Still the two sides do not quite duplicate each other, or march in step. The grounds shift slowly as advisors and advisees misstep or choose not to follow each other exactly. Each introduces new material into their interaction, altering the areas of concern and contention. Each makes feints, finesses, and dramatic shifts, to some extent recognized and justified by the other. When there is a leap that redefines what's up, a leap that changes the kind and topic of discourse, then trust in a human story about us can act as a bridge. A person goes along for a while with someone else and sees what happens.

Advisors are likely to end up enacting roles filled with dilemmas, distant from the ideal of advice-giving. We have tried to understand these roles. Next we want to explore the problems advisors work on, the manner in which advice becomes an appropriate activity for working on problems, and how breakdowns in this activity lead to our viewing problems as autonomous, as puzzles that we are welcome to solve if we can, rather than as situations in which we, as persons, may participate in advice.

## Problems

Problems are claims we make upon each other about the situation we are in: that something has gone awry. In general, problems cannot exist abstractly, outside of being claimed. We encounter difficulties, similar to the ones we came upon in considering roles, when we deny the claim character of problems. Having a problem is a way of being in the world, and it depends as much on who we are as on the conditions we are in. We have problems by working on them, by telling stories.

Still, there is a temptation to treat problems as if they were not claims, but merely objective statements of our situation. In a dialogue between a hypothetical sensible advocate of this position and a critic, I describe the dilemmas we get into when we take such a stance. In this way we explore the limits of formal problem-solving systems and how we try to patch up those limits. Instead of being haunted, as we were in the previous sections, by modern bureaucratic roles, here we are haunted by efforts to make machines operate more intelligently and formal problem-solving procedures be more explicit. Of course, the issue is not whether bureaucrats can be human or whether machines can think, for we know of many

*cases where the evidence is encouraging. The issue is whether
we need to be persons in advice in the crucial marginal
situations.*

## 9 PROBLEMS

The problems we have, like the advice we ask for and receive about
them, arise out of the extraordinary aspects of ordinary life. We can
feel uncomfortable or lost in a situation, and our discomfort is articulated into a problem, a problem that can be made explicit, and worked
on and transformed, as a consequence of the advice we give and receive. Advice helps us to figure out what to do. Then we can go on
with what we are ordinarily up to or initiate a new task.

Not all our discomforts lead us to seek or offer advice. Advice is not
needed if we can follow some ordinary procedure to work on our discomforts, even if we are unsure of the procedure's outcome. We know
what to do now. Or perhaps from previous advice we have figured out
what we should do in these cases. Nor do we need advice if it does not
matter what we do; perhaps all outcomes are acceptable. On the other
hand, advice may be sought at just those moments when we should
know what to do. It is a way of avoiding that knowledge, at least temporarily, or of gaining support for what we must do. Usually we do not
seek or offer advice or have explicit problems, but sometimes we do.

Problems are claims, claims on others about our world. Calling a
situation problematic tells them that our situation is not an ordinary
one. It suggests that advice may be needed to figure out what to do. Of
course a problem does not claim, as such. Someone claims that there
is a problem. Others may agree or deny that the situation is problematic. The formulation of our problem, if there is one, implies a constellation of relevant actors and a way of thinking about our situation.
And the set of actors may be incorrect or the conceptualization may
be inadequate.

Saying that I have a problem is a claim about claims, for the description of the problem is a set of claims. Saying I have a problem, I ask for
or give advice. I say: the world is like this, it is not the right way, and
we need to figure out what to do. As contrasted to a misconception on
my part, the problem comes to be understood as our problem, as a
problem we had felt before but perhaps not explicitly. And we now engage in a process of advice-giving, continuing the sequence of claims
upon each other.

The process breaks down if we ignore or forget that advice requires
us to act as persons who make claims on each other. Problems then

can become objects that are processed in a manner called solving. Problems are treated as if they were textbook problems, with little chance of being reformulated, having definite right answers, and actually being given and written out by someone else rather than discovered by us in the course of life. We do not treat the supposed problem as if it might be denied as a problem, as if it may be out of our world, irrelevant to it, making no sense, or as if the problem is not ours (but yours or no one's). Sometimes this is an appropriate stance. Some problems are well formulated and manifestly ours. A textbook solution might be just what is needed. But how do we know if this is the case for all but the most obvious of problems? We need to understand how problems come to be.

Before going further, I want to point out explicitly the recursive nature of advice. Advice is an ordinary activity about the extraordinary that makes the extraordinary ordinary again. Claims are about other claims. Advice may be about advice. But these self-referential series are not infinite. We are not infinitely lost. We more or less know where the relatively solid ground is. So we do not give advice about advice about advice about . . . *ad infinitum*. Most of the time we have a good feel for what is ordinary in our lives, and we know how to return from the inquiries we pursue in advice to everyday ordinary taken-for-granted experience. Most of our lives are not so problematic. Also, we know how to settle our claims against each other and to resolve what to do, and we accept that resolution as long as things go along smoothly. We look for advice, make claims on each other, and bring up problems when we are lost, but for the most part we are not lost.

Persons have problems. They work on them. Asking for or giving advice, they make that claim, that *this* is a problem. Yet they change the *this*; they change the problem. After several changes they may find that they do not have a problem, at least for now. They do not need or want advice.

When persons have a problem and try to figure out what to do, such figuring out will depend on who they are, what they have been up to, and what is being claimed as not quite right about their situations. Admitting that many problems are universally shared, we also note lots of differences. Since people lead different lives and have had different previous experiences, situations (what they are, whether they are problematic now) may also be seen differently. A situation that seems problematic to one person may seem ordinary to another. And even if a situation seems problematic to two persons, and both think it is worthwhile to seek advice, each may define the problem to suit his own purposes. Persons with different cultural backgrounds who seem able to understand each other may still define problems differently. They may have different languages for describing situations and so for revealing problems. And they may differ as to which are the choices that matter and are valued. In giving advice to each other they will admit that their problems are personal in origin. That becomes the basis for making authorized claims, legitimately convincing others, and going on together. Being personal is not being idiosyncratic or irrational, for problems are shared by others and we can explain a problem to those who may not share our own, and perhaps bring them along to our point of view.

Problems do not come from nowhere, from some great textbook in the sky. They are part of our lives, a way of understanding what we are up to. When they are defined outside of our lives, outside of a context of advice-giving that involves other persons like us, they can easily be used to manipulate us. When a problem is presented as an object, as part of an objectified environment that is given to us, we cannot know whose choices are being faced, or whose alternatives for action matter. Problems defined by an unknown someone else as abstract objects, out there, which we then accept as part of our work, are likely to be disconnected from us. Unless our acceptance is informed and allows for rejection, we are not acting in terms that need make sense to us, but only to someone else.

Problems are, of course, objectified to varying degrees. Rarely are we accepting of a problem without its having some connection with us, without our having some chance to shape it to fit ourselves. Even some textbook problems allow for variation in comprehending them and answering them. A city plan may present a problem of urban development in what seems like a monolithic way, but we know that people interpret the direction of a plan and the way it is to be fulfilled in different ways depending in part on their own interests and in part on the kind of actions they can take.

To be able to have problems is an aspect of being an autonomous person. In having a problem a person sets up a claim to his own world, a world that, in general, is not so different from other persons' worlds. Insofar as we each can have our own problems, we can have a picture of the world that encompasses our own lives. It is a picture that we may speak about and convey to others. So having a problem is a claim on others, how they ought to think about our situation and how they ought to act. And in advice actors make claims, and not just speeches to no one. They are not even actors who read a pre-written script that suits their character. Rather, persons express, articulate, and discover themselves in making such claims. Having a problem is working on it.

We need to reconcile the last two paragraphs. We want to have our own problems. We also want to convince others that our problems are theirs. But they also want to convince us that their problems are ours. The claims and counterclaims we make on each other lead us to modify our understanding of what we are up to and what we might do about it. Now, our own problems gain their content and meaning from the community we are in. We share our lives. So we might believe that we can come to a common core understanding of some problems, or perhaps two or three major versions of the problem. We might come to some agreement. Autonomy and community can be consistent if we can treat each other as worthy rational persons, and through argument try to bring each other along.

In the practice of social research we can see how problems are defined outside a context of genuine advice. Outsiders will enter a community, study its operation, and then define its problems. They take over, perhaps unintentionally, the community's image-making capacities and its processes of legitimately having and working on problems. The researchers may even note that the community's ability to define its own problems is weak, and therefore the community needs the aid of outsiders. But that help has often proved to distort the realities as much as reveal them. And since hierarchies of racial or sexual domination seem to be reproduced in the relationship of researchers to those studied, it is not unreasonable for the community studied to question the fairness and competence of researchers who represent those hierarchies.

Researchers have become more aware of the difficulties of their position. Political conflicts over their research reveal the conflicts between the norms of their research work, their own interests, and the interests of the community. Full disclosure and scientific accuracy, abstractly conceived, may not be consonant with the possibility of a community's retaining legitimate control over its own image, even if it has invited the researcher to work there. A community always manages what others can find out about it, so the issue is not simply one of freedom and liberty as opposed to control and distortion. It is fair for the community to ask how full is the disclosure or how scientific is the accuracy. Research is used to define problems, and problems set political agendas. Research is central to, not outside of, an advice situation in which we determine what to do, so researchers who act as if they are "only looking" cannot help but appear inauthentic.

In some cases experts may claim to know what to do, and advisors and researchers are often treated as if they were gods. But problems defined without the interactions characteristic of advice-giving will not be our problems; they will not have our allegiance and commitment. I, as an outside advisor, may claim that a society or an organization has a problem. I am saying that, using my experience about some aspect of that group, I have defined what I believe are the possibilities available to the group. But the problem is posed by me, and unless others feel it or can be made to feel it, it will not be a problem for them. They may concur in my definition or choose another one. But my saying that the society has a problem is not a claim if they cannot deny it. It is an act that limits the set of possibilities that can be designated by the members of the society. I have attempted to take over the problem-defining process, and the society's politics.

We can begin to describe how persons work on problems once we note that to have a problem is to be in a situation. A problem is posed at a certain time, and we may view it, its posing and presentation, as a critical point in a sequence of actions. The actions previous to its statement are the experiential base for posing the problem, while our anticipations are what make the problem problematic. Our working on the problem is a choice about our future made by articulating our understanding of the possibilities we can conceive. For a while our situation is problematic. We're not sure what to do. But then we seem to figure it out, at least for a while, and we go on with our lives. Advice begins and ends with persons going on with what they ordinarily do, including giving and receiving advice.

In asking for and giving advice, our work is to tell a reasonable story that claims to be a way of looking at the situation we are in. The story will say how we might think about what we might do. At first we might try to salve the irritations and discomforts that brought the problem to our attention. But the story we tell in working on the problem may bring up different irritations, ones that should more appropriately concern us. We might not appreciate the extent of our difficulties or we might disagree with others' assessments of them. Still, eventually, we want to bring the problem to a resolution. This is not to say that we obviate the deepest sources of the irritating, extraordinary situation. Rather, our description of the situation incorporates means of working on the irritation and, eventually, a way of acting as well as a reinterpretation of the sources, so that the new situation is more ordinary, more under our control.

The situation we are in is not given, but is something we discover and describe. The problems we have and work on depend on how we understand our situation. And the stories we tell depend on the situation and the problems we are dealing with. We seek advice to work through this sequence of situation, problem, and story. But sometimes a variety of good stories can be told for any problem. Our description of our situation does not preclude or exhaust the possibility of other ones. We do not always have a simplified, agreed-upon set of abstractions (such as exists for much of physical science or everyday life) in which to fit each situation we encounter. This does not mean that each situation is absolutely unique, nor that we cannot have some small number of archetypal stories that work most of the time. Even if the world is comparatively wild in how it might be described (if we could have such knowledge about its describability), cognitive anthropologists and literary critics will point out how tamed that world becomes under any particular culture compared to possibilities revealed in all the others. But we seek advice just at those times when there is no formula to plug our problem into, or at least when we do not yet understand the problem in that manner.

Of course, the formulas of, say, physics, with their comparatively clean abstractions from the complexities of life, are a product of a long history of hard work and subtle delineation, internal to the discipline, of what have come to be called the important problems. Lots of aspects of ordinary situations are ignored by the physicist's formulations and are considered irrelevant for the moment. The success of a science, such as physics, depends on its being able to keep the irrelevant factors from becoming important. For the complex political and personal situations we ordinarily encounter in advice-giving, it is hard to control the irrelevant factors. They can protest or become powerful, and then unseat you and your explanation.

The stories we write or tell should provide a sufficiently rich description of our situation so that it is clear what is most important in figuring out what to do. A story is a world in which we can project ourselves and understand who we are, and a world that makes it possible for the problems we feel to make sense. If a story does not fit us, then we will recognize the strains and tightness. We may make counterclaims and offer revised versions so that a new cut might suit us adequately. How might a story be judged? We should recognize ourselves in it, it should be relevant to us. If the story seems factually correct and does not leave out important aspects, that too will help. If the story connects with other stories we know and trust, then even better. And if the story helps us through our problem, then we may feel as if we are on home ground at last.

## 10 PROBLEMS WITHOUT ADVICE

In advice-giving, problems are well defined. They always have solutions, for they are part of complete stories about us and what we should do. Even our dissatisfaction, our unsureness, our anxiety about the story may be incorporated into the story. And so the story is meaningful for us. The problems we bring up and discover in advice are already-there, and to discover them is to discover who we are in the community. Of course, we may develop more satisfactory stories with better solutions as we go along. Our problems are not unchanging. Advice-giving is an appropriate activity because we cannot go on as we would ordinarily, not because a problem cannot be solved.

This description of problems should be distinguished from the textbook notion of an abstract problem that needs a solution. No, our problems are part of our situation and we work on them. They are resolved as a byproduct of doing our work. Sophisticated descriptions of how scientists work on problems, say in mathematics or physics, read similarly to descriptions of how advisors work on problems. They play around and eventually they may be able to formulate the problem so that it might be said to have a more conventional solution. But the solving at that point is often a comparatively minor achievement. We have already worked hard to re-set the problem so it can be conventionally solved. We might say that we have two kinds of solutions—a kind that incorporates all the complexities and difficulties we experience in the middle of a problem, and the cleaned-up kind we present to others afterwards. The problem always comes with a solution, including the one that says we are not sure how the problem works out but we have some idea.

If problems are treated as abstractions, as not already-there in our situation; if they are separated from the persons who find them and are figuring them out; that is, when we forget we are in an advice-giving situation; then we find there is a breakdown not unlike the one I have described in talking about the roles of advisors. In taking the abstraction as the concrete reality we end up with a set of dilemmas.

The dilemmas appear as we describe how abstracted problems are solved. Paraphrasing many such descriptions:

A problem is well-defined [Note the change of definition.] if a specifiable way of working on the situation is available that leads to a satisfying prescription for action for the person who posed the problem as well as for others who may be involved. Well-definedness of a problem requires that the method of working be automatic or at least sufficiently well specified, so that we can give a person an explicit set of rules and instructions that he can follow so that he and others can work on the situation. Such systematic procedures for working on the situation may permit us to give a set of criteria, to be searched for in the problem statement, that tell if the problem is well-defined.

This prescription comes from formal logic, some work in artificial intelligence, and general notions (which have a long history) about mechanically determinate processes. It seems that problems are treated very much like textbook or logical problems. They can be stated in some formal representation, in which they are straightforward. Then advice for solving those problems might also be given in that formal representation. And the human, personal, and social interactions that occur in advice are potentially also describable in formal terms. Of course, logical, mathematical, and mechanical problems are worked on and discovered in a much less neat fashion than their retrospective proofs would indicate.

In any case, if we believe that we can treat problems abstractly and perhaps formally, then advice-giving must be set into a framework that provides automatic procedures, formal rules, understandable and clear instructions, and criteria for examining a problem and finding out if it is well-defined. These requirements say virtually nothing explicit about a relationship among persons who tell stories, and who understand each other, which is our original notion of advice-giving. Still, it is reasonable to expect that persons who are at home in our world will be able to follow procedures and rules that are neither automatic nor formally and completely stated, and they can understand the instructions we give them and appreciate if a problem is reasonably clear. But it is much harder to specify these formal desiderata so that a logical machine of comparatively little "experience" will be able to handle them, unless we simplify the world so much that we only dimly recognize ourselves in it. Usually there are no persons in these pictures to supply the rich context or world in which what we are up to makes sense. But it still may be true that these abstracted versions of our problems and how we work on them are a good model of what we do. But there are difficulties. Continuing the paraphrase:

> Most of the time the criterial set for deciding if a problem is well-defined does not exist. We usually deal with systems that are self-organizing, that can exhibit goal-oriented behavior, and that are self-examining. (These are ways of describing what

persons ordinarily do, but in mechanical and biological terms.) Consequently, we never can give a simple rule for saying when we have worked a problematic situation through to solution; nor can we say that we have a solution that is true or false in the sense that it logically follows from the problem statement; nor can we say that we may automatically apply a working method we have developed in the past to the present situation. But most of the time we more or less follow the rules, we can give a logical reconstruction of what we are doing, and we have some general method we apply almost universally.

Sometimes we will have rules, logical entailments, and methods that do work. But problems are moving targets, situations that may resolve themselves by our changing their structure, their goals, or their purposes. We can find definite formal or mathematical equivalents for each of these changes. So we can make a formal picture of what persons do in the terms of mechanism or of biology. But these pictures do not seem to capture the vital facts of life. In general, persons who ask for or give advice do not need rules to tell them when to stop or if a story is true. And most of what we need to know about advice comes from what we have done before.

A second major difficulty with formal models of working on problems is that we do not have a good language for describing most problems. There is no canonical form for posing them and so there is no obvious way of limiting our set of solutions. For a similar reason, the set of permissible operations that we may perform when we work on a problematic situation is not defined. The set may arise out of the statement of the problem. There does not seem to be much hope for problem-working systems. But there are interesting exceptions. The law (curial, talmudic, secular) is one of the canonical modes of limiting our description of problems and their solutions, and for that reason it has been powerful. Not all or most problems fit comfortably under its purview, and it requires that persons interpret it and judge among its applications.

When we ask for advice, we ask in language that is a mixture of technical or formal language and of our ordinary everyday way of speaking. We expect advice to be in a form that does not completely alienate us from our everyday lives, even if it sometimes does need to be expressed in technical terms. But in the end, we live our lives as persons and not as technicians, and our problems are no more controllable than the rest of our lives. So the effectively controlled environments of technical advice are unlikely to suffice much of the time.

The dilemmas in the above description of formalized problem solving are a product of its assumptions about our inadequacies. But in ordinary advice-giving, on the other hand, we manage the dilemmas quite well, for we, as persons, know how to be in the world.

There are problems that can be formalized and objectified, and then worked on technically with good reason and effect. Advisors still note the dilemmas, and their responses to them are almost, but not quite, correct. We shall first look at a response, again a paraphrase, that emphasizes the active subjective (but not personal) quality of problems, and then another that more richly describes mechanical problem solving (but again not by persons). First, the active subject:

> Many problems seem poorly defined since the persons who work on problems are self-organizing systems, and they use a descriptive language insufficiently powerful in the formal sense to provide for a canonical treatment of situations. So there is no neat description of the problem. If a person believes that he knows how to begin to work on a problem, his personal experience is involved in his working technique. He defines the problem in his terms. The technical procedures he uses are not external to him, but part of his way of being in the world. He is at home with them. He understands where he is within a situation, and then abstracting his understanding, relating it to what others understand, he can apply technical procedures to work on the problem.

When we ask for and give advice, our problems depend on who we are, although they may be stated in less subjective terms. But we know how to do this only after we have figured out what the problem is.

> We are not only concerned with how well defined a problem is, but also with the possibility of changing its definition. Changing the definition is one of the most powerful tools for working on a problem. Having a large number of ways of representing a problem is very much like having a variety of seemingly two-dimensional aspects for reconstructing a three-dimensional situation. And in some problem areas there exists a representation of the problem that immediately suggests a suitable solution of the problematic situation.
> When people work on a problem, they may try to tell others

about it. In conveying the essence of the problem to someone else, it may be redefined by either person. Their interaction, it seems, increases the likelihood of developing new representations, in part because of the experiences of the listener. And a problem that is malleable to redefinition, to playful talk, is also one that is likely to be worked on.

The recovery of advice, but often in a weakened form, continues:

> Are problems ever solved? A solution to a problem exists when we have a situation in which a series of choices for action are posed and one is taken. In this sense few problems are solved, most are not. Some of our solved problems are solved only formally. We do something. Snap judgments, if we do not have time for deliberation, or the roughest of guesses, for those that are resistant to redefinition, substitute for careful working on a problem. Sometimes the solution to a problem may not be a product of working on it. The original reason why the situation became problematic fades away; or, the problem is reposed and weakened; or, sections or parts of the problem may even be solved. We may not wish to solve a problem, but only to work on its solution. Working is an active process that may be beneficial of itself.

This revised description of working on a problem is attractive. It describes the feelings and experiences we have in solving a problem, but we still treat it as an object out there. The description does not say much about how persons find their meanings in a community of others like them whom they have to bring along, and go on together, in advice. Problems are still thought to be outside of us, even if we define them.

At another extreme, problem solving is described in terms of the powerful formal mathematical and mechanical models of some psychologists, computer scientists, and operations researchers. Paraphrasing their descriptions:

> Given a problem statement that is fairly precise and descriptively complete, how does a person work on it, or how should a machine be programmed to work on it? It is almost always assumed that a solution exists in the sense that a short statement can be given that "solves" the problem. I quote: ". . . A problem solver exists in a task environment, some small part of which is the immediate stimulus for evoking the problem

and which thus serves as the initial problem statement. (Its statement form is clear when given linguistically, as in 'where do we locate the new warehouse?' Otherwise, 'statement' is to be taken metaphorically as comprising those clues in the environment attended to by the problem solver that indicate to him the existence of the problem.) This external representation is translated into some internal representation (a condition, if you please, for assimilation and acceptance of the problem by the problem solver). There is located within the memory of the problem solver a collection of methods. A method is some organized program or plan for behavior that manipulates the internal representation in an attempt to solve the problem. For the type of problem solvers we have in mind—businessmen, analysts, etc.—there exist many relatively independent methods, so that the total behavior of the problem solver is made up as an iterative cycle in which methods are selected on the basis of current information (in the internal representation) and tried with consequent modification of the internal representation, and a new method is selected."

This description makes sense if certain automatic or heuristic methods will work. Research suggests some ways formally defined problems are worked:

Sometimes the problems are just solved, because the way we have described the problem immediately leads to a solution. More frequently, we have to try a variety of ways of describing a problem until we find one that solves it. Another possible technique is to assume various simplified forms of the problem, for which solutions are clear, and then apply such solutions to the more complex problem.

But how do we mechanically recognize immediate solutions, or generate various ways of describing a problem, or think of a simplified form of it? Persons have these skills. They figure out solutions; they recognize when problems are related to each other or when one is a simplified version of another, and so forth. They have some good sense about what is important in their world, and what is most important for the situation we are in. If a person could not do all of this we should wonder if he is a person.

Problems are recognizably ours because we have had experience with ones like them. By restricting our purview to particular areas and developing a set of archetypal cases, we might design a mechanical equivalent of experience. Then a machine could match new problems to old experiences, taking into account context, representation, and knowledge of the situation, making small changes to obtain correspondences. But for the matching procedures to work at all, problems have to be presented in a highly stylized fashion, much more restricted in form than persons usually need. We are quite flexible and adaptive.

Abstracted problems worked on mechanically are not the same as advice. The two technical formulations of problem solving that I have described, the active subject or the formal machine, are attempts to construct a notion of persons in a community out of bare objects, that is, objects (a subject, or a machine) apart from a set of community conventions. We try for objectified problems and actors in advice for the same reason that we try for objectified roles. We demand that claims be certain and exhaustive, rather than just obvious and complete, just as in the case of the breakdown of roles. But there can be no guarantees as to certainty or exhaustiveness in our lives, nor need there be. Persons can handle failure, and all they need to go on in the world is a way that is obvious and complete. If there are alternatives or uncertainties, that is all right.

The formal guarantees we develop for deciding when a problem has been done with or solved, ones that surrogate for personal judgment, are no more worthy of belief than is professionalism, especially in the monstrous situation. For both roles and problems, the difficulties we have encountered seem to be an artifact of advice without persons. The past successes of the un-personal tradition, with its seeming guarantees and powerful calculative methods, would encourage us to continue in that vein. But that makes sense only if we realize that it has built-in limitations as a product of its artifice.

## Persons Telling Stories

*In advice we tell stories to each other about our problems. Stories are narratives with actors and settings, and I mean to keep in mind these dramatic and literary associations. Stories are addressed to an audience and they allow for some controversies but not for others. Advice can then be about us and make claims on us. After describing how stories work in advice, I show how we can forget that stories are told in advice, not abstractly. An institutional profession tries to finesse advice's requirements, especially of claims and coun-*

terclaims, by treating stories as ideologies justifying the profession's hegemony, describing technologies for its practice. But this viewpoint turns out to be workable only as long as the profession has no challengers and no new problems. It is not so resilient and responsive to contest as a true advice situation.

It is possible to describe science in terms of advice, problems, and storytelling, for science's universality and seeming objectivity is a product of the very limited range in which its stories are meant to apply. Because scientific stories seem universal, they are attractive to institutionalized professions— even though the limited range in which scientific stories make sense does not usually apply in professional practice. Advice is generally much sturdier than science, and professions pay for their scientific stance.

## 11 STORIES AND STORYTELLERS

The stories we tell to each other tell us about ourselves and what there is and how to be in the world. We are the actors in these stories, and so we find out what we might do and what that could mean. If the stories we as planners tell did not work as stories, if they did not help us get around in the world, if they did not tell persons about themselves, that is, if the stories were not claims upon us that we could recognize, then professional claims about trust or expert claims about public understanding would not hold up either. Stories provide a foundation for trust and a political theory for understanding.

A person tells a story to us and so establishes a setting for our situation. He describes the situation and the kinds of acceptable controversies about it. Controversies outside the setting, which cannot fit into the story, lack meaning, since relevance and significance is given by the story. The story also determines the kind of evidence that would support it. Other evidence is irrelevant or has no theoretical foundation.

Stories are told as part of advice-giving, an ongoing activity of persons. They are not told to no one. The story makes sense of the extraordinary situation that occasioned the advice. If it does make some sense we may change how we go along in our lives, even changing our conception of ourselves as persons, and so changing the stories we tell.

Advice is a serious business. There is a competition to tell the most convincing story because rewards of money, status, and power may come to those whose advice prevails. So economists will conflict with lawyers and politicians in claiming their stories as the exclusively best ones. We want to understand how and why those stories work, how they become detached from their tellers and strive for hegemony over all the others, and the consequences of this separation and breakdown.

Advisors, such as in the professions, will try to divide up the universe into separate realms, each of which is suited to only one kind of story.* This division controls competition and maintains stylistic purity and uniformity of product, creating a sense of reliability. For example, legal problems and stories are separated from medical and pastoral ones. Each story is a reflection of a theory of how the world works. If the theory is to help maintain a particular profession, it must provide a genre that guides persons to tell stories that make consistent and effective claims about how the world looks and about what to do next. A theory must be rich enough to permit the advice to be lively and helpful in figuring out what to do, yet it must be sufficiently patterned to suggest something specific and distinguishable from other theories. We have to be able to recognize what we hear as, for example, "medical advice." Now we often think of theories as being universalistic and instrumental, as if they were tools independent of who uses them, rather than the basis that persons use to make claims about the world. But theories are developed by persons who are up to something. They are as much ideologies, systematic justifications for action, status, and role, as they are formal cognitive structures for understanding and predicting what people do.

Advisors, such as professionals and planners, do not provide interpretations and stories where there were none before. It is not a matter of light after chaos. No, the world is always fully interpreted by us, even if some things are mysterious. We always have a story to tell about what we are up to, although we may seek advice if we feel that our story is not good enough for what we want to do. The battles for hegemony waged by the professions are attempts at reinterpretation. Each act of interpretation is a claim against the interpretation we already have.

A profession is thought to be successful if its theories become objectified, seemingly detached from persons, and if its reinterpretations are not taken as claims but as what there is. Let us see what happens when success hits.

---

*In the rest of this section I shall be especially concerned with the planning role of telling stories as engaged in by members of the formal and institutionalized professions. Hence I shall use "advisory group" and "profession" interchangeably here.

A profession has an associated ideology, which among other things justifies its way of acting autonomously. The group or profession gains the authority to make its claims unchallenged. It develops problems and technologies such that alternatives become meaningless. The problems are usually esoteric, which guarantees that the profession retains control of them for some time after it has defined them. It takes a while for others to catch up.

It is difficult for others to define and claim new alternatives if we use the old descriptors. The institutionalized thought structure created by a group to command the problems of a society become pervasive.

In advice-giving a group maintains its authority if the stories it tells could be explicitly denied by other persons. But in the institutionalized profession the challenges either are meaningless, for the advisors control the turf, or the challenges shake and destroy the false authority of the advisory group (in its planning role). Institutionalized professions, such as medicine, law, or architecture, actively deny that they are claiming anything. They can escape the demands of others, because they have effective techniques independent of others, or so they say. Since certain techniques almost always work, such as medication in medicine, procedures in law, and natural science in engineering, this is a viable absolute claim as long as the situations we deal with are straightforward. A profession may claim the prerogatives of advice—trust and public understanding of what the problems are, for example—without fulfilling its prerequisites.

Advice becomes a process of those whom we call confused consulting the knowing. The profession in its expert role presses its formulation of a problem, which then puts the problem under its authority. The everyday activity of a profession is not colloquy but problem solving. It goes something like:

> Our irritations can become common complaints because others have similar ones. These common complaints are directed, perhaps by the advice of others, to professional experts, who tell us what our complaints really are, what we should do, and why we should trust them. They transform the complaints into their own language and so they identify them. They offer a description of our situation that is amenable to their professional actions. They can remediate or ameliorate the original irritations if the problems are understood in a certain way. They may then translate their knowledge or practice into a

more common language, still perhaps highly technical but not in their sole possession, that prescribes what to do about the problem they have created. In the process of transforming the common complaint to an understanding of what to do about it, the norms (ideologies) and procedures (technologies) that define the profession become part of the problem and its formulation.

An ideology or theory, as a matter of course, establishes what is significant and relevant, what is worthy of note and why. And it says what is real, both what are the real objects and what are the effective agents or actors. Of course, not any ideology will do, since, given an ongoing community life, some will not make sense, they will not be effective, or what they say is important just will not hold up to such elevation. And not every ideology will offer a way of life that people want to lead, that is sufficiently appealing so that they are willing to make choices and sacrifices so that the way it describes could come true.

Technologies are the modes of action associated with ideologies. They are deliberate and distinctive interventions that make it possible for our intents to be realized where they might not have been otherwise. Technologies limit and create their associated ideologies. If the technology is not reliable, the profession that administers the technology will not seem competent. Its justifying ideology will not feel to us as if it has a grasp on reality, and then it will become just ideology in the pejorative sense. On the other hand, if by using its ideology a profession has convinced others that something is significant, then a technology that can do that something makes the profession look good and be effective.

The profession, its ideology, and the technology support each other. Agent, belief, and action work together, and if they can march in step well enough we have a viable world. But we might expect that if they get out of step and cannot catch up with each other there will be some changes made.

As long as a profession can deliver or look good then it can act as if it does not depend on an advice situation, but rather is a matter of technology and understanding (now a polite term for ideology). But say that a new technology develops outside of its fold, one that seems to do what the profession claims it does, only better. If the profession cannot rapidly incorporate the technology, it loses its comparative effectiveness. Then the merit of its ideology, no longer supported by the technology, becomes dubious.

In an advice situation, the trust, reasonableness, and understanding that have developed will make us think twice before we abandon an advisor just because a new technique has emerged. We realize that advisors provide more than fixes; they provide ways of organizing our lives. Just what does the new technology offer? we might ask. On the other hand, the advisor's profession is likely to be subject to much closer scrutiny as to its authority and legitimacy. It will never enjoy the secure, but brittle, status of the institutionalized profession.

Even if there are no technological changes as such, the service that a profession delivers could go out of fashion. New stories are being written (and in a sense they are the technologies) because that urge to make sense of our lives is a recurrent one, and people keep asking for advice. A profession that acts as if its stories are not a product of its relationship with others may lose contact with these new stories. The technologies a profession can effectively use may no longer be relevant to what we want to do.

Even if it survives, an institutionalized profession, which has separated itself from persons and advice, may not be autonomous. Its technology will reflect larger societal forces and social investments that direct invention in particular ways. So medicine may benefit from a big space program but not from a nonexistent organizational-studies program. The profession's ideology seems to reflect the powerful interests of others, not only those of the practitioner or his clients. For example, if advisors buy into a scientific ideology, then all sorts of crucial, seemingly irrational, factors will not receive much attention, except as nuisances. But those factors may be more than nuisances; they may be the source of revolutionary change. Finally, there are the philanthropists and theoreticians who can wait as long as necessary for the right time, and then alter the profession's practice in the guise of helping it.

Professions and stories may no longer have much to do with us. The claims that are made become unjustifiable, internal to the profession, and unstable.

There are vast differences in our attitudes toward the blind. The nature of their stigma, its severity and kind, vary substantially. We may concretely summarize what we have said so far with a quote from a study that examined the manner in which blindness is handled in a number of countries.

> These considerations suggest that the conceptions of stigma contained in professional ideologies are only partly determined by empirical knowledge derived from direct experiences with and scientific studies of stigmatized people . . . . The meanings

of stigma that experts construct are deeply influenced by values, attitudes, and beliefs that are central to the society. These values affect the expert in several ways: they are a part of the language he uses to express his meanings; they are an integral part of the assumptive world of the culture against which the meanings of his conceptions of stigma are judged; and they are critical elements in decisions concerning the willingness of laymen to give financial support for programs.

## 12 SCIENCE AND ADVICE

Science, such as doing physics or biology, is a human activity. Scientists work on stories and tell them to each other, much like the rest of the advice in their lives. Science is also an attitude toward life and a way of thinking. A scientific argument or story will have a special tone and logic. Outsiders are tempted to think of actual scientific activity as being mathematical and formal and logical, the proper way of reporting on scientific work in journals and giving scientific explanations in textbooks—just as we give elegant retrospective reconstructions of our reasons more generally in life. But science is more like everyday advice than any esoteric or mathematical form. There are decisive experiments in science, for example, just as there are decisive facts and reasons in advice—if we choose to permit anything to be decisive. And the regularities and repetitions that scientists look for are not so very different from the regularities and repetitions in our ordinary lives. So-called law-like formulations of our knowledge are only one way to describe regularities. We wake up each day roughly on time; we conduct ourselves consistently and repetitively; we stay in character.

Science arises out of a particular kind of advice-giving. In modern times we want to tell universal stories about the mundane and material world, while at other times we have told universal stories about the heavenly and spiritual. Science has replaced theology as the province of the universal.

Advice depends on the community to which we belong, and on the common sense we have about the world. We refer to that common sense when we try to bring each other along so that we may come to agreement. We can make up a scientific story in advice if we can systematize this common sense into what seem like universal patterns and make those patterns explicit in our stories. But how does advice, which at first seems so different from science, become a scientific activity such as physics?

The activity of science, as an ideal, represents a commitment to universal understanding, a natural ontology, causal models and quantitative abstraction, and an instrumental orientation. But advice, in general, is concerned with the particular situation we are in, is oriented around persons in a community, is based on historical and narrative models, and has expressive as well as instrumental purposes. Now actual science, as practiced, embodies its ideal, but taking into account individual capabilities and idiosyncracies, political and social constraints, and economic limitations. Because of these constraints and limitations, actual science becomes a form of advice. Science is the special kind of advice-giving for situations where we can get away with a universal law replacing the particular, where the stories and narratives may look like mathematics, where the personhood of the actors may be comparatively ignored, and where our expressive urges can be made to look practical.

Science may be described in terms of advice. Science requires a relationship of persons who do science in a community with a basis in the world which they find out about and make sense of, and who understand our situation and what is important about it. Science is no solitary activity. In doing science, persons give advice to each other. A scientist telling a scientific story is playing a political role, saying which are the important features of the world. And personal interest and biography influence which problems get explored in science. Actual science requires these advice-like properties. Otherwise, who would do it and how would they decide what to do? Science, like advice, requires ambiguity, conflict, politics, and subjectivity, even if it denies this under the veil of universal truth.

But if doing science arises from an advice-like activity, scientific explanations are such that we can delineate situations where the personal interactions characteristic of advice are not so manifestly important to the final outcome. Science may be objectified, at least part of the time, with no loss. The goings on of persons in a scientific community do not directly affect what we could explain about atoms or pith balls or even trees, although the scientific theory and what we choose to explain is a product of those goings on. Scientific stories that we offer as explanations are quite special because they can seem to depend on no particular persons. They depend on the whole community. The community supports those stories and does not dissent from them, at least for a while.

In advice-giving in general, we cannot afford the fiction that advice does not depend on who is asking for it. But science has selected out those situations in which the fiction works well enough. The questions we ask come in a very stylized form; the situations we are concerned with are sharply defined; the answers we offer can be only of a certain sort. But this fiction holds up only when the science is well understood. In its early stages, if I read the historians correctly, science looks even more like ordinary advice.

Let us look more closely at scientific stories. To recall, we tell stories and invent technologies about the extraordinary situations in which we need to figure out what to do. Just when our usual modes of understanding what to do fail us, telling stories lets us articulate where we are. We want to preserve the potentially saving ambiguities, wild guesses, and fantasies, at least until we know what to cut out. We need not have a single universal story, since each of us can comfortably hold different stories that need only mesh at the edges, at least for a while. Our typical and sensible stories make use of this room to explore alternatives and leave space for human choice and action.

A well-established science will try to tell a single, coherent, universal story. The story will be less roomy than the usual one we tell in advice. But there is a rich metaphoric content in most scientific theories that suggests how they can become more articulated and complex. They depend on everyday pictures and models, and so the stories are actually much less universal than they look. Still, science must tell a trustworthy story about us that says what to do in a convincing and confirmable way. If a universal science has no explicit room for persons, its ideal still requires the actual community of persons to advise each other, to test findings, and to agree that they are universal. (That community could even represent a universal Godly truth, embodied in particular persons.)

Sometimes we may adopt a scientific story when we give advice outside the scientific arena. Scientific stories are powerful, although they are limited in range and wide open on their flanks. But it is not only their power but their relevance to our problems that makes them attractive. Scientific stories deal with important parts of our lives and may affect what we would think possible biologically or physically, for example. Historical studies show that scientific stories reflect our ordinary life and problems projected into the cultural form called science. Scientific stories are metaphoric transformations of our ordinary stories. Persons naturally borrow back stories from science and adapt them to advice.

A scientific story may not be appropriate for advice in our situation. Its relevance and appropriateness are automatically checked by the scientist when he does science and follows its protocols. But in more general advice these stories may be like wealthy visiting relatives who do not know how to draw well water. Their universal parentage and powerful origins do not guarantee their compatibility with what we want to do. And there is no reason to believe that the scientific claims should receive attention over political or economic claims.

An institutionalized profession would rather tell scientific stories than ordinary ones. Scientific stories may be presented as if they were logically true, independent of particular persons. They seem to remove the risks inherent in the usual claims to professional usefulness and competence. Now sometimes a profession can tell scientific stories, or we can surrogate for trust a notion of rational expectation of benefit. This is so attractive that it is not surprising that a profession would want a fully scientific theoretical basis for what it does. As long as it could ignore the fact that science depends on a scientific community, the profession could forget its foundation in a relationship of persons who ask for and give advice to each other. The profession could act autonomously.

However, un-personal universal scientific stories do not work in general. A scientific basis for advice should structure its stories and say when that scientific basis might not be applicable, when things are too wild. But persons who ask for and give advice can step out of the ordinary situations of their lives, and risk becoming monstrous. When they do step out, there seems to be no science available that will work, that will make advice scientific in these extraordinary situations. Science knows very little of the monstrous—by its nature.

Ordinary advice looks strange from the point of view of science because it so explicitly depends on a relationship of persons. It seems unclear and unsure. But that is the way things are. Advice is what we do. It is a sensible way of coping with a situation that is unclear, unsure, or not immediately like ones we have been in before—or so it seems. Science may be helpful at these times, but it is not the only or best way of coping. Trust and rational expectations for benefit are not interchangeable.

Scientific procedures of advice-giving are helpful for delineating some of what is known about the world and for tending to a body of knowledge. Sometimes they shake up our conceptions. But science is a less than helpful form of advice in the middle ground, where our problems are not well defined. Science is concerned with problems that most people most of the time do not care about. If people care enough, then science is directly subject to our larger community's politics and stories. It then becomes un-scientific, and not universal.

Persons tell the best stories they can, relevant to what is going on, as well supported by the current universal understanding as they can make them. They tell the stories to others, who must understand them and judge their trustworthiness. When those stories are taken to be just that—stories told by persons—advice can make sense.

## Understanding with Others

*We are tempted to think of knowledge as detached from the persons who understand the world. We desire something beyond our selves. But knowledge without persons is of limited value in advice. In fact, our understanding of the world is expressed in imperfect but adequate narrative stories, roomy enough to accommodate us.*

*Still, it is remarkable that some of the time we can tell more general stories that seem to be good enough for advice. And, conversely, even though the less general stories we usually tell are imperfect and manifestly filled with lacunae, they still work. I describe how we use our understanding in advice so that these two extremes are possible.*

*Our judgments about what we ought to do depend on the stories we tell about our situation. We can make those stories quite un-personal and get away with it, as stories based on universal rules with simplified pictures of the world, or stories that apply some general laws to a specific situation. And then our judgments will seem scientific and objective. We can tell un-personal stories as long as we realize that they do not always work, and that it is persons who recognize when they fail.*

13 UNDERSTANDING IN ADVICE

In giving advice, persons develop and tell a trustworthy story about us. Their authority for doing so comes from the trust others place and re-place in them, not from God or science or some empirical studies, although all of these may be important. When advice fails, it is a failure of the persons in advice: of trusting mutuality, of rational verisimilitude, and of public understanding. The claims persons make risk being unfulfilled, and they accept that. How else could they tell stories that are believed to be trustworthy, in situations that are also claimed to be potentially extraordinary? We are able to live our lives in these situations and judge them by our selves.

This is what we do in advice. But it is easy to misconstrue what goes on when we seek advice. We forget the situation we are in and the persons who we are. Then we tend to ask: How can we be sure that we are right? What do you know that absolutely qualifies you to give advice? Knowledge tends to be separated from the persons who know it and use it. We create an apparatus for checking and confirming certainty and truthfulness of knowledge (and not so much the persons involved) in order to test our advice. Formal, mechanical systems for testing knowledge resolve the problems that come up in advice. Advice becomes *un-dramatic*, lacking in persons, in roles relating to each other, in a story that defines them and their world. Advice now comes to depend mainly on systematic, technical, true and verified knowledge.

But even if knowledge is treated as advice's most fundamental component, advice need not ignore the moral and political dimensions in giving private and public account of our lives. Knowledge of the good and the right and the true may be pursued systematically and technically, especially when we act as theorists and philosophers, although those roles may make it difficult for us to actually give advice. But we may be able to do better, to step back and reflect on those values as persons, and as advisors figure out what to do according to them. Advice can then be dramatic and personal as well as concerned with knowledge, surety, and truth. There is a conventional distinction between knowledge as being technically informed about facts and truth (*technē*), and knowledge as being aware of or understanding the meaning of something and its implications (*epistēmē*). Advice bridges this distinction, for the facts are always facts in a story.

When advice breaks down, understanding becomes in part a matter of abstract scientific knowledge. But insofar as advice is dramatic, understanding is situational and rich, rather than abstracted and thin. We can better appreciate this distinction when we know more about the kinds of understanding we have when we ask for and give advice.

## 14 THE QUALITIES OF UNDERSTANDING

Our understanding of who we are and what we might do is the foundation for the advice we seek and give. We understand our potentialities and how we might realize them. The persons who participate in advice have that understanding, and through their actions they make actual what we understand as possible for us. They want to affect the world purposefully and intentionally, but their understanding and their capacities for action are limited. They do not know just when and where their understanding of the world becomes a less than adequate guide in figuring out what to do, even if they are on solid ground most of the time. There are misunderstandings, and we may learn new things that alter how we understand what we are up to.

Our understanding of the world is expressed in a style we use when we tell stories and write history and literature. It is a generous style and so in the middle of the story we may shift to algebra and then back to a more conventional narrative. The narratives and stories come in generic forms and what we might call archetypal plots. We select one (or find ourselves using one) and then make it specific and articulated enough so that it helps to explain what we are doing and why.

When we give advice, we exhibit our understanding by the stories we tell to work on the problems we find ourselves in. Our understanding is an understanding, as well, of the meaning of our situation for other persons, persons who are like us. Our stories exhibit that understanding, too. Most of the time we know what to do and what is likely to happen. We have been brought up more or less properly to be members of this community and this world. But we need not be perfectly knowledgeable. Problems are difficult and imprecise in their statement. Usually we do not have a guaranteed-to-work way of thinking about what we are doing and guaranteed procedures that go with that mode of thinking, but our way of going about in the world need not be so demanding. We make guesses and trials. We patch up and make sense of what happens as we need to. We have some tried-and-true ways of going about things that have worked for us in the past. Also, persons are aware of how they work on problems and tell stories, and they try to improve their methods and their rhetoric. They know that some of the time their armamentarium is incomplete, insufficient to resolve the problems we come upon. So they keep on working.

Social scientists have tried to describe this use of our incomplete understanding for solving problems in advice. They say that we have heuristics, useful but unsure rules for figuring out what to do. Still, rules conceived in this vein tend to look like scientific laws or logical systems, rather than like biblical commandments or everyday life's catechisms. But our understanding may not be expressed economically and explicitly, with high deductive power and generality, or logically completely, as we might hope for from some formal scientific set of rules. It may be a mixed bag, as it is for actual science, that includes hints, standard operating procedures, and archetypal cases.

In advice, understanding is not necessarily a matter of economy, explicitness, sureness, completeness, or generality—the ideal of a parsimonious science. This list would be a poor aesthetic for stories and histories, which must be commodious and comfortable enough for persons to fit into. Rather, our understanding must be appropriate to the situation and problem we face. We want a rich, generous, and open, yet specific story that we would understand. One that might mix in as they are needed the findings of a parsimonious science without pretending that they are the whole story.

Our understanding of what we are up to is sometimes exhibited in intuition or wisdom. Both show themselves when we work on a particular problem in a particular situation, rather than as more generalized or absolute knowledge. And both depend on a person having them—a person *has* good intuition—rather than on being somehow objectively there.

Intuition is not mystical. It is exhibited when "an individual approaches a new and inexplicit problem, and solves it without the aid of what would be considered to be adequate information. In this process, the thinker or problem solver is seen to draw on his store of knowledge, experience, and habits, to vary these, to carry out covert and even unconscious trial and error behavior." Archetypes and instantial cases, if we have a rich enough set of them, make for good intuitive power. They help to fill in the inadequacies in our particular knowledge and our general laws. A person must be able to use these cases and appreciate when a case is sufficiently close to the question at hand that it may be applied. One way of thinking about good expert advisors is that they are good at selecting the relevant cases. A more experienced person can more effectively explore the available possibilities and choose from among them.

Wisdom is a holistic appreciation of the significance of what there is in the world. The sense of balance, of proportion, and of the way things seem to go comes with maturity. It depends on an accumulation of past experiences that leads to a richer understanding. Wisdom centers not on information and technique, but on the meaning of information and the consequences of technique. Wisdom is not easily transferred to others, for it is a personal quality dependent on having lived a particular life, your own. Stories are often used to convey wisdom.

While it is hard to make a person wise, it seems possible to develop intuition in another. We can tell someone how we think intuitively, and so act as a model. Natural scientists develop good intuition in their students. Students begin to think as if they were a speeding electron. This does not come solely or mainly from systematic studies. Imitation of the teacher is crucial. That both student and teacher are persons seems to be a condition for imitation to be possible and successful. They know the other is like me, and they appreciate each other and so understanding is possible. They share a world.

Persons with good intuition or wisdom are among those who are said to exhibit good judgment. In advice-giving we use our understanding to make judgments of our situation. A judge evaluates various statements and stories concerning a situation. Are they true and relevant? Which are the significant or interesting points? What story can he tell that reflects his judgment? Studies of judgment in clinical and legal situations, as well as in literary and art criticism, often try to find characteristics of situations that predict the stories and the ultimate judgments we make. Might it be possible to design a set of criteria that we could check off and so predict judgments, including judgments of the best outcome? Sometimes, especially when the situation is defined narrowly and well, good predictors of judgment can be found. But when advice is most crucial, the predictors usually are not so good. For then our situation is not so well defined; that is why we sought advice in the first place. There is often no final judgment, but only a sequence of revisions. And the story we tell depends on the judgment we want to make. If our judgment requires trust, complex stories, and a rich understanding of who we are, we seem to be outside the range where the check-off criteria are so helpful. In fact the criteria can become monstrous, ignoring what is most important about a situation in order to have a neat description of it.

Many models of how understanding works in advice try to exclude capacities specific to persons, such as intuition or wisdom, aiming instead for a more explicitly (and perhaps mathematically) expressible picture. But these models seem to be inadequate for just those situations when advice is most needed. In particular, they tend to exclude two aspects of being a person. First, understanding (like a claim, which it is) is exhibited by and resides in persons, and not in the object or in the situation that advice is about. A person's apprehension of what is going on in advice depends on what he is doing, what he is up to. The meanings we derive from our observations and exhibit in our understanding depend on the way we organize what we have seen and what we now see. Since persons will have different organizations of their understanding of a situation—they are up to different projects—we might expect that there are no general ways of systematically ordering the understanding we have in advice.

But our understanding of a situation cannot be so idiosyncratic that others do not recognize the claims we make. Trust will not bridge absolute incomprehension or a sense that another person completely misconstrues what is up. We do have a shared history of similar situations that we can recall together, and so we can make sense together and reconfirm that our trust in one another is reasonable.

It turns out that much of the time we can have general notions that are applicable to a large number of situations. Still, a person must understand just when they do not apply, when the situation is out of hand, out of the ordinary.

The second aspect of being a person that is often excluded when advice is most needed is that understanding makes sense only in a community. The social and political context and the common sense that is accepted as "the way things are" limit the kind of doubts that persons express. A claim will be accepted as a claim if it follows naturally from the common sense that we share. A story need not be impervious to all doubt, for only some claims are likely to be challenged. It can be vague or even wrong in part without being poor or useless.

Some advisors are more experienced and expert, and claim their judgment is superior to others', which is based merely on the common sense. The different and differentiated lives we lead are the basis for this specialness. Access to experience is controlled by class and status requirements, and racial and sexual prerequisites, and professional rules reinforce the differences. The differences create the esoteric, and so the justification for some to assert that they ought regulate access. Thereby they maintain their esoteric knowledge.

We shall be especially concerned with the claims of experts who say they understand us. These claims are reasonable if understood properly. But when we deny or ignore the fact that it is persons who make those claims, then we wonder how knowledge is applied, rather than how understanding is exhibited.

## 15 UN-PERSONAL MODELS OF UNDERSTANDING

We are always tempted to create explanatory models of what we do that employ a simplified notion of a person. A person is like a logical system, or a computer, or an expressive non-human animal, for example. This is often a fruitful strategy, but sometimes it unduly limits the models or makes them ineffective just when they are most needed. What we are up to when we ask for and give advice has been modeled in a number of these simpler ways, which, although powerful, turn out to be filled with inadequacies. In each case, we find that some of the inadequacies of a model are generated by its exclusion of full-bodied persons. As we have seen before, adding on a bit of personhood as a patch-up may not help. We shall examine two such models, one that assumes that our understanding is based on some (innate) systematic universal rules, and that we may usefully simplify complex situations, and one that treats understanding as a matter of applying a more abstract theory. Each model has essential difficulties in linking its simplified picture with the actual advice-giving situation we are in—unless we say that the persons in the models know when to apply the rules, how they are relevant, and when they probably do not fit, and then of course the models are no longer so simple.

By analogy with the simplicity of the fundamental physical laws compared to the complex variety of the natural world, we might hope that we can give some deep underlying rules for what we do and expect that the complexities of life would derive from the application of these rules in varied ways. Chomsky has argued, for example, that the apparent complexities of natural language hide some simple and general underlying universal rules that are embedded in our cortices. Could we use such an approach to account for the understanding we exhibit when we give advice? We would have to account for trust, self-doubt, and tragic failure, which are crucial to advice-giving, as well as for straightforward knowledge of the world. But systems of universal rules seem to be less adequate in accounting for trust than for arithmetic. So we might wonder if we can account for understanding in advice in these terms.

The understanding that makes it possible for us to ask for or give advice depends on an accumulation of experience. But how does the accumulation take place? What is the adding machine in our lives? How do we learn? It seems that we develop through already-there models around which experience is articulated and so comes to make sense. When we are born we have the capacity to get along in a world largely defined by mother. Through formative experiences our models become more complex and adequate. As we get older, we develop methods for self-consciously improving our models and we search out experiences that will enhance both the models and the methods so that we can do what we want to do.

We might be able to describe these processes in terms of quite general, formal, and seemingly universal rules, rules for learning, listening, and telling stories. As I have said, we are tempted to create the kind of rules that do not depend on the relationship of persons that makes for trust in advice-giving. We want universal un-personal rules. We want a kind of explicit rule that we sense must exist in the heaven of mathematics or physics, one that is as general as possible, not particularistic or situation-dependent.

But rules function in a community trained to follow them, to question them when appropriate, and to realize that they sometimes fail spectacularly. These contextual factors make the un-personal and universal rules personal and particular. There is a trade-off between rules' generality and universality and their ability to account for the context in which they are used. When we abstract away from the advice's interactions, we need only a comparatively small number of rules to generate the stories we might tell. (In fact, such rules turn out to be useful for describing the structure of narratives, especially the more formulaic ones found in folktales.) But it is much harder, under this abstract regime, to account for our understanding of why a particular context demands a certain kind of response. We understand a situation because we recognize its structure according to rules, but how do we recognize a situation?

The community and "we" aspects of advice are expressed in how we follow and understand these common universal rules that we share. We make claims and counterclaims on each other about their meaning. The rules, the story, and the appropriateness of engaging in advice-giving are all up for grabs when we are giving advice, although most of the time we do not contest them all at once. Universal rules need our understanding of them if they are to apply to tragic failures, the cases you thought you understood, the ones you did not expect to be absolutely wrong about. Otherwise each failure challenges your whole understanding of the world. For under the regime of universal rules, exceptions destroy the rules. But under the regime that says, ordinarily, for the most part, you know what to do and how to handle exceptions, how to get around some and ignore others—there is room for you to say as well that you are not sure of what to do in all cases. Most of the time you can manage, for you do understand most ordinary situations. Persons learn from experience, recognize situations as similar ones, know why we are like each other, and manage and deal with errors and failures.

This picture has none of the elegance and simplicity of a proper mathematical formalism. But it does permit us to concern ourselves with context, situation, persons in relation, expectations, and particular facts. We put the persons back into the rules we need for understanding in advice. Still, our understanding may not be so complex as it first may seem. Complex situations may sometimes be epitomized by a small number of features, and our advice may follow from a comparatively straightforward examination of those features.

Being a person depends on having and learning specific substantive knowledge of one's own community, and recognizing other persons and the important aspects of life. Mechanical models, such as those used for artificial intelligence programs, tend to need these recognition and substantive capacities as they become more adequate.

Advice is not only a matter of having an understanding. It also requires that we apply what we understand to a particular situation. Actually, we demonstrate our understanding of our situation as we use it to figure out what to do. "Having" and "applying" go together. Sometimes we think of knowledge or understanding as just sitting there waiting to be applied. We confuse objects in which we put the memoranda we need to act knowledgeably, such as books, with understanding itself. But still it might make sense to speak of applying our knowledge when we move to a new area from one in which our understanding has developed naturally. As an example, let us examine a model of how theoretical scientific knowledge informs policymaking.

A practitioner, such as a physician or an applied social scientist, can effectively translate scientific theory into practice. The basis for his knowledge and understanding includes professional creeds, case studies, rules of thumb, technical modes of description, and scientific laws that he might apply. The basis is only partly scientific. We apply scientific laws by first performing an exploratory inquiry, then developing an understanding of the problem, then conducting a confrontation wherein the practitioner explains his understanding of the problem to the client, then discovering solutions, and then giving scientific advice. A competent practitioner is a problem solver who consults with clients to make sure that he understands their problem and then tries to explain his solution to them.

The give-and-take of advice-giving is converted into consultation and translation. Storytelling and understanding become problem solving and explaining. Some of the time this abstract reduction of advice-giving is just what we ought to be doing. But if the problem is controversial or the theory is not well established, this picture cannot fairly account for what we do. For then the nature of the problem is what is to be contested, and the solution is not at all clear and authoritatively known. Persons, who engage in the give-and-take of advice and who tell stories to each other so as to work out their problems, are needed to enhance this model so that it is sufficiently realistic.

The model must also say more about how we make use of case studies and rules of thumb. We recall these cases and rules in generic stories that allow us to understand our situation in their terms. We solve a problem by analogy, by telling a good story and claiming that it is a reasonable way of thinking about what we are doing. Of course, even when we apply theoretical scientific laws we are telling a story, claiming they are reasonable and relevant. It is not surprising that the laws should be applicable—at least no more so than the case studies and rules of thumb. The theory itself arose out of problematic situations, involving exploratory inquiries, picking out crucial features of a situation and relating these to previous theoretical understanding. The scientific laws should have an intimate connection with the situations we are concerned with in advice. That is where they came from. But we need persons who understand our situation, whom we may trust, and who can tell good stories, to show us the theory's intimate relationship to our situation.

The un-personal models I have sketched—universal laws and applying science—are less than adequate for explaining how our understanding of the world works in advice-giving. What is relevant to a problem? When is it extraordinary? What is applicable to this situation? In sufficiently narrow areas, these models are helpful. They provide a neat picture of understanding. But we are tempted to forget that the picture is no longer about advice, but about simplified, less problematic situations, not like ones we often engage in inadvice.

## Coming to Agreement

*While we may have come to agree in the past, when advice is called for we often discover that we differ and we must find a way to come to agreement again. Those past processes of agreement and argument have shaped us and we know how to continue enacting them. So our coming to agree will be a matter of our interacting together in advice. Bargaining is a model of coming to agree that is both procedural and rational. It is a way of acting together that is committed to developing effective and true stories. But we are tempted by un-personal models of coming to agree, models that control our interactions so as to avoid undue personal influence and that treat us as isolated individuals who never agreed before. These undramatic models include Delphi methods and statistical decision theories. But when we improve them to make them more realistic, they begin to look more like personal advice—a path we have seen before. We have to be persons in advice to know how to use these simplified models and to know when they lead us astray.*

*We can train people to bargain more effectively and to tell better stories. But the stories still depend on our human capacities to understand them. For example, syndromes are stories that must be in a form that physicians can relate to the patients they encounter and the therapies they employ. Considering the usual complexities of advice, it is still possible to have these fairly fixed universal abstractions that we are at home with.*

*Truth is needed for advice, and there are technologies that make it more likely that we give true advice. Again it is interesting that the truth may sometimes appear in a universal form, such as science. But looked at more closely, as we have earlier, science turns out to be more like everyday advice than any of the ideal pictures presented of it.*

*Finally, I argue that advice is real, that we actually do engage in mutual interaction as persons. Larger cultural and economic forces will set limits on what advice we engage in, but it is a property of advice that it rearranges those limits as well.*

16 CONFLICT AND SHARED UNDERSTANDING

Persons will find that within their community their understanding of what to do will eventually conflict with that of others, even though they have come to agreement before.

One way we work this out is to ask for or give advice, and try to bring others over to our side. This process should reveal errors in the conflicting views, shore up the weak points in each story, invoke foundations of trust, and remind others of the public understanding we take to be among us. We limit the time allowed for working on conflict, for the exploration of claims and counterclaims. We always have something to do and the limit is part of that. The conflict and our working on it reflects how persons live their lives together. So not only must we come to agreement again, we must agree on time, creating and dissolving deadlines as we need to.

The conflict about what we understand is unavoidable if we go on living together. Rarely can we coherently add up what each of us understands, and come to a common claim the group or community might make. Usually we have to thrash it out.

We could avoid thrashing it out by having a group of non-overlapping specialists, each of whom trusts the others. They complement, rather than interact with, each other. There is effectively only one legitimate expert claimant at any time. But specialists do not act this way. They argue over borderline cases, they want dominance over other specialists, they do not trust each other. In part they do not know each other's turf well enough to know if it is being properly cared for. And in part, specialties are rarely so sharply separated from each other, so specialists will naturally conflict.

In an organization, the process of public confirmation of what is claimed, the consensual agreement to act as if something were the case, involves more than people agreeing individually that something is so. The consequences for the organization, and the relative positions and relationships of people within it, will influence the process. We may be able to create fairly separable islands of belief and understanding within the organization. An island retains its cohesiveness partly on the basis of the beliefs its members share that are exclusive of the rest of the group. So the structure of the organization will affect the degree to which a claim is shared. Coming to agree is an organizational and political process, and rarely are our islands stable.

We may not be able to come to agree. Conflicts may be unresolvable if we are so polarized in our positions that we share no common ground, or if to give in to the other has no saving graces. In actuality, having no common ground or saving graces means we cannot tell a story that accommodates all of us. Sometimes that may be so. Yet we know that members of a community share cognitive styles and experiences to some extent. Their differences may be better described in terms of what they share, than by starting out with their individual positions and then seeing if they have some common ground. We have been brought up in a community and our common sense about the world is no mere coincidence. We can come to agree when we engage in advice-giving because we agree for the most part already. Individual positions are drawn from our common ground.

Conflicts are unavoidable in a community. We must live together and we do differ. But it is also in a community that we share enough to resolve our conflicts in a satisfying way, and so we are able to live together. In effect, conflicts we work on among ourselves affirm that to a large extent we share an understanding of what to do, even if we differ in certain areas. Through conflict we come to realize there are claims that we understand yet we would not make, and hence our own understanding of the world and the claims we make about it may also be understood but not assented to.

Our work on a particular conflict within a community can result in a new shared understanding, the ending of our need for advice for the moment, and in our going on together. Each conflict and each occasion for advice has preceding ones in which we have had to relate to each other as persons in a conflict-filled, necessarily shared story about who we are, and then try to figure out how to go on together. Our current claims in advice are based on past claims and how we have resolved them.

So advice may be said to be historical and dramatic. It depends on what we have done before, what we have said, and the kinds of persons we have become. It depends on what we have done together, what we have said to each other, what situations we have been in. We play full-bodied characters in relationship to each other. Conflicts concerning advice are not merely disagreements about what to do, but whole scenes that must be played out as we figure out just how we disagree and what we might still do. Positions are not fixed or determined ahead of time.

Pictures of advice-giving outside of a dramatic context seem strange. They have difficulties not unlike the ones we have already examined for roles and problems. But it is possible to sketch pictures of conflict in advice that are both simple and helpful in understanding what we do when we conflict.

## 17 DRAMATIC MODELS

How do we come to agreement? Sometimes we bargain with each other. We make exchanges, up the ante, give and take. We need not be exchanging goods or monetary equivalents of them. We may be hammering out an agreement in a labor negotiation or in a joint communiqué. Even when we sketch abstracted models of bargaining, as in a mathematical theory of strategy, we must have ways of representing crucial qualities of persons, such as trust and distrust, and the previous history of the bargainers.

One disturbing aspect of bargaining as a way of coming to agreement is that if we believed there were a truth, then bargaining seems like a poor way of getting there since one seems to have to give up part of the truth to come to agreement. But it turns out that even in scientific research of the most theoretical sort, most participants have to come to provisional agreements, and so they may well be giving up an aspect of the truth in order to continue their work. Only a few are so independent that they pursue their own path without appreciating and acceding to the strengths of other approaches. And there is no reason to believe that the holdouts will do better in the end than the compromisers.

Hegel appreciated this problem because he knew that in our ordinary mundane actions we seem to sacrifice the absolute and concrete truth for the abstracted particulars of the moment. But he also believed that the truth reveals itself in time, that our compromises seem to serve the interests of the truth almost despite ourselves. He called this the cunning of reason. As for Adam Smith and his invisible hand, the order of the world depends on individual actors who in acting out their own little dramas seem to fulfill a much higher purpose. One does not have to share this divine belief to appreciate our capacity for recovering a coherent strand of truth and meaning from our various actions, whether it be in history or science, and so reconciling ourselves to our own lives.

More mundanely, let us return to bargaining as a way of coming to agreement. Analytical descriptions of bargaining have been useful in thinking about what we ought to do. In bargaining, "the ability of one participant to gain his ends is dependent to an important degree on the choices or decisions that the other person will make." We can describe how interactions and influence occur, and how setting up a problem in one way precludes a whole set of other ways of thinking about it. The range of behaviors in bargaining includes feigning, secrecy, threats, arbitration, mediation, and even mutually acceptable bargains. Since we are tempted to think of advice in much more benign, less conflict-ridden terms, a model of advice-giving as bargaining can make us aware that the stakes are large some of the time, and under an umbrella of trust we can play hardball.

In advice-giving persons bargain about their differences and especially about how to understand what's up and what is up for grabs. We might think the advisor controls the situation, and he has such inordinate power that there could be no fair bargaining. That may be true. But advisors must deal with those who consult them, fully realizing that the advisee may ignore them or go to others. And professional advisors do need their clients. Hence the process of coming to agree can be, and I believe ought to be, much more a matter of an equal mutual interaction than we usually assume.

Why should persons bargain, rather than ignore each other? They have no choice. They must go on together; they conflict; and bargaining is a way working on that. Advice takes place under these auspices too.

What is the currency or barter persons exchange with each other? In advice-giving it is the bargainer's personal commitment to his claims. When people bargain in advice they are dealing in their selves and statuses, their reputations and the esteem in which they are held by others in the community. Say we assume that we are what economists call rational actors. Then bargaining, besides resolving conflict, provides one means of converting personal understanding and a sense about the world, into socially determined rates of risk. These rates of risk concerning the likelihood that some advice will lead in an appropriate direction become the surrogates for advice's truthfulness.

If someone were to bargain with his life when he is about to be shot, we might doubt his assessment of the situation. Authentic bargaining requires that we have some degree of voluntary choice about when we might bargain and over what. We must have the option not to bargain and just go away, to deal with conflict in other ways. Then our entering into a bargaining procedure suggests that we are justifiably committed to what we say. We must be able to put our reputations up for grabs. We must be able to be responsible for what we say. We must be able to respect others, and they us, as persons in our community.

Bargaining is a way that persons can work on the conflicts we come upon in advice-giving. But how is a particular position built up into a coherent whole that is potentially convincing and effective? We need to create stories that others will believe, that reflect our understanding of the world, that cash in on the trust we share with others and the evidence all of us have in common. The story, our way of describing what we are up to, is rhetorical. It will be addressed to others who should find it appealing. It will help us pay attention to some features of what we are doing and ignore others. It will suggest proper modes of agency and causation. In coming to agreement our problem is to find a way to agree, to have a sense of common order and purpose. We might call it a problem of politics. What would be an adequate political theory from the cognitive and narrative point of view? How would we approach such a theory?

A political leader creates a story that helps persons structure their experience. He draws from their stories to make his more perfect, more encompassing, more capable of attracting a wider following and gaining greater allegiance. Such a story will make it possible for persons to describe what they desire, and what has happened to them, in a way that makes them more effective and more capable of dealing with each other. The archetypes and experiences the leader emphasizes in his story must be sufficiently rich so that others can see themselves in that story, yet at the same time the story will transform how the others see themselves. The leader's story is not simply his own story, but it must be that of the group trying to come to agree about what they understand.

It may be useful to think of a political leader as a teacher trying to gain collective assent to a way of thinking about the world, a way that may not be obvious to others. The teacher develops a shared understanding of what we are up to by cueing others to significant experiences that play a primary role in the story he wants to tell. And he must show why the conventional cues may be ignored. He must emphasize that the important new features are not accounted for in the old stories. The new story and its experiential cues go together. The story makes the cues interesting and the cues give evidence for the story. Others may reject a story or tell their own, so that leaders and teachers depend on those whom they lead and teach for their authority. Students will tell better stories than their teachers and retire the teachers prematurely.

When persons come to agreement they jockey with each other to find a mutually acceptable position, but that position must have its own integrity, be logically justified, and give an account of the world that we can respect. Advice cannot be simply a matter of winning a bet, or of insisting on the unique logical force of your argument. How you win counts, and it turns out there is more than one good argument around. But we can come to agreement.

Being members of a community, we do not start out without some agreement. Each person, in his role and character, understands the general flow of the drama we enact together, and how we go on together. He knows when he is out of role or lost. At times we are not sure where we are, which stage we are on, what is up for grabs. Anxiously, we may search for a story to organize our lives, but others understand that we can be anxious. So being anxious, we are not absolutely alien even if we are unsure of where we are. Advice is that curious activity that depends on our not knowing what to do, but at some other level being quite at home with our condition, and knowing how to go about finding out what to do next. As I have said, advice is an ordinary response to the extraordinary.

Now we might try to avoid the drama I have sketched, the need for bargaining, the need to create new stories, and the risks these needs entail. To avoid the uncertainties (ones I believe we are made to manage—that is what makes us persons), we search for modes of guaranteeing understanding, of making our coming to agree automatic. Then advice-giving becomes mechanical. And, it turns out, it does not seem to work too well.

## 18 UN-DRAMATIC MODELS

In the dramatic model of coming to agree to an understanding with others, the actors have meaningful roles in their interaction with each other. They are not simply individuals given parts that they then act out, waiting their turns to do their lines. What they say depends on what has gone on already; and who they are and how they show themselves in the play depends on what others do. That is why bargaining and story creation are dramatic.

There is another tradition of analyzing how we come to agree, or, more generally, how we come to act together. We already discussed it when we looked at conflict in organizations. Start off with independent individual actors. Surely they will interact together, but let us control or specify those interactions with some care. Then identify characteristic collective behaviors dependent on these controlled interactions. The neoclassical synthesis of microeconomic theory or the physics of crystalline solids is roughly of this form. (But, in general, much of economics and physics involves cooperative and field phenomena not at first glance amenable to such an approach.) These pictures have proven extraordinarily powerful and productive, especially because of their tractable mathematical structure.

We might try for a similar approach in describing coming to agree on our understanding of what is at issue in the advice we give. Could we combine our claims in such a way that their dependence on and interaction with each other is controlled and well defined? Could we then tap into the mathematical formalism that has developed for handling such interaction? To some extent the answer is yes.

The Delphi method for combining the wisdom of experts is an interesting form of controlled bargaining and story creation. A series of questions is asked of a panel of experts. They indicate their answers, giving both an estimate of the answer, and perhaps an estimate of its error. The manager of the Delphi exercise then combines the panel's answers, averaging them in some way, to obtain a measure of the mean answer and its dispersion. The manager may formulate new questions on a second round, if that seems appropriate as indicated by the answers and suggestions of the panel.

The manager feeds the questions and the panel's averaged first responses back to the panel, and asks each expert to re-estimate his own answer to each of the questions. It is expected that the differences between panel members, revealed to each member as a result of the first round, will cause a member to take the difference into account in his second estimate. He may rethink his way of coming to the initial answer he gave.

The Delphi method controls bandwagon effects, illuminates differences of opinion, and suggests modes of coming to agreement. If we can set up our differences in terms of this kind of schedule of questions, and if the coding of the answers is fair, it just might work. But if we differ very substantially in how to approach the problem or if we need to personally confront each other, then Delphi will not speak to us.

The manager of the Delphi exercise intervenes between the panelists. There is no direct personal interaction among them. This is considered desirable since it is felt that personal influence and prestige may get in the way of more adventuresome or unorthodox answers. But from the perspective of an ideal of advice-giving (think here of Plato or Machiavelli, too), personality and commitment are the foundation for proposing claims that are out of the ordinary. Delphi methods are distinctly helpful, it seems, when we do not have a relationship of persons who are like me, but rather a relationship denominated and dominated by power that prevents our making claims.

Where do the stories used to compose a Delphi exercise come from? How are they put together? To a large extent they come from the common knowledge in an area as synthesized by the manager. So we must provisionally trust the manager to produce an effective and fair set of questions, although the respondents can reject questions and change the tenor of the exercise if the Delphi stories are insufficiently flexible to encompass what they understand, and if they are belligerent enough.

Where do the stories come from in a drama? The Delphi participants come to the exercise already in role with their own powerful interests and their own cogent stories about what's up. The playwright (or manager) gives us the script, but the actors give us the story. The actors in a drama are defined by the story they enact, and they give it life.

Say the Delphi participants directly argued with each other. And say that one person tried to steer the argument in a certain direction, "to clarify a point." The participants could address one point, then another. The moderator could deal with overbearing interlocutors and participants. There would be moments that would be unfair and the powerful would exercise inordinate control. We might want to shift to a Delphi method for a while to break that control, or we could have subtle politicking to go around it. We need not treat the effects of bias as matters that can be eradicated only by restricting our personal interaction. For by increasing that interaction we may be able to control bias as well as to clarify the personal source of advice. Claims are made by someone on others and that legitimates what we do. Making those claims explicit and public may make advice fairer and more encompassing of a wider view of ourselves.

Statistical decision theory provides a procedure that further disentangles and formalizes the mutual influence of experts, yet permits them to schematically indicate their personal commitment to and belief in a direction for action. Experts estimate the likelihood of particular events' taking place and say how much they would bet on their estimates. These bets will depend on the financial consequences of each outcome (to the expert or to his client), as well as on the expert's certainty in his probability estimates. For a group that wishes to come to agreement there is a set of systematic procedures for combining these probabilities and bets to obtain a most likely set of probabilities. One can also derive a betting strategy that should give the largest returns. This method explicitly takes into account the expert's commitment.

A simple case would be a parimutuel system, which assumes that all the bettors are expert to a degree weighted only by the amount of their bets. The odds at any time will determine, in part, future betting behavior. In this sense, experts' judgments are pooled and indexed. This system would be sensible if bets were proportional to actual knowledge, which might occur in a long-term equilibrium by eliminating irrational actors, the ones who do not know a horse. But the interactions are meager, and that too leads to paradoxes and surprises.

An example may suggest some of the potential difficulties: Say we have a group of experts, each of whom is asked to choose between situation A or situation B. Each expert makes his own independent estimate of the probability that A or B is the winner, and of the odds and what he would bet on each choice. It is possible that each expert would have different estimates of the probabilities and betting odds, and different bets, yet all would agree that they would bet on choice A. If we averaged the bets at this point (the Paretian method), we manifestly would find that the group bets on A. However, it is possible to construct plausible cases wherein if we averaged the probabilities assigned by the experts (a seemingly not unreasonable thing to do, the Bayesian approach), and then averaged the bets they would be willing to make, choice B would turn out to be the best bet.

A prisoner's dilemma situation can also develop. In this case each of the actors in a collective situation, acting in what he perceives as his own interest, is likely to end up in a position that is less advantageous to him than if he acted in others' interests. In this case, a smart expert would take into account others' betting postures, make some assumption such as that the others are smart, too, having the collective self-interest at heart, and then make a sensible bet. This is a kind of bootstraps altruism, lifting oneself out of a morass created by immediate self-interest into a world where one's self-interest is more adequately provided for, but using altruism as the initial justification. Our picture no longer has individual actors who do not take each other into account. The model becomes more dramatic as it has to deal with more complex situations.

In our actual ordinary lives the interactions between individual actors are complex and ambiguous. Actors go around the rules, anticipate feints, assume sensible group behavior on the part of the others in their community, and so forth. The dilemmas in the simple models point to the talents persons have in getting around them. (Formal mathematical models can often encompass these complexities.) These talents are just the ones that are important if advice-giving is to work. A person giving advice can talk about and change the rules, cheat on his bets, even decide he is not a betting man, without becoming less of a person. Violating some of the formal rules does not exclude you from your community.

These un-dramatic models describe institutionalized places for action, for placing bets on our claims. They transform our personal understanding and ignorance into socially appreciable claims and risks. Now, it seems as if one first has a position, and then one places a bet behind it. Unlike bargaining, where the claims we make on each other define who we are and what we say, the original positions in un-dramatic models are thought to be held without necessarily making a claim on others. This abstraction, a split between a position and its claim, has actual consequences. The trust, reasonableness (or story quality), and publicness that defines persons in advice-giving, can be reduced in these models to matters, respectively, of betting odds and stakes, consistency, and a notion of shared information. But, for example, our picture of who we are, the nature of our public life, does not seem to be adequately surrogated for by the information we share. Would we want to reduce personhood or citizenship to matters of information storage and processing? We might imagine that some of the time these formally powerful un-dramatic models would be useful for characterizing how we come to agreement, but often there is too much at stake to allow us to so simplify our picture of what we are up to.

"There is too much at stake" suggests however that sometimes we do think in terms of betting behavior, with utilitarian measures of goodness, when we try to come to agreement. In this case, "there is too much at stake" says that the alternative, no matter how efficient, would never be worth it. Some of the time the choices are quite comparable. And then we do balance outcomes and costs, and choose a most rewarding strategy given our resource limitations and constraints. Often, however, the different paths we pursue have very different rewards, and comparing them on a single scale makes no sense. Rather we choose a way of life with its good and bad parts and pursue it the best we can.

Obviously we try to learn more about what we are up to, and then modify our desires, values, and estimates of the likelihood of an outcome, by what we have learned and how well we have achieved our aims so far. So we might say that not only are we sometimes utilitarian, we are also cybernetic. But if we do think in these terms, we do so quite generously and metaphorically. So we may not be so clear or explicit or complete in specifying just what we are betting, or how we learn, or what our goods are. We change the actual specification of these to fit the situation we are in and the quality of the available calculus given the problem we face. We try not to adopt a calculus that will force us to denude our picture of our situation of its most crucial details, even if the calculus is temptingly powerful or elegant.

When we solve problems together in groups or work in coalitions, our coming to agree is characterized by the workings of personal influence, bluffing so that we take positions we do not necessarily hold, pushing in one direction to get movement in another. Histrionic ability counts, and people will sometimes cheat or lie, perhaps just a little. But we, as persons in a community, can monitor unsportsmanlike behavior, control deceit, and not be fooled all of the time. We are not always taken in by others, and of course others are suspicious of our motives too. Most of the time we can trust each other, knowing that we will recognize a false move or at least be able to think twice when one occurs. And even if we are deceived, we may eventually recover and lead an ordinary life.

An analogy might be helpful at this point. Scientists are usually deceived by magicians and psychics because they look for natural scientific means to explain tricks and what they believe are supernatural acts. They do not immediately think in terms of deception and illusion, and human means for accomplishing tricks. But another magician will always search for the most ordinary devices, such as sleight of hand or selective control of others' attention to explain an effect, rather than turn to a revision of nature's laws. The magician, much more than the scientist, is committed to human nature and the well-understood natural science of the time. Similarly, dramatic models allow for all the devices human beings tend to use when they are persons in a relationship with others. Un-dramatic models are comparatively blind to these human capacities, even if they are more elegant and computationally more precise.

Un-dramatic models have incorporated more of human device as they have become articulated. The mathematical strategy theorists are ingenious. These models try to account for human behavior with the least amount of the irrational modes. But dramatic models take those modes as fundamental. Dramatic models start out with human device already built in. The difference between the dramatic and the un-dramatic is not only logical and cognitive, but moral and political too. It is a difference between a mode of exposition that uses a style that is conventionally rational—straightforward, clear, logical—and another that uses that seemingly residual style, the non-rational—the wily, the "feminine," the political.

Un-dramatic models are powerful because they use simplified actors, but their dilemmas and inadequacies, including the ones we have discussed, derive from these un-personal actors. Advice incorporates calculation and action, but it is the story we retell and rewrite that makes advice worth doing and our understanding meaningful, a human story that makes advice-giving civic and real.

## 19 DRAMATIC TECHNOLOGIES

Dramatic methods of combining our claims to understanding and of coming to agreement show how persons change as they enact their roles, and how they remake their notions of their community and their selves as circumstance forces them to come to agreement. The un-dramatic, un-personal methods obtain agreement using calculationally powerful, but abstracted and simplified, notions of actors. It is difficult to understand how our richly understood and articulated experience plays itself out in these methods. We do know that the subtleties provided by experience are crucial in finding a way to come to agree. Un-dramatic methods are sometimes quite useful. But persons may not need these abstractions to come to agreement. To be a person in a community says that we already know how to understand things together. We bargain with and tell stories to each other, to whom we are committed and with whom we live in the community. We come to agreement because stories must make sense to others, claims can be countered, and new stories can be offered.

There are technologies that make us more effective bargainers and storytellers. Much of the mathematical theory of bargaining has been developed to understand these processes better and guide us strategically as we bargain, especially in international affairs. Schools of labor relations and arbitration train persons to be more effective actors in formal bargaining situations, just as the Sophists and the rhetoricians once had their schools.

Persons can be trained to be more effective storytellers, too. That training may come from an oral tradition and require a mastery of the rhythmic and rhetorical forms and of the major story types and myths. Or it may come from a written tradition, and that will require a mastery of the proper narrative and logical forms, suitable character development (although the "character" may only be a mathematical concept or a physical notion), and effective stylistic devices. A book on how to write a dissertation or a novel tells one quite explicitly the minimal requirements for creating an effective story. Whatever the story, the persons in it will have to have a full repertoire of human capacities and failings, and metaphorical or conceptual analogs (such as "electron") must do more or less what we expect them to do in our ordinary lives. Hence the electron as a particle has to act as would a billiard ball, and the electron as a wave must act as would a water wave. The story has to have a recognizable style, plot, and characters, all sufficiently detailed so that we can project ourselves into the story and feel at home there. Now we may decide that it is impossible for us to project ourselves into some stories because they do not make sense, or they seem contradictory or unrealistic, or they are just not good enough. These stories may be innovative in style or substance and the avant garde will suffer until it proves itself. But if the new form proves rich and fruitful it will eventually gain adherents who understand it, whether it be the novel or quantum mechanics.

One kind of story we often tell is the syndrome that describes medical disease. These stories have highly stylized forms. They depend on our assuming that the physician has a very good idea of how persons manifest health and illness, how various single factors or symptoms are likely to combine in human beings, and when a treatment may be said to be not working so that the physician does not blindly apply a therapy. The stories are too schematic to specify everything. A good physician already knows most of the usual details from the patients he has already seen. The syndrome must describe the disease in terms of a distinctive set of characteristics that other physicians will recognize, preferably a small number of characteristics that are in accord with how a physician examines and assesses a patient.

We might think it would be possible to generate all the syndromes and classify people's states of health with respect to such syndromes, using systematic combinations of the various symptoms. But most such combinations would not be realized in our actual lives. We become ill in only certain ways. Describing illness in terms of syndromes becomes useful in practice when the syndromes are archetypal disease entities that make sense to physicians, persons whom we have trained to recognize other persons in sickness and, residually, in health. Physicians know what a syndrome means in terms of diagnosis and therapy. So a syndrome is a rhetorical device, a way of addressing physicians, that permits them to understand what is going on. A syndrome is not a list of properties but a situation, a running together of those properties in which we, as professionals, clients, and relevant others, play our roles.

Archetypes and myths are similar to syndromes. The myth becomes a way of accounting for what happens and of telling us who we are and what we are to do. Yet at the same time it is a synthesis of what people know, historically and personally, and it is a way of talking about and improving that knowledge.

It may turn out that certain syndromes and myths are so structurally uniform that we can explicitly specify the cues or indexes that persons use to recognize the meaning of a complex of properties. A warm forehead means a fever, and tragedies usually end with the demise of a character we call the hero. This capacity for cues should be especially robust if the myths and syndromes have been around for a long time, and uniformities and redundancies (biological and cultural) have developed to facilitate communication. As I have mentioned, when we analyze the structure of folktales and oral narratives, we find they have formal logical structures that are so well specified that we might believe the structures especially suit our cognitive and emotional apparatus. So stories may not be simply orderly confections, but confections that are in accord with how we live our lives, and some stories are so much in that accord that we can take them to heart and be at home with them.

It may be helpful to have another example of something we put together so we can be at home with it. Designed objects often are confections of uniform or standard parts, but the objects then acquire an integrity so that we think of them as having their own wholeness. That wholeness may be cued or recognized not by any single one of the original parts or a simple combination of them. The object has become unto itself. Now, designers produce a thing to do a set of tasks. They have to synthesize in order to fulfill the requirements of the design. The distinctive methods they use involve breaking down a problem into sub-problems and then, by selecting from sets of stock answers for the sub-problems, putting together a working design. An overall conception, chosen from a stock of overall conceptions, guides the breaking down process and the selection of stock answers. The process is sequential, since the solution to a current sub-problem depends on the preceding solutions. It is also tentative, in that a particularly difficult sub-problem may force rejection of solutions chosen for already-solved sub-problems. Stylized, straightforward sub-problems will alternate with ones that in their development require great invention and advice-like consultation with others. We have to come up with a design that makes sense, that we can recognize and naturally use (or be trained to use) in the intended way, and so we may be at home with it.

To summarize, persons in these dramas rewrite their stories as they enact them. They may refer to themselves, their situation, and the drama itself as they figure out what to do. They may ignore the rules, at their peril. They may talk about them. They are reasonably comfortable with ambiguity. They always understand what to do, yet can feel uncomfortable in a situation. They have the full repertoire of human capacities. Conflict, shared understanding, and coming to agreement are not ultimate problems but ways of going on together when they ask for and give advice.

## 20 TRUTH

Stories are about our world and our selves. They are not fabulous fictions. We claim they are true. If we, all of us, deliberately and systematically cheated and lied, and so could not honestly feel others' claims upon us, it would be hard to give advice or even to have a community. Similarly, if we could not understand each other, or if we needed infinitely explicit accounts of situations—always asking, "What do you mean by that?"—then, too, we could not go on together. We need a substantial, shared, reliable basis in experience, knowledge, and convention among ourselves in order to maintain our community. Yet the basis is not foolproof, nor is there a way to avoid its potential traps. No prophylactic technologies or rules, such as formal logic or experimental tests, will prevent the monstrosities that arise when we lie or when we systematically misunderstand each other—for in our devilish work we seem to be able to get around the prophylactics if we want to, and even when we do not. And falsehood does not always lead very far into monstrosity. No method will catch all liars or cheats, or eliminate all misunderstandings, without also destroying the substantial texture of our lives, sacrificing it to total control and a simplified denuded existence in the name of the absence of error.

Still, technologies of inquiry such as science, legal processes, and even checking the grapevine, can reveal our unintentional biases and prejudices, as well as deliberately hidden ones. This should increase the likelihood that trust is warranted, stories are real, and understanding is fair.

The technologies also force us to reexamine our everyday practices so that we might act in a more generous way. For example, we know that when people work together in a group to solve a problem, in the name of group solidarity they are likely to muffle dissent and to maintain illusions and presuppositions without carefully checking them out. This has proved costly in invention and in foreign policy. If we had a technology that could maintain a reasonable level of group solidarity and yet break up these intellectual logjams, we would want to adopt it. Similarly, in psychotherapy or social research, the professionals may play out their own problems and interests, rather than serve those of their clients. Professional training attempts to make practitioners aware of how they do this and so, hopefully, they are less likely to act out or to blindly follow their own interests.

The technologies do not eliminate our interests and biases. Persons are constituted by their interests and what they care about, and if a technology eliminated those, there would no longer be persons. Rather, technologies of inquiry enable persons to maintain a community by maintaining the truth, by keeping it up. None of these technologies could guarantee much if persons were not concerned about trust and the truth, if appeals to these values would not make persons think twice and act differently if need be.

Advice may be said to be true insofar as it enables all of us to go on together in our community. Our understanding of our situation can be true because it makes true advice possible. And statements can be true if they guide us to fulfill our intentions. This practical notion of truth applies to a person, in a situation, concerned with a particular action. But there are some classes of situations for which a very large number of people do agree on what are the true statements. The sky is blue. Seven plus six is thirteen. Some of these, such as a political constitution or scientific problems, can be remarkably well-defined areas of concern in which our community comes to a very substantial and effective practical agreement. More careful examination of these scientific and political situations shows that dissenters are often surgically excluded from the community. They are said to be crackpots, or astrologers, or traitors. Agreement may be an artifact of such violence as well as of politics and thoughtful argument. Another class of situations where we have wide agreement is based on the common-sense ideas we have about the world, the ones that are so pervasive that we assume them without question. But sometimes even common sense is questioned, perhaps by the philosophers or the theologians or the scientists. But their questions, even when they eventually prove useful in new realizations and discoveries, are often labeled impractical. And it is not unheard of for us to label as insane those who do not share our common sense. So common sense, too, is constructed and manufactured.

Truth arises in advice. Scientific truth, for example, is not more abstract than political truth. It arises out of complicated scientific situations that require that persons advise each other about what to do. Only afterwards do they settle down to the more narrow, seemingly universal, formulations laymen hear about. Logic also has a cultural history, with rather different formulations in different societies. These observations do not mean that science or logic are not true. Rather, I want to recall that what we call the truth with all of its wonderful properties arises out of some mundane human processes. And there is a variety of true stories, depending on our situation and what we are up to.

In seeking and giving advice we find the truth by reformulating our understanding of our problem and of our desires and aims. Such continuing revaluation permits many truths and good stories, depending on our picture of our situation: How do we conceive its history? What actions do we think of as permissible? How do history and action alter our conception of our situation and of our problem? When we evaluate what we are up to, we are not only trying to decide what should be done, we are also concerned with what should have been done in the past. Evaluation is not a process of finding a most desirable truth as such, so much as a process of creating a rich true story, and perhaps a set of doable actions related to achievable goals that meet our needs.

Persons do not try everything they can conceive of. We try those stories that are close to ones we already know, or that seem likely to get us closer to being able to go on in our lives. We have richly articulated model stories that we try to apply, although those stories may become blinding myths if they are not appropriate.

When we do research we build up a point of view, articulating it both in its own terms and in contrast to alternative theories and ways of thinking. Certain kinds of evidence are more supportive of one way of thinking than another because they confirm the one and not the other, or because they do not seem relevant to the other way. Once in a while the armies are suitably marshalled, and rather than exercising them on different battlegrounds, we can arrange for a confrontation between them. Our armies are sharply defined, the uniforms are of different colors, and each person belongs to one side or the other. After the battle, perhaps one side is victorious and it may eliminate the opposition's leaders and elevate its own. But we know that some of the wounded losers remain unconvinced, and they work as guerillas in the bush for a hundred years, eventually to triumph (perhaps in only a small way) the next time around.

We more or less aim in research for these sharp confrontations that demand resolutions. But rarely are documents or experiments so definitive, so clear to everyone. There really are guerilla groups, sometimes quite hard to snuff out because they are on to something substantial. More importantly, we must realize how much political and economic work is required to build up each position, how much this historically commits persons to a side, how much the strength of a position depends on the resources available to maintain it, how much having the best persons on your side does count.

Persons are constantly making commitments to each other within the framework of finding the truth, but they seem to have no trouble in sincerely committing themselves to different sides. Of course, the resources available to a position are limited. The commitments of the best persons are justified and not arbitrarily made. But it turns out that there are good justifications for various positions. As in legal processes, the various sides make their best case and, through judgment and appeal to each other and to bystanders, a resolution is found. Each side shifts depending on the moves of the other. Perhaps they can settle out of court or bargain a plea or arbitrate the case. Along the way the relevance and factuality of the evidence is argued out. It is sometimes hard to determine the truth of some evidence without determining whether it is relevant, since the theory or case we make sets the context for deciding if something is true. The confrontation is on a muddy field and not only is it hard to maintain your footing, but uniforms get dirtied, obscuring their colors.

Advice depends on persons. And inquiries concerning the truth depend on the persons who perform them. The problems we think worthy of investigation and the results depend on who is ransacking the archive and doing the experiment. How we act, which byways get explored, and what is concluded may be different for different researchers, although the profession will train people and conform them into some fairly regular mainline behavior. The social and political milieu affects the directions for inquiry and the kinds of conclusions that are acceptable. Conflicts are conflicts carried on about interpreted facts, not conflicts of facts themselves.

But inquiry, like advice, is not idiosyncratic, for the most part. Persons may be sinful and imperfect, their foibles are multiple and recurrent. But persons are mostly decent, fair, inventive, and civic, too. They are polluted by their imperfections, but they have hearty guts and seem to be able to get along quite nicely anyway.

It is possible to train persons, as I have said, to be scholars and scientists, and to professionally certify them so that idiosyncracy is controlled. Although inquiry depends on who does it, that dependency is not so outlandish as it first might seem. Objectivity, disinterestedness, and universality, values that suit a hegemonic science and society, are not so difficult to instill in some souls. And so we've eliminated the crackpots and magicians. If such a discipline or science is esoteric, it is also seemingly clean, and uncontaminated by pandemic irrationality, caprice, and bias.

It is a curious fact that mortal and flawed persons can produce almost universal art and truth and godly understanding, that fleshly individuals can be saints and salvific figures. We might understand this if we note that we appreciate the universality and perfection of what we do from within an endeavor. Scientists, artists and critics, and religious believers are the ones who most effectively proclaim the transmundane character of their or their predecessors' work. To others, it may be just another person doing his work, work that might be pretty good, but there is no reason to believe that it is produced by divine genius residing in that mortal soul. Yet his work appeals to many others' sense of universality and truth, and by its practical effect in this world it confirms that sense, at least for a while. Art and religious ceremonies make us feel special and extraordinary.

So the stories we tell are true for the persons who ask for and receive advice, and for others too. As persons, they can act decently and fairly because they are involved with what they are doing. And they can affect each other in both small and transcendent ways. The monstrosities of lying and nonsense are controlled by our personal involvement in advice and our concern about being true to each other. But they are always present, never to be completely effaced.

## 21 IS ADVICE REAL?

The picture I have sketched of coming to agreement may seem quite benign. Do persons actually try to understand their situation, and then in advice-giving convince others of what they understand, and thereby go on together? Do they not have more sinister purposes? We know that there is a politics of truth and advice-giving, and I have described some of it. But many discussions of communities and social systems argue that there is some real power, such as economic power, that determines what we might understand and so how we come to agree. Our world is quite limited by the resources that are available to investigate it, and that economy determines what we know. To some extent that is so. But advice seems to have its own autonomy. I am not so sure that we are all marionettes, nor are the claims we make actually made by a ventriloquist in the employ of the boss.

Surely economic power is important. And surely our capacities to conceptualize are culturally bound by our language and common categories. Limits and language set the rules and possibilities for how we could be persons in the first place, and how we can be free at all. Yet limits and language are made by us, although not arbitrarily, and by what we do. So economics and the economically powerful are overturned by the facts of depression, transformation, and invention. Within our culture we develop new facts, new modes of discourse, new theories that supersede, perhaps in a gentle way, their seemingly exclusively correct predecessors—only to be succeeded in time themselves.

There are repressive regimes and inflexible modes of thought, and within any regime or thoughtway some ways of being seem never to come up. What is important is that within a very wide range of regimes and ways of thought we do have the opportunity to give advice and come to agree in a manner that suggests that we are free, that we are not dehumanized and controlled, that we can recognize when things are out of hand and are monstrous and oppressive. I doubt we can be simplistic about deciding if we are marionettes and who pulls the strings. The question is more subtle. For the marionettes control their puppeteers much more than the puppeteers would like to believe.

People make the world for themselves from their experience. Sometimes they do the unexpected or find themselves in very different positions than they planned on. Still, they come to provisional agreement and so make their way in the world.

## The Conditions for Advice

*Advice depends on the feelings we have for each other. Those feelings permit us to be convinced by others, to sense what they mean by their stories, and to care for them. Feelings are primary, and our surrogates for feelings, such as betting odds, are secondary and abstract. For it is persons, with their everyday ordinary capacities, who participate in advice. But feelings have a poor reputation, as to both their reliability and their trustworthiness, although we seem to be able to handle feelings just about as well as we handle our rational knowledge. People deny that their feelings play a role in advice in order to claim their advice as universal and independent of its source, a claim that only undermines their advice.*

*Persons are just what we need to give advice. They are sensitive, flexible, sturdy, and, most importantly, they understand our world and each other.*

## 22 FEELING PERSONS

Our feelings make advice possible. The feeling of trust is the foundation for a relationship of persons; being convinced by a story and being able to feel your way around in it makes a story rhetorically effective; and empathy and being able to feel at home in someone else's situation let us understand one another and believe that we do understand. These feelings of trust, and of being convinced and at home, are means by which we confirm to each other that we are persons who care for each other in our community. Conversely, the expression of these feelings, like the expression of our knowledge, is stylized and controlled by the community.

We may develop un-personal equivalents for these feelings, such as probability measures of reliability to surrogate for trust or hypothesis tests and logical proofs to surrogate for rhetorical power, but we may rely on these equivalents only so long as they represent our sentiments reasonably well most of the time. We may abandon these provisional surrogates when they do not adequately represent us. And if they cause us to revise our feelings, perhaps to be more rational or to abandon an illusion that no longer serves our interests, so much the better. Still, we may trust people irrationally, and we may find logically defective arguments quite convincing. In these cases our trust may be quite warranted. Our trust may make others more effective, or it might lead, eventually, to more sturdy arguments. If we confuse the surrogates with how we do feel, we'll no longer understand what we do when we give advice to each other. Advice will seem irrational just when it is most human and personal. The difficulties are not unlike ones we encountered when we explored roles, problems, stories, and understanding.

Our feelings and moods are subtle and highly articulated. They are the basis for good and sensible advice. They set the conditions for the relationship of persons when we seek and give advice.

Affective relationships and bonds, whether political, social, or intimate, motivate and suggest why we engage in advice: We care for and empathize with other persons like us. If we were to deny the role of feelings in advice-giving, we would destroy the possibility of genuine advice. We would have un-personal and depersonalized persons who advise for no reason.

## 23 ADVICE AND FEELINGS

Advice is a personal activity, and the feelings persons have toward others, such as anger, hurt, and love, are the condition that makes advice possible. What role do these feelings play in advice-giving? Let us look at how feelings work in dramatic, sexual, and social situations, as models for how feelings must work in advice.

Artists, writers, and pastors convince us of the reality of their stories by evoking feelings of being at home, and of passion and melodrama, among others. The power of most claims in advice, no matter how well argued and rational, depends on these feelings. The feelings must be based in a believable story, not a fantasy, if we are to act on them effectively. We are usually sensible enough not to follow a story if it is a confection made simply to evoke those feelings. An adult understands his feelings and appreciates when they are appropriate. Sometimes we will be confused, especially in the middle of an unstable situation, and we may misinterpret feelings as well as arguments and data. But in general, feelings are not beyond our regulation and deliberate use.

Persons also have feelings of empathy for other persons. They understand how others feel. The claims we make on another person in advice make sense because we know roughly how he or she will feel about them. We understand how to act so as to affect others who are like us, to touch them, to make a claim they will recognize. And a person recognizes that others in his community are like him, not only by what they say and do but by how they respond emotionally to various situations. They must have appropriate and adequate affect, and their feelings are usually ones that he can conceive himself as having.

Empathy is based on our cognitive and our affective capacities. We know what others might think and do, and we appreciate how they might feel as a consequence of what they think. Similarly, their feelings affect their thought. In certain technical or professional situations, our capacities for empathy might be restricted to limited aspects of another's experience. Our ability to give evidence to another that we do understand him might be limited to particular areas. This would be especially true if the others we deal with are only marginally like us, at least in our own minds, as is sometimes the case with physicians and their patients or social workers and their clients. Empathy can become merely knowledge of how my treatment of you will affect you.

Most of us do not like the idea of being treated, unless the treatment is quite specific in its effect and side effects. Otherwise we might justifiably feel that we are being treated as objects, or used for experiments by a person who does not share the risks we endure. No one wants to be investigated.

Empathy depends on truth. Our commitments to others and our treating them like us requires that we have realistic pictures of each other, that we be aware of when advice does not work despite our best wishes, that our treatments be effective. Sometimes empathy will be based as much on systematic and scientific studies, where we know what will happen in an objectified way (say, predictors for schizophrenia) as on intuitive and particular feelings.

Empathy is a way in which we appreciate one another when we ask for and give advice. Feelings of eros and sexuality suggest how and why we might be attracted to and care for one another. Desire and love can be expressed in the advice we share, in the trust we find possible, in a story that is considerate and roomy enough for all of us, and in the understanding of another that truly takes him into account.

In sexuality, eros, and love, we expect that the other person will have the feelings we have and the capacity to feel as we do. We come to know that by what we say; we may sense the glow in the other person; and we feel it in ourselves kinesthetically. We choose our erotic involvements to some extent, but some just come our way, such as with our children and parents, and others sneak up on us and take us over. Our seemingly casual choices are sometimes quite difficult to shake off. We express eros in varied ways, from rather chaste love, to sexual intercourse, to the production of great works of art or science.

I have described erotic involvements in this way because it is just these erotic features of our mutual interactions—how they feel, their degree of voluntariness, and the ways they are expressed—that we display in advice as we are attracted to and care for each other. In advice we feel desire for another person, we are sometimes taken over by that desire, and we are moved to great acts by it. It is in these senses that advice is erotic.

The completeness and mutuality of erotic involvements is a measure of their quality. Satisfaction and caring are part of these measures, as they are for advice. Our sense of satisfaction or care is rational, not only a matter of hormones, and we feel eros or advice is good because it is good. We are sometimes tempted to reduce eros to heterosexual intercourse as conventionally conceived, or advice to problem solving. These surrogates are likely to fail us just when eros is most powerful and advice is most needed, when they are most encompassing and vital and extraordinary. The breakdown of trust and mutual understanding, our modes of unfulfilled desire in advice, takes place when we treat the other person as an object, when we make unclaimed assumptions about our shared understanding, and when we give abstract care independent of whom we are involved with. But these features also characterize less adequate erotic relationships. Advice and eros are ways we matter to each other, caring for each other in the community in a necessary way. Advice can go on because we are persons, and in the mutuality expressed in advice and eros we reconfirm that to each other.

Empathy is the way we treat others like us in advice, and eros suggests why we would want to engage in advice. Our education in our community, as we grow up and develop, gives us the repertoire of feelings that makes us articulate advisors. We learn how to love and hate, how to express anger and approval, how to modulate these expressions in ways that will affect others. And we learn how to respond to others' expressions. We find a mode of expression that is not only effective but also satisfying for ourselves as well. The expression of our feelings is not only communicative, it is also a means by which we live our own lives, in our bodies. Talking, thinking, and the expression of feelings are metabolic activities and, like all metabolic activities, they are to some extent under our conscious control. We learn when our feelings are inappropriate and how their expression must be modulated if we are to be civil with each other.

We need just this repertoire of feelings if we are to be able to participate in advice-giving as authentic persons, using the repertoire to say what we mean with sufficient subtlety so that we have room for tacit doubts, quiet encouragement, and strong feelings. We learn how to play the polyphonic capacities of human interaction. And in advice we improve our play.

Our feelings are fundamental conditions for advice: how we could give advice and make claims, why we must do it and care for each other, and how it is a continuing process that is growing and educative. Empathy makes it possible, for we can understand each other; eros and mutuality make it necessary, because we care for each other; education and development make it coherent and viable as we learn to express ourselves effectively in a community. Still, we may believe that feelings are dangerous, that they too readily lead to the monstrous, even as we concede their fundamental necessity.

## 24 CIVIL FEELINGS

We, as persons, have feelings and those feelings are the conditions for advice-giving. Our affective capacities make us sensitive and articulate. Most of the time we are capable of being civil and decent to each other, and our systematic knowledge and our feelings contribute to that. Yet we are rightly concerned about how knowledge might lead to technical monstrosity and how feelings might lead to mass emotional hysteria or totalitarianism. A reasoned commitment to knowledge and civility could make less likely the diabolical takeover of our human being. But we can have no absolute assurances, no truly preventive measures. If we desire humaneness and respect for individuals, that we treat persons as persons, we need to have a primary commitment to these values in our institutions and in how we act toward each other. Our feelings and justifications can reflect this commitment.

For example, our feelings change in both psychoanalysis and in thought reform. But in one case we respect each other, while in the other someone is treated as an object. Will we question identity, rather than assault it; will we accept another's self-image, as well as be critical of it; and will someone be able to re-form his self from many alternatives, rather than accept only one possible choice? But even after we make these distinctions, we may still fear that our feelings will lead us astray. Surely they may, but perhaps no more so than will our other human capacities.

Persons care for each other. If technical methods, or eros and sexuality, are separated from that care, then they may be twisted to inhuman ends. Yet if we think of advice as a matter of objective data applied by legitimate experts who logically resolve our difficulties, then care and feelings seem to destroy so-called rigorous advice. But advice is a way we care for each other. It is not simply a matter of objective data and legitimate experts. Advice is not fragile; it is buffered by the generous capacities of persons to treat each other as persons and not act monstrously toward each other. Our human capacities, whether they be cognitive, rational, affective, sexual, or merely for hurting each other, will be out of control unless we realize that they are capacities possessed by persons who care for others in their community, and even for visitors and aliens.

These considerations may help us understand dilemmas of the professional role advisors sometimes take. City planners, for example, have been described as "predominantly universalistic, affectively neutral, collectively-oriented and functionally specific, as well as achievement oriented." It is almost as if professional planners want to forget they are persons. They would seem to prefer neat situations, which are unlikely to be reality tests, to the complex and ambiguous ones, which are always under contest and modification. All the sterility and impotence frequently associated with planning may serve the planner's deeper needs and fears. Yet only by rejecting this un-personal image of themselves can professionals be truly effective. Only as persons can they legitimately take the risk of planning for and making claims about the better society.

Effective advisors can be hard-nosed, play politics, yet treat others respectfully as persons. Even if they worry about health policy or profits or war, and not directly about justice, pride, and freedom, the human consequences of what they do as professionals, planners, and experts are what count in the end. Feelings, understanding, and trust are not luxuries, but the foundation of our relationship with each other, as much as are liberty, justice, and the law.

### 25 PERSONS

Throughout this essay I have depended on the notion that it is a person who asks for, gives, and receives advice. Persons know, understand, and feel when situations are human and when they are not. They recognize likeness and monstrosity. They understand our ordinary lives and extraordinary situations, and they recognize lives and situations that are beyond what human beings could live in the community, if they are still to be human beings. Persons may talk about these situations and about themselves, and change and modify the rules by which they live. No doubt there are many ambiguous cases. Boundary and extreme situations are rich with information about ordinary situations, and so they occupy our attention yet we are comfortable with them. But most of the time our lives are quite ordinary. That makes it possible to investigate the extraordinary without losing ourselves completely.

Advice can make sense because persons know how to get along in the ordinary everyday world. Were their understanding of the world a fantasy, then advice would be absurd. Were their relationships objective, based only on technical performance or on the plausibility of their stories or facts, then advice would become potentially monstrous, easily losing its connection with the stuff of our lives. Our capacity for feeling and for understanding lets us be human and sensitive, actually comfortable in being persons, in ambiguous and problematic situations. We know what to do. We can comfort each other and seek advice from each other.

Scientific procedures turn out to be quite useful for codifying some of what we understand, and some of the time they help us in giving advice. Science itself arises out of advice. But if a science does not agree with what we understand, we are as likely to rethink our science as we are to rethink our common sense. Scientists are one of a variety of political experts who help us figure out what to do.

Persons can make errors, and their advice may be distorted or wrong. Systematic procedures—such as methods or professional certification, which delimit personal involvement—can control error and distortion to some extent, but at the high cost of denying the personal foundation for advice. Sometimes that may be necessary, as when charlatanism reigns, or when survival is at stake, although this is usually crying wolf. But systematic procedures are not the only way that we root out charlatanism and monsters. Persons can be suspicious of what is out of the ordinary and can recognize what seems wrong to them. They then may make further inquiries, checking up on their suspicions. They are quite flexible and varied in their sensitivity to what might be out of kilter. So by stalling, asking further questions, consulting with others, checking up more often, and the like, they can sniff out the rotten cases.

Through our upbringing in the community we are trained to question and be suspicious. We learn to ask appropriate questions, and we learn that some questions are, in general, overly suspicious. We seem to know how to tread a middle ground, and that ground is rich enough to do most of the work we want to do in life. We can make claims on each other that articulate our doubts and concerns in an effective manner. Advice is not improved when we bring our personal feelings into it. Rather, only then does it become possible, necessary, and viable. And then we may go on in life together.

**II**

The two essays in this part show how ideas and ways of thinking characteristic of humanistic study of history, philosophy, religion, literature, and art help us understand what we do when we plan, design, make decisions, and judge what is good. This connection, between humanistic study and planning and decisionmaking, is suggested by the fact that our activities of this sort, whether in our personal lives or in government, are conducted by us, the humans who are the foundation and subject of humanistic thought. But the humanistic tradition is not an abstract one. We could trace it back to the Hebrews and the Greeks, but its contemporary form in the universities is very much a legacy of the German Idealist tradition—think of Kant and Hegel. It is no accident that perfection and an ideal play a central role in the models I describe. Considering the late-eighteenth-century origins of these problems, it is reasonable to expect that they will be Christian and Romantic, as well as Idealist problems. The basic theme is that in this mundane world absoluteness is represented by an imperfect shadow. How do we reconcile the rift between the mundane and the transcendent, the same and the different, the body and the soul, the absolute and the particular? This is the Protestant Lutheran issue, for there is no church to perform the reconciliation. We must do it ourselves. And we must do it in our earthly community—through a Romantic self-realization, a self-fulfillment and recommitment as our own proclamation of God's word . . . and so we are justified. We must heal the rift, although it is through God's grace that we might do so.

How can we make our peace with the palpable presence of our dirtied, polluted, mundane world and our alienated, from God and each other, Romantic selves in that world? Most of us are not still Jews nor can we return to being Jews, who lived in this mundane world—managing legally by interpreting the Scriptures, staying righteous through daily ritual and practice, yet without having the most recent sign of truth. The Jew has no mysteries to which he alone has special access. Luther and the kingdom of heaven on earth make heaven more mysterious by keeping it on our minds. "All German philosophy is but an attempt to remove the kingdom of heaven to a transcendental space and time which is inaccessible for mortals, but which nevertheless stimulates us constantly to make a new (though hopeless) effort in the direction of the ideal." (Rosenstock-Huessy.)

But the issues I address here are in actuality entirely more ordinary and un-theological ones that have already come up in "Advice": about how we stop and think, as Arendt puts it, and make a decision, how stories and narratives work, how persons in a community bring each other along. In general, the humanistic modes and models assert the continuity of our ways of being in our ordinary everyday lives with those in our bureaucratic and transcendent ones.

While I make much more direct reference to philosophic figures here than in "Advice," my main concern is to develop descriptions of what we do that feel right and familiar. We'll pick and choose from the thinkers, as long as they serve these descriptive purposes. And while I borrow from anthropological and religious thought, my concern is to be faithful to the world rather than to those literatures. In the first essay I give a fairly straightforward description of some humanistic models, while the second begins and ends with a demonstration of a way of thinking that tries to be consistent with those models.

# ✌ॐ Criticism, Conversion, and Confession

*Evaluations often seem fudged; we keep planning even when our plans rarely work out; decisionmaking has components of anxiety and ecstasy. I believe these are not unrelated observations. If we view evaluating, planning, and decision-making as somewhat like the everyday activities we engage in ordinarily, and then examine descriptions that have been developed for them in the humanistic tradition of criticism and religion and art, we may understand why. We find that these processes share features of magic, rites-of-passage rituals, and sacrifice. They appeal to perfection and ideal values, just as religion and art often do. What bureaucrats do and what we do in our everyday lives share some of the most central features of our cultural tradition.*

*It is not difficult to see some of these features exhibited in actual situations such as the Bay Area Rapid Transit System. (I use the example not so much to decide whether it was a good project, as to show how these considerations might help us think about its goodness more effectively.) In evaluating such a large project, the most natural description of what we ought to do comes from how critics of art and literature work, how they point out the important features of a work, develop rational justifications for their judgments, and make those justifications into the truth about the work. It is a form of magic. Evaluations seem fudged not because they are faked, but because they must be confected by the person examining the work or the project. They do not come from someplace else. Because evaluations must appeal to others' good sense about their world, they are about what we have in common, even if evaluations are subjective and depend on who is doing them.*

*Perfection seems to play an inordinately important role in our lives. Although never to be achieved here on earth, we refer to ideals and perfection in evaluating projects and in de-*

*ciding what to do. A careful examination of how converts to an ideal vision make their peace with the actual world suggests how the ideal and the actual may coexist and play against each other. I have given a rather detailed description of conversion because I believe that it captures the experience people have when they commit themselves to an ideal vision. I will also want to argue that such commitments and conversions need not be totalitarian.*

*Decisions may be viewed as conversionary experiences, which would account for the anxiety we feel when making decisions. The description I give is both logical, about justifying decisions, and psychological, about how we feel in making them. It turns out to be a phenomenology of what happens when things are not going quite right, just when we seek advice. And the description helps us understand error and forgiveness, stigma and grace, as well as the fact that decisions often require irrational costs or sacrifices. There is a substantive continuity between what the anthropologists and theologians tell us about our world, and what we view as bureaucratic and social science practice, and what we do ordinarily every day.*

Critics, historians, and philosophers are our contemporary representatives of the humanistic tradition of thought that tries to say what is good, what is whole and perfect, and what is worth being responsibly committed to, and why. They analyze the great works of human art and artifice and figure out what makes them so special.

When we plan and make public policy, many of the activities we engage in may be interpreted as humanistic activities. Policy evaluation has close logical and procedural analogues with literary and art criticism; the themes of ideal and utopian designs correspond to the conversionary tradition in religious thought; and decisionmaking is a rites-of-passage ritual that we describe in confessional terms. As we explore these humanistic models of what we do we shall want to have a concrete example in mind. The history of the Bay Area Rapid Transit System is exemplary for our purposes.

### BART

The Bay Area Rapid Transit System (BART) is a two-billion-dollar rail rapid transit system that covers much of the San Francisco Bay Area. It opened in 1974, and service was gradually extended over the route and to longer hours. A study and evaluation of BART, examining behavior before and after its opening, concluded that B A R T must be considered a failure. Yet it also concluded that B A R T may turn out to be a success in the long run. B A R T is a failure because its ridership is proving to be too low. Its cash flow will be insufficient to pay for operating costs, without even considering retirement of bonded indebtedness. B A R T's planners underestimated people's allegiance to their automobiles and their unwillingness to wait for trains or for connecting buses. The study also claims that B A R T has not contributed to economic growth and is funded disproportionately by the poor.

B A R T's advocates agree in part with the evaluators, especially with the observation that the system was never designed to match the grand claims made for it. The general manager points out, "It's hard to explain to someone who voted for something that he was told would be wonderful . . . and 15 years later someone comes along and tells him, well, that wasn't all quite true." (*Minneapolis Tribune*, March 3, 1978.) But many of B A R T's problems are intrinsic to the economic structure of large-scale projects. For example, since public finance tends to be regressive when it is supported by property and sales taxes, the disproportionate but not absolutely large share paid by the poor is not surprising. Still, the system works. In case the automobile highway system fails (because of jams, bridge difficulties, or the like), the secondary system of rail rapid transit provides backup, the extra cost of which may pay for itself over the long run. Other arguments are offered, especially concerning the hidden costs of the entrenched infrastructure (roads, automobile manufacturers) that make the automobile look efficient compared to other modes.

The evaluators suggest that it might be fiscally prudent to junk B A R T and return to a bus system. Yet at the end of the report, Melvin Webber points out that the situation is a bit more complicated:

> B A R T has been heralded as pacesetter for transit systems throughout the world. The evidence so far suggests that it may also become the first of a series of multi-billion-dollar mistakes scattered from one end of the continent to the other.
>
> But in the long run, say in 50 years when the bonds will have been retired, when everyone will regard B A R T as just another built-in feature of the region, rather like Golden Gate Park, perhaps no one will question whether B A R T should have been either built or abandoned. It will then be regarded as a handy thing to have, a valuable facilitator of trips that would not otherwise be made by the elderly and the young, a blessing that enriches the quality of Bay Area life. And who will gainsay then the wisdom of having built a white elephant today?

In the long run B A R T may transform the Bay Area and its people's habits. It will change the life space of those who cannot use a car. It alters the image of the Bay Area, reinforcing other development plans as well. But it seems that no reasonable discount rate could financially justify such a large investment with such a long-term payoff. This should immediately make us wonder about the model of evaluation (cash flow and economics) used to evaluate B A R T in this study. B A R T may well be uneconomic, but there are other reasons for entering into projects, and the financial modes of analysis may be insensitive to them. The B A R T evaluators' main conclusion should be that they do not understand why B A R T was built. Actually, of course, they do appreciate its developmental and prescriptive purposes, but wonder if they are worth it. Presumably a cost-benefit tableau will be illuminating, retrospectively, once we appreciate what are the costs and the benefits.

We need a way of thinking about long-term consequences that does not simply reduce them to their discounted present cash value, and that acknowledges the pressing importance of short-run, seemingly technical, problems of finance and management. Positively, this might be called a matter of leadership; more ambivalently, it may be a matter of sacrificing the present for the future.

We know that a large-scale transformation must sacrifice some entrenched interests. As Schumpeter argued, this creates the liveliness we associate with capitalism in its freest form. But the transformation will make short-term financial sense only in some sub-markets. Usually it is in the market of the politically powerful that the transformation is pecuniarily profitable. But if an innovation is particularly inventive, it can destroy the political power of some group by robbing it of its fiscal advantage. So far B A R T's influence on the Bay Area's political economy has been quite tame. It has performed only the usual sacrifices.

Everybody knew that B A R T would benefit downtown interests, but everybody also knew that they did not want another Los Angeles in the Bay Area. Hence, the benefit to the downtown interests seems in fact to be a benefit to the public interest. The political desire to avoid Los Angelization converted a selfish set of benefits into a public set. Of course, this does not mean that such a public set of benefits is fair or does not unduly harm the poor.

Let us say that we have an evaluative scheme that makes B A R T seem more reasonable, so that it is not merely a fiscal mistake. Say it is a matter of the shape of the Bay Area. Then we may discuss the political economy of the project. Is the meaning and justification we find in the project politically good? If BART is justified by long-term downtown development, we then want to ask whether downtown development is good, and so put BART in question.

Having a justification for a project permits rational discourse about it. If it is treated as a failure because it makes no sense according to an analytic procedure (for example, it is uneconomic or illogical), we do not know why it exists. Put differently, if we are going to consign some of our actions to hell, it is useful to have as an analytic procedure an articulated theory of sin that says why they belong there. The analytic procedure must be rich in its understanding of failure (for example, market failure, paradoxes) if we are to go further in our discussion of what to do when things go wrong.

If BART were merely an innocent plot by the wealthy downtown interests to help themselves, it would be nonsense from a larger point of view. But we can incorporate it into a rational political economy. We can view BART in terms of resistance to the culture of the automobile, or in terms of aggrandizing metropolitanization. We can then see it much less idiosyncratically and be more universal in arguing for or against it.

Perhaps after all our analysis we agree that it was a mistake to build BART. Who is responsible for the decision to build it? The voters who approved the bonding, the politicians who promoted it, or the professionals who planned and designed it and estimated its costs and ridership? All are, to some degree, and systemic accounts will say just how. Today we argue that professionals have a special responsibility. But how can we blame them for defects in transportation theory (of the modal split) of twenty years ago? Perhaps they could have known better. But say that they did their best. Is that enough? A model of evaluation must incorporate a moral theory that says more about the nature of failure and responsibility for it. Is atonement or redemption possible?

HUMANISTIC MODELS

I believe we need more realistic and recognizable models for the practices of policy analysts and evaluators, planners, and decisionmakers— public affairs actors, or "actors" for short—as well as for our everyday judgments, plans, and decisions. The models should incorporate features that help us think more clearly about what we are doing when we work on large projects such as BART, projects that require our most general capacities for judgment and that are phrased in terms of overarching transformations. Critics, scholars, artists, and theologians are centrally and explicitly concerned with judgment, and with perfection and wholeness and transcendence. These values are quite important to public affairs actors, even if they say they are just being practical. Ultimate values haunt their models of policy evaluation, ideal plans, and decisionmaking. In their work, as we shall see, actors use concepts and modes of thought characteristic of art, criticism, and religion when they make sense of what they do.

Perfection and wholeness may be thought of in several ways. The world might be perfect and whole if it had no flaws and no missing parts, and coherently fit together. Or perfection might refer to an ideal by which we reckoned our own world. Or, it might describe a sense we have that our world is coherent and intelligible for us; we fit into the world or it fits us fairly well. That fit may be expressed using the notion of rationality, or by a kinesthetic sensation of being in touch with the world. As I argue further on, neither rationality nor being in touch necessarily mean that we could not change and develop in time, with new parts of the world becoming whole and perfect for us. At each point in our development we know how to get along, but there are also aspects that offer the potential for growth. In this view, the perfection and wholeness of one way of being does not imply that it is the only way, nor that it will not have successors that are also perfect and whole. If there were an end of time, a judgment day, development would no longer occur then, and perfection and wholeness would have the more static meaning implied by a flawless world.

I shall discuss three models concerned with perfection, wholeness, and transcendence. The first describes how connoisseurial skills function, and how we criticize and evaluate works of art or literature so that we appreciate and make sense of them. We can apply the model to understanding the analysis and evaluation of programs and plans. The second model is one of transformation or conversion. It shows how formal unity works in art and literature, and how ideal situations work in a religious context. We can then see how formal unity and ideals work in everyday planning situations. The third model is a description of a rite of passage, the transition to a new status, and how that status comes to feel whole and proper and filled with grace. It is an account of the experience we have when we make a decision.

These models can incorporate actors' technical procedures, such as cost-benefit analysis, experimental design, program planning, and statistical decision theory. But they put such procedures in a place that suggests how they are in a continuum with the rest of our human activities.

## EVALUATION AND CRITICISM

When we evaluate programs, policies, and plans, whether in business, government, or our private lives, we try to say if they are good. We find out how they are working, whether that is satisfactory, and why they turn out the way they do. Sometimes we can be quite sure of what we expect from a plan (or a program or a policy), and so we can decide ahead of time how to determine if it is working. Usually we are not so sure, and evaluation is not so simple. The intentions of the designer, even if we can discern them clearly, may be a poor guide to deciding if a plan worked. There will also be surprises, and some of them will be quite pleasant. Does the plan deserve credit for those surprises, or are they due to extraneous factors? And are the so-called extraneous factors, say, exogenous economic developments, actually extraneous?

If the plan did not work, we have to figure out why, find any saving graces, and determine how to do better next time—and make sure there will be a next time.

In genuine political evaluations, and political evaluations are the effective ones, people want to take credit for pleasant surprises, even if they do not deserve it. Politicians do not believe that deserts are determined by causal factors, for their constituents will not excuse them for errors that are beyond their control. Evaluations must find out if a plan or decision did work in some good way, even if the outcome is not the one we wanted. They take credit where they can. Effective politicians and natural scientists have great respect for the vagaries of the world. They are willing to believe that a push here and there can save a disaster, even if the save may involve transforming the program or the experiment.

This description is guided by what critics of art and literature do. Critics describe what is good and what is great, and what fails and how. They try to convince others of their judgments, and help others to see why the judgments are reasonable. They appeal to others' prejudices, if only to change the prejudices. They must be educative and persuasive.

But what do critics literally do? They pick out features of a work or a performance and say they are important. They link the features with others and show how they form a coherent whole. And so they open the audience's eyes to what is going on in the work.

Critics must also say what it is they are examining. Usually that is straightforward: it is a poem or a play or a painting. But not always. New works often mix forms or cut across the established boundaries.

They demand to be evaluated in terms other than the obvious ones. Imagine a scientific paper written in verse form. How would we decide if it is good? Some might say that the verse quality is irrelevant nowadays, although it was not irrelevant in the past. Then I might point out that scientific papers, plans, decision memoranda, and the like all have proper forms and rhythms, and when they do not fulfill those rhetorical and poetic requirements they are much less effective than they might be. So the formal or poetic quality is relevant. We might ask, does the verse form make the scientific paper more effective?

Deciding what something is has direct practical consequences. If B A R T were seen, not as a regional rapid transit system, but as an elaborate monument and advertisement for the Bay Area, it would be evaluated in different terms than it has been. If it were seen as a long-term attempt to control economic development, as are land-grant colleges, highway systems, and VA loans, we would again evaluate it differently.

But original intentions do not fully determine how we think about a work, as I have said. While it is sometimes clear enough what the artist or writer intended, the quality of a work may not be related to his intents. It may be great despite what he thought he was doing, a failure in his terms but not in ours. A critic may be more capable than the artist of understanding a work, and of figuring out what is good about it.

An evaluation of a work or program must say what it is, say something about its quality or goodness, and point out significant features of the work or program that will convincingly support those judgments. Critics also have to locate a work in history, and in the biography of its claimed author or designer. They create the idea of periods that have certain themes and values. And they show how a particular work exemplifies those values and is consequently of high quality. Saying what something is will affect our estimate of its quality, and identifying the appropriate aesthetic and social values for a period will affect our judgment of a work. In this sense, policy evaluation is always political, never merely an indication of what worked. When we evaluate a policy we use a political theory of what are the appropriate values and processes for the society. Even when we simply describe how something works, we are also saying what is important, which ways are interesting, significant, and worthy of attention and resources.

Criticism and evaluation affect how we act. They become the history that says what worked, and why and how. They justify as rational and sensible what we want to do next, whether it be a form of literature or a social program. This kind of justification is required before we embark on a large public program. It is also important for artists and writers. Critics help to prepare audiences for their work and can perhaps suggest how the artist might improve, just as they accommodate the public to future social developments.

Like coaches in sports, the critic may be able to pinpoint where an artist or a program is going wrong. He can suggest ways of thinking and exercises, new conceptions and practices, that lead to improved performance and an appreciation of just what the artist or program is up to. The critic can be therapeutic and supportive.

Evaluations are effective if those who commission them are powerful and those who do them are capable. But the political effectiveness of an evaluation also depends on its being rationally authoritative. Critics and evaluators must refer to the important literature and documents, and to the observations and data that are available about a work of art or a program or a plan. These references ground their argument. They suggest that the critic is aware of the current discussion of the issue, and of what is at stake in taking a particular position. The footnotes, and the names and topics he brings up, contribute to his authority. But of course all of this might be faked—dropped names, falsely adduced evidence and support—all just window dressing. Yet we cannot have authoritative evaluations without these signs that the critic or evaluator is aware of the context and facts about a work of art or about a situation. So we need procedures for distinguishing proper references from false ones. These procedures, which have been best developed by humanistic scholars who do textual criticism and write history, are derived in part from problems in the exegesis of sacred texts such as the Bible. They are talmudic, legal, philological, and paleographic skills. They use texts to understand what is true.

We may summarize our discussion so far. The connoisseur judges works and is an expert on their provenance and quality. The critic offers larger-scale rational reconstructions of what is going on in a body of work. The humanistic scholar knows how to manage texts, how to determine their authenticity and to write histories from them. The connoisseur, the critic, and the scholar write books and articles that make sense of part of the world. These roles have direct analogues with the work of the policy evaluator, who also writes a report to make sense of another part of the world. He judges projects, justifies them, and puts them in a larger context. These are people who use words to make things so.

Words that make things so, that form a history that becomes part of what we come to think of as the past, are magical. Magic is effective words, words that affect our actions. In Indonesian historiography, for example, one problem is to decide which priest was using words to legitimate a previous king, rewriting history to suit the current holder of the throne, and which was telling a more comprehensive truth. Historical writing was a form of magic for making the current king legitimate. Even properly done evaluations of policies may be magical in this sense, justifying what we do.

There are many magics, as there are many evaluations. The allegiance to any magic depends on its effectiveness. A magic may be considered effective if it explains what has happened or if it guides us in making something happen, although the guidance may be simply a matter of passive prediction of what we are fated to do. Not all magics are equally good. We like to believe that evaluations and magics that are more comprehensive and better founded will be more effective, and some of our experience confirms that.

Magics are usually ritualized. An evaluation is magical, and it, too, is ritualized, with certain phrases and judgments, such as positive cash flow or good chi square, being the imprimatur of "it works" and "it's real." In evaluation rituals we perform educational and political actions that bring people along, that convince them of "what is so" through their own experiences and judgments. Of course, not all rituals will work. People will not be convinced by everything. Just as there are better magics, there are more effective rituals.

Evaluations are almost always in words, and they fall heir to some limitations because of that. For example, something may be of great quality or a program may work well, but we cannot quite say why. Our technical apparatus and scientific tests may be insensitive to just how the program is effective, or it may be politically unwise to say what is true. Conversely, we may concentrate on aspects of a program that we can say the most about, even if they are not the most important. It often takes many years to find a measure of a program's success that is both tractable and also fairly reflects what the program does. Measures of the power of armaments or the effects of racial desegregation have had this long and complex history.

There are similar problems in criticism. Art historians may concentrate on the symbolic meaning of a second-rate work because it gives them lots of opportunities to exercise their scholarly skills. A great work may not receive comparable attention because there is not much to say about it—at least now, for this work, with our talents and interests. Works of art can sit around and wait for a critic to rescue them from obscurity. But in business and public affairs, we may lose the benefits of good programs for lack of a successful rationale, while poor programs may endure because they are supported by our analytical apparatus.

Experienced people can make good judgments that, at first, they may not be able to articulate. They have a sense that "this is it," but they may not be sure why. Subsequently they may give a good account that justifies their judgment, although the account may cause them to alter their assessment. There is a play between experienced judgment and rational justification.

There is also a loose but still influential play between our evaluations and what we do, between our judgments of success and what is successful, between what we try to educate people to believe to be good and what they support and think is good. The subject may be paintings or novels or investments or plans. In each case, the play between what we say and what we do is regulated. Evaluation, judgment, and education are not arbitrary. We can convince people to believe only some things. Certain arguments are much better supported than others. Yet we also have differing well-supported judgments of a work or a program.

Connoisseurship, criticism, and scholarship in the humanities, and analysis and evaluation in business and public affairs work roughly in the same way. There is as well a similarity between the logic of criticism and that of evaluation. The logic of one of the dominant modes of criticism, derived largely from Kant, goes something like the following.

Critical judgments are subjective. They depend on my experience, what I see with my own eyes. This, of course, does not mean that such judgments are arbitrary or idiosyncratic. They cannot be replaced by a set of criteria or determining rules that will reliably and automatically pick out the good paintings or successful programs. Still, rules of thumb may be helpful in guiding our judgments: Pay attention to color and line and organization. Check cash flow and solvency; look for leadership; be concerned about unserved demand. These checklists remind an experienced judge of the important points, and they are useful for training the novice. But they are not enough, for there are many exceptional cases. A good judge shows his skill in how he handles them, finding new rules and new ways of applying the rules.

We act as if others should agree with our judgments, that the judgments are true or universalizable, independent of our selves, even if they are subjective. We believe that other judges with similar training should make similar choices and for roughly the same reasons. We act as if we had a common sense. If there is disagreement, we should like to be able to have an argument with the other critic or evaluator, in which our reasons for holding an opinion would be cogent ones for him or her, even if they were not ultimately convincing. Our reasons should be educative for others. Yet having made our points, we may find we still do disagree. But our disagreement need not be a sign that our judgments are unreliable. For we may disagree for good reasons and continue arguing with each other, trying to bring the other over to our side.

We want to be able to presume that our evaluation of a program or a painting does not depend on our having an interest in it, a personal stake in its being thought a good program or a painting of high quality. Our interest would seem to pollute the universality of our judgment. We should be disinterested. But that is rarely the case, although our interest may be merely a matter of supporting our own previous position or judgment. Still, the reasons we offer to each other can be comparatively unbiased and open to discussion and disagreement. Once we display our arguments, others can pick at and choose from the various points. So interest and self-interest can become a less crucial factor in the evaluation. In any case, as I have mentioned, we might agree with all the various points that a critic makes and still come out on the other side of his judgment. Other points may prove more important, or our interpretation of certain features may be the reverse of his.

For example, even if I agreed with all the details of the BART evaluation, I might still decide that the context for thinking of the project was wrong, that cash flow was an interesting but incorrect measure of the liveliness of urban places. The number of fortifications or baths has been the true measure of liveliness at other times, for example. I would then bring out a set of very different aspects of BART—say, a study of the national perception of the Bay Area—that shows that BART actually does work by maintaining the sense of the region as successful. Or, again agreeing with the fiscal facts, I could argue that all public projects reflect the dynamics of our taxation system, which is geared to the maintenance of private enterprise at the cost of losses in the public sphere.

We like to think that if we are rational and systematic, our evaluation will be convincing and true. But that is not quite what we are warranted in expecting. It is a bit too much. We can hope to produce an evaluation that is worthy of attention, that others will have to take account of in their position. It will be recognized as a necessary part of the community of thought about how we ought act together. It will be an "enlargement of mind," as Hannah Arendt puts it, following Kant. Recognition and enlargement mean a great deal. We can use them to establish a political space where we can meet and act.

Evaluations, whether they are of artworks or of policies, are rhetorical, educative, historical, and subjective. This does not mean that they are arbitrary or irrational. Rather, their logic depends on a mode of persuasion based on our seeing ourselves as members of a community who have a shared common sense that we may appeal to. The ways we have developed for judging works of art, works that exemplify perfection and wholeness, prove useful for judging policies and plans because we require that policies be harmonious and not wasteful, and that plans hint at a more perfect and whole world.

## UTOPIAS AND IDEALS

In the public and governmental sector, grand designs and plans are often the organizing themes. They require the broad political support, the high tolerance for substantial risk, and the capacity for absorbing large losses and distributing windfall gains that especially characterize that sector. Grand designs and plans inspire inventors and private enterprise too. But the private sector must be more circumspect. The market discourages large overarching schemes because they are usually plagued by cash-flow problems, although government often does provide some insurance to these risk-takers.

Capitalism and the market mechanism itself are based on a sense of a seemingly designed coherent order. They were originally hailed as a means for providing the world with a sense of order and peace unavailable to the feuding monarchies, and as a means for controlling catastrophic risk. This design and regulation were to be implemented not only through the invisible hand, but through people's shared sense of the rational human world.

So visionary and utopian plans and large-scale, long-term designs play an important role in all kinds of enterprise. They provide a framework for our judgments, as well. For example, the perfect market is one of the most enticing utopian models. Surely our world is imperfect. The market, or, by contrast, a communitarian society, will not be achieved on this earth. We know full well that their prerequisites are not available to us. Yet we insist on invoking them as models.

We keep making plans, even if past ones have not been achieved. Utopian plans and designs are everpresent in city planning and architecture. We know they are likely to fail, but we need them anyway to guide our actions. A sensible corporate planner knows that there is much about the external environment that he cannot incorporate into his models. All sorts of internal factors, both structural and personal, are likely to change. He knows ahead of time that the plan will not work out. He knows as well that the success of his corporation has depended substantially on these environmental and changing factors.

He does the best job he can, but it is often not enough. Still, he makes a plan. We need to have larger conceptions of where our enterprise will go, even though we know it will not quite go there.

We seem to guide ourselves by falsehoods or impossibilities. Rational men and women might say that these are provisional modes of guidance, the best we have right now. Carefully done, they are more likely to be true than random expectations. But studies of utopias suggest they are meant as more direct guides, not only provisional ones. We take them seriously. Classical utopias, for example, attempt to discern man's essential qualities. Distant from our present lives, they serve as a standard of judgment of them. Modern utopias are, rather, a development of a particular viewpoint. They recognize that there will be other utopias with large numbers of adherents. Still, even modern utopias set an ideal for us to follow. They are not simply provisional. In each case a problem remains, that of interpreting the standard or ideal. To follow the utopia we must figure out how it guides us, now, in our present lives. These are the usual problems in biblical and talmudic interpretation. But rather than there being a single method of interpretation in those fields, as we might wish, we find a set of often conflicting methods. The problem of interpretation remains open.

Utopias, ideals, and perfection play a much larger role in our lives than their impracticality might suggest. We might understand this role if we examined how the experience of religious conversion is described in confessional literature, such as in Augustine and Dante. Conversions always take place here on Earth, in this imperfect environment. Yet conversion refers quite specifically to a perfect heavenly world. How are these two worlds reconciled and brought together? The story goes something like the following (see Figure 1).

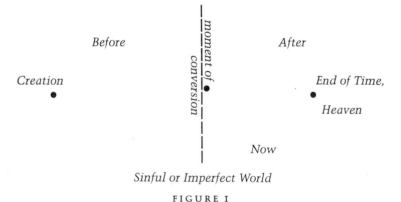

FIGURE I

There was a (moment of) creation when all was perfect. But Creation was shattered (by Eve and Adam?) and the flow of historical Time, under which we now endure, began. Now we live in a sinful imperfect world.

Before conversion, you [shifting to the voice of the experiencing person] thought that this world was all there was. There was no truth or perfection or, even worse, you thought that this world was the best you could imagine. You did not even appreciate the meaning and promise of creation. Although others may have written about it, you could not understand what they said. You were not ready.

Then there is a moment of conversion.* Perhaps you are touched by a certain person, or act, or situation. It may be God's grace. It may be an appreciation of what the truth is, so that a scientist will speak of a discovery, such as that of the double helix, in these terms. From then on the world feels different. You now know that Before was only that, a time before you could have had an idea of what was true and perfect. You did not even know the meaning of what you were doing. Your interpretation was systematically self-deceiving. Now, After, you can see Before, that is, the Before interpretation (which you once thought was all there is, which you did not even know was "before"), in terms of falsehood and sin and misapprehension, for now you see, perhaps only roughly, what is true.

When you write the history of this experience, a confession, you have to rewrite what you had once understood in Before terms. From the perspective of After, that Before understanding is a misunderstanding. Perhaps you can show how it was a systematic misunderstanding, since it was not a matter of casual error but of an intentional interpretation that was wrong. The new, After, reading of your past should show how the systematic misunderstanding (of Before) led to your being ready for the discovery of the truth at just that time when it happened, the moment of conversion, although you could not have known that ahead of time. Before, you might not have believed there were such a thing as a conversionary moment, although you may have heard of others who have had it or have had one yourself already. Still, you might have had an inkling that you were getting close. There is a certain excitement, anxiety, or feeling of prehension that people re-

---

*Reports of conversion include both fast and slow conversions. In the latter case, there is continual deeper implication into the new way of being. There seems to be no single moment of conversion. But people who have these slow conversions often identify *a* crucial moment. Fast conversions may well be slow ones with a more decisively described moment.

port—but always after, when it is then clear what those feelings must have meant. (They weren't *just* a matter of an upset stomach.)

Others who claim to have experienced that moment can serve as models for our lives. They may be great scientists or writers or entrepreneurs. It might even be Jesus, whose coming (for Christians) is that moment, where Creation is what Genesis talks about, where the Before story is the Old Testament, the After the New, and that final moment, the End of Time, is not yet here. Mohammed, Sabbatai Ṣevi, Joseph Lewis, and Mary Baker Eddy are other models.

After the moment of conversion, your life is different. It is informed and suffused by the truth. Perfection (or an ideal or utopian model) gives meaning to your life. You now have an understanding of what you are up to. When you go wrong you can know why, and give an interpretation of your action in terms of the proper way. Errors are not just random, they signify the order of the universe. They are a matter of our fall from the ideal, an ideal you now can have a conception of.

Ideal plans and designs lead to an interpretation of how we live and how we err. They say how we ought to act, and show why we cannot act as well as we should. They account for the failures of the Before past, as well as excuse them if we, only, finally, at this penultimate time, acknowledge the truth. So rather than saying that we guide ourselves by falsehoods and impossibilities, once we have experienced conversion we say that we may still live in falsehood and impossibility but now guide ourselves by the truth. Utopias are real. Our current world is only a shadow, intermittently interrupted by the clash and thunder of that reality. Ideals and plans guide our lives here in this imperfect time. They regulate and give meaning to what we do. They provide a norm and a moral ideal for us. But it is not at all clear just what the ideals and plans mean, or how they are to guide and regulate and provide a norm. Theories of practical and political interpretation, often biblical in origin, are needed to figure out the implications of an ideal. Institutions such as churches, planning agencies, and politicians are also needed.

Still, returning to our story of conversion, the perfect world is not yet yours. You are not in heaven now. You shall fail frequently, although not always. You have only an intimation of the true and perfect world; you do not know it. Your interpretations will not always be right. But you have a handle on what is perfect and it guides you. At the End of Time, we shall have a meeting of our mundane lives with the perfect world; there will be no difference between what we ought to do and what we do; time will come to a halt. We will speak the truth as clearly and easily as we speak today. Utopia will be here. We will understand the structure of the world.

Of course we cannot now know what it would actually be like to be in heaven, to have a grasp on the truth that was firm and without tension. So although we speak of perfection, and guide our lives by models of it, we cannot fully articulate what it would be like. We cannot conclude that we know what is perfect, at least right now. And perhaps we will have a second or third conversion in our lifetime. Converts will find it impossible to conceive of something like this, for isn't the first sufficient and isn't a conversion a conversion to the one truth? Even scientists, who have a reputation for being open to new evidence, seem to find it personally very difficult to experience more than one theoretical revolution in their lifetime, and for many of them even one is too much.

So we cannot insist that our vision is the one that must be imposed on others, although we unwarrantedly tend to. We might also believe, although we almost never do, that others who disagree with us might have as strong a vision as we do, and we might be wrong in part.

There are a number of ways that we identify those who believe that their mundane vision or plan is the only one, with no subsequent conversions or alternatives. In the world of research, we call someone unscientific, or dogmatic or ideological. In religion, it is a matter of intolerance or the sin of pride. In politics, we call it totalitarianism. There are more generous descriptions of these absolute behaviors. A scientist is persistent in exploring the consequences of his theory; the religious person is devout; the political actor is committed and willing to struggle. Ways that we decide whether a believer deserves the less or more generous designation and interpretation of his actions include the quality of his evidence, his degree of self-awareness, and his capacity to acknowledge doubt. But these are not infallible indicators. Some fanatics deserve a more generous reading, and some coolly rational, persistent researchers are simply pig-headed.

Certain interpretations of modern totalitarian movements and states suggest that the urge for perfection is the foundation of totalitarianism. That may well be true. Transcendent commitments (to perfection, say) made immanent would seem to be potentially totalitarian.

But in general, an urge for perfection need not lead to totalitarian beliefs. For a plan or a vision of perfection is a guide to how to live now in an imperfect world, a world not to be made perfect by any finite activity of ours. As I have suggested, that guide cannot be interpreted with certainty by anyone. It cannot justifiably be used as a cudgel, any more than can any system of belief or law. Rather, it provides a meeting ground for rational argument among those who share the commitment to perfection. In other words, an urge for perfection is one foundation for a liberal rational world.

The model of conversion shows how this world and another more perfect world (actually created in this world, by us) might be reconciled here and now. Heaven, doomsday, truth, and perfection are signs of the future, and if properly interpreted they indicate to us what we must do now to make a better world. They regulate and guide our lives. They interpret error and give meaning to what we do.

For example, perfection is often measured by the maximization of something, whether it be returns on investment, the amount of output, or, as in physics, quantities such as free energy. Maximization models interpret waste, failure, or not-working by saying that the situation is less than maximal. Similarly, a perfect heaven gives meaning to our earthly defects by causally relating the defects to our previous transgressive actions. So it shows how we might be different. Models of formal unity play a central role in criticism of works of literature and art, for we may argue that works are poor because they are defective and not unified.

The dynamics of conversion help us to think rationally about the relationship of B A R T's current financial difficulties to its future possibilities. Say we believe that B A R T will become a means of reorganizing the economic geography of the San Francisco Bay Area over the next fifty years. Say we also believe that if others agreed with us, if they could see the sensibleness of our claim, then it would more surely work out. Proselytizing is not simply madness; it is necessary for the success of ideal visions. More radical visionaries might believe that those who do not see the truth will eventually be dragged along, but usually the impulse to gather co-converts is sensible and irresistible.

If we hold these beliefs about B A R T, then it is clear that cash-flow measures miss the point, that B A R T does not succeed by paying off, as would an ordinary investment. Rather, B A R T is a sign of the future. Of course it will need financing, but measuring success in terms of financial viability misses B A R T's essence. Bankruptcy or default is only sinful in terms of finance; in terms of long-term large-scale development, it is part of a kind of transformation we have seen many times before.

Continuing in this vein, development and consequent reconceptualization of the Bay Area is the long-term meaning, the true meaning, of B A R T. We must look for signs of this future, even small ones. For these signs are the authentic signs and are indicative of what is really going on. We believe that in fifty years this view of what is real will be manifestly true. Surely we shall have to deal with finances and keep the bankers from the door, but such problems need not be the central ones in evaluating B A R T.

Under such a scheme of thinking, B A R T's evaluators should be historians, novelists, and developers, as well as the economic geographers. Not all signs equally signify what might eventually happen. Selecting the ones that are more likely to be the actual forebears requires a good sense of human nature and of narrative possibility. You would want to be Moses and Robert Moses.

In any discussion of conversion there will always be doubters, those who find that the conversion and the new After interpretation, and perhaps the whole idea of After, is a sham, a sham that will mislead us. It is a sham because there is no such thing as a conversion or because the truth has already been discovered and we are After already. They may be right. But doubters cannot argue against the proselyte simply in terms of the presently accepted values. To the proselyte these are merely Before values, even though to the doubter who has already converted earlier and is now resisting a second conversion, the currently accepted values are already the embodiment of the After vision. How do we know that the current values are more likely to be true than the future ones? And why should we treat current values with more hallowed respect than some alternative set? That current values "work" makes sense as a criterion if we are willing to enshrine the nature of their work. And why should we do that unless we are intrinsically conservative? The argument for conservatism and against conversion cannot be only about the usefulness or necessity or provenness of what we have now. The argument must be about the kinds of worlds offered by the various visions and the evidence offered for them, and about the power of a vision to reinterpret the action and error of the past and make sense of it.

It may be useful to recall that many men were candidates for the Messiah in Roman times. How were the Jews to decide who to follow? These were times of great instability in Judaism. Jesus's success awaited the first hundred years after his death to be more or less confirmed, and four hundred years to become established. From the point of view of Christian history, the difficulties of the early stages of Christianity, its problems of survival and of differentiation from the rest of Judaism, all point to its ultimate success. But for a secular history that success is not foregone. Usually, in fact, the early trials and difficulties lead to failure.

I should note that my description of conversion has been deliberately designed to be similar to current discussions of change in natural science. Although scientific theories are often said to be provisional, in practice they are usually treated in the same way as utopias and ideals. They function as the truth; they suggest the nature of our errors; they determine the appropriate signs for confirming their truth; and they often are adopted and rejected in much the same way and with a similar tone as are utopias and ideals. In the Appendix to this essay I want to pursue this in greater detail in a somewhat different context.

In models of conversion, perfection is not something we have here and now. In fact, it is specifically for another time and place. But it guides what we do, it is the standard for our critique, and it is the basis for our shared argument. We believe in models of perfection not because they are realized already but because of their promise, and because of their effectiveness right now in our lives.

Confession literature offers us a model for understanding what we say about large-scale transformations. We reconcile the past, the present, and the future in the same way the After story or theory accommodates the Before. The ideal is not achieved yet, and perfection and wholeness can be compatible with a liberal, rational picture of the world.

We can go further and describe the structure of the experience of transformation and of decisionmaking. We may then see why decisionmaking intrinsically involves making responsible moral and resource commitments, commitments that we regularly recommit ourselves to.

## COMMITMENT AND DECISIONMAKING

We make a decision when we initiate a project. In choosing a particular path we commit ourselves to a line of development. How do we do this? Are the various commitments we make, whether they be about how we are to live our lives, to invest our resources, or to fulfill a certain role, roughly of the same sort? I think we can describe a common model of commitment in government and business and in our personal, political, and religious lives. The model is quite faithful to what we actually do and feel when we make a decision. And it accommodates the technical apparatus of formal decision theory as well. Yet it does not permit the technical decisionmaker to lay responsibility for his choices simply on his technique. His selection of a technique is a foundation for his responsibility.

We want a conception of decisionmaking that feels familiar. When we enter into a project, do we actually initiate it? Or do we find ourselves in a certain place, already up to something? Then we might look backward, project forward, and explicitly sketch a project, a project that permits us to identify a point of initiation. What makes us stop and think this through? Sometimes it is the need to justify what we do, to others or to ourselves. Sometimes, what we thought we could do without stopping does not work out as we expect. We have to rethink what we are up to. And sometimes we actually do initiate a project, actually decide to do it, actually choose a path and follow it, rather than find ourselves on what we discover to be a road and then call it ours. Retrospectively or prospectively, we commit ourselves to a line of development, and then see it as a path involving some initiating decision.

A decision may be a matter of choosing from a well-defined list, as in examinations, position papers, or a series of cost-benefit–evaluated projects. We try to do the best we can by a fairly straightforward measure of success. But often our decisions, even if they are retrospective reconstructions, are manifestly a matter of commitment, of entering into and continuing a way of life and articulating its possibilities. Even if we were presented with a set of choices, we might find that the different choices are in no way simply comparable, even on a set of scales. They involve different ways of living. Each way may be good, but good in a very different manner. Even if we believed there was an essential unity in our notion of goodness, its realizations could emphasize diverse aspects of the notion. When we choose a way of living, we examine it as a whole, fitting our selves into it. Does it allow room for what we think is important? How will it work out for us? Surely we can compare parts or aspects of ways of living, and those comparisons will bring out important features of each way. We may combine ways of living to develop alternatives that are more suited to our desires, as well.

But decisions may not involve a set of alternatives. They may require our forging ahead in one way and figuring out, again and again, what we are up to as we go along. We may branch off from where we thought we were going without having much sense of the terrain we are entering, but knowing that we must grow, and grow in a different way.

A decision requires more than selecting or discerning a path. We need to justify our decision to others and to ourselves. We want to make sense of what we are up to. We want to organize what we know about how the decision or path will work out. But sometimes our original reasons for selecting a direction no longer seem cogent to us, and these original reasons may become hidden or forgotten.

Various procedures are useful for organizing the argument in a systematic way. Economics and statistical decision theory make up one powerful mode. Other ethical theories and legal arguments are also helpful. The procedures help us to be more careful, and, being canonical forms of thinking about decisions, they make our decisions seem less arbitrary, at least until we question why they are the canonical ways.

In time, a systematic procedure or method may come to be seen as the proper way of making and justifying decisions. We may use it to determine retrospectively just what our decision was. For example, an economic historian will rewrite conventional history in terms of market-like decisions. The method, because it seems objective and independent of us, may permit us to forget that we may not have actually originally chosen using the method, or that the processes of justification mold the structure of a particular choice. It is hard to believe that we could forget how creative legal processes or decision analyses are, but sometimes we do. Then the decisions and commitments do not seem to be ours, but are a matter of following the rules, of paying allegiance to such values as justice or efficiency. Following the rules can make us less aware of our responsibilities, even if the procedures permit us to do better and more fairly in the world.

If we see the method itself, rather than ourselves, as having gone awry, we inherit a number of problems. We cannot take credit for the successes of a method, only for having applied it correctly. We find it difficult to understand why people undertake commitments and projects that we all know will not work out. Consequently, we may split our picture of decisionmaking into one about rational sensible choices and one about transcendent and irrational ones. (Note how this split feeds the needs of both the scientist and the preserver of religious transcendence; it is Kant's legacy to us.)

Summarizing, decisions often do not feel like methodical and rational choices. If they are rational, they may not be among commensurable or comparable alternatives such as are required by most methods. Also, we may want to select a path that will require more substantial commitments than our reasons will permit us. And some of the time we may follow a method, and manifestly do poorly or incorrectly. Are we to understand that as a matter of ineptitude, stochastic failure, or something more tragic? Finally, some decisions involve extraordinary experiences of anxiety, and these experiences seem intrinsic to the decision, and not likely to go away when we try to be cool and rational. How might we understand these phenomena?

Our discussion of confession and conversion showed how we might give an account of a major transformation. We may also describe in a parallel fashion the experience of the transformation and examine its logic. Are the extraordinary feelings we experience when we make a decision logically necessary? What is the status of errors that are spectacularly wrong or strange or gone awry? How do we manage extreme cases and seemingly incomparable alternatives? Can we use systematic methods, yet treat them as part of the process of decision and commitment? How do we allow for the historical and personal development character of making a decision?

Descriptions of rites of passage in cultural anthropology, of religious commitment in theology, of anxiety in psychology, of the heroic voyage in literature, of mystical experiences, and of what we might call existential choice, suggest a model of the process of decisionmaking that incorporates the features we need. The model is a synthesis drawing from all these fields. It is consistent with our model of confession, articulating the details of the moment of conversion.

A few caveats before going further. Rituals are ritualized. Rituals control the path of transformation. Anthropologists note that rituals tame and encapsulate change. Sometimes nothing happens as a result of the ritual. So the model of the rites-of-passage ritual incorporates conflicting tendencies. Internal to the ritual is the experience of dramatic transformation that it allows. But externally it is quite conservative, and its political implications are ambivalent. It allows for incommensurable changes, but then, by means of a retrospective reading of what happened (the After story), the transformation is tamed, and future changes are said to be precluded, at least until the final salvation. When we are in an After situation, there will be tremendous resistance to embarking on another transformation, unless, as in the life cycle, the final state is still further off. As I have mentioned, new actors and a new generation will be needed to make a next transformation. They are persons who have not gone through the previous transformation, convinced that that was "it."

There are three aspects I want to describe: the nature of the experience, the quality of being in the middle of making a decision, and the kind of world assumed by the model.

For the most part we live in an ordinary everyday world (Figure 2,

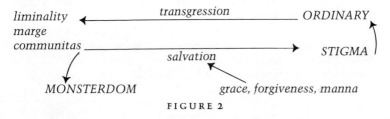

FIGURE 2

upper right). We know how to get along, how to deal with difficulties, how to manage. At times there may be dilemmas or problems, but we are able to figure out how to handle them using the skills we have. The world is tame for us. But there are other times that are not ordinary, when we do not know how to manage, when we hit a snag. We see ourselves as having to make a decision. We have to change our course. Entering the world you experience . . . .

Perhaps to others [shifting to the second person to describe the experience of going through a transition] you are just going through a stage, but to yourself the transition is novel, its outcome is not obvious or sure. The seamless web of life is not so seamless. Correspondingly, for conversion, you find a moment when the way you thought adequate for living your life no longer seems to be. You are stopped in your tracks. Suddenly there is the possibility of a Before and an After.

Obvious examples of this kind of transition are such rites of passage as marriage, ordination, bar-mitzvah, and a change in career. Religious conversion, the development of a new theoretical model, or embarking on a heroic voyage are other similar transitions. In each case, the way you have been living proves no longer viable for you. The way you organize your life no longer makes the sense it once did. You not only find yourself going along a new way, but you act as if that transition was a marked one.

When you step over the line or find yourself in an extraordinary situation, you have *transgressed* the usual way of doing things. Transgression does not imply bad or evil action, but a situation in which sacredness, of this or another world, becomes a possibility. Even if you have heard about the event before, for example, marriage or development of a large-scale project, you cannot treat it as ordinary. Even if you are sophisticated, you are taken over by the dynamics of the transgression and transition. Marriage becomes holy; decisions become gripping.

Having stepped over the line, you enter a middle ground, what you eventually see as between Before and After. But you do not know which characteristics of before this time will mark it as Before, and which of the subsequent time will mark it as After. You do not know what it is that you are between.

Of course you have some idea of what will happen. You know what has happened previously and to others in similar situations. What is distinctive about these transitions is that you feel a high degree of anxiety about the middle state. It has been called *marginal* or *liminal*, to designate the fact that it is on the border of experience. You might fall off, never to return to an ordinary state. The marginal state is not incoherent. Studies of the structure of mystical experience and heroic voyages, for example, show that the structure of the marginal state is a reflection of our ordinary past and future, perhaps not surprisingly since it is reported on after you have returned to an ordinary state. These reports may read strangely and be filled with seeming contradictions, but they are actually quite veridical. They are a summation of where you have been and a preview of where you will go. But this account we have only afterward. During the period of transition or decision, you are much less sure, much more aware of your distance from what you thought was the ordinary world. You are outside of yourself: in a word, ecstatic.

*"that it is"*                                                          ONE

FIGURE 3

The distinctive characteristic of the *ecstatic* state (Figure 3), when you are in-between, on the marge, is that your ordinary usual world seems as "one." The dichotomies and polarities—analytic, conceptual, political—that we think of as most natural now seem to you to be part of a unity. The incommensurables that make it necessary that we choose, sacrificing one thing for another, are comfortable with each other, not even ordered in a hierarchy. Paradoxically, the dilemmas that forced us to abandon the ordinary world are temporarily transcended here. The one-ness presages a resolution of the difficulties or dilemmas that initiated the transition.

You look back and down on your everyday life, and can see that the unity you sense now is sundered by the fall from unity to separation, by the mundane and contingent demands of everyday life. So you might believe that you can transcend those demands and resolve your difficulties, with a new, and what we eventually call After, way of living. But this moment in heaven, this sense of Aha!, this feeling of comprehensiveness, is not available to you for all time. You are not in heaven yet. You see the fall from unity to dissipation, from wholeness to mundanity, as necessary, not contingent. Eve's eating the apple was unavoidable in this ontology. Our errors and everyday problems will not go away; rather, they define us as human beings. The fall is part of the one-ness of the world, too, so you see not only the one of unity, but also the fall from one-ness to separation as part of the one, and both are intimately connected. (We could not have a notion of the one without separation being also present.) The fall from the grace of unity is not a matter of choice, but the way things are. In your experience there is a hint of the End of Time, of the unification of all, of the grace of God, of the fulfillment of plans and designs—but you are still in this world. This experience gives you hope in despair and strength in defeat. It makes you see problems and their resolutions as intrinsically intertwined.

And finally, in ecstasy you are distant from it all, outside. You feel: that it is. You actually experience ecstasy in the ecstatic state, although in my description I have deliberately emphasized the cognitive aspects of the ecstatic. The one-ness feeling of ecstasy is the realization of the conceptual unity you know at that time.

In the marge, in-between, you break the role boundaries of the ordinary world for a while. It is a time of play. Action and awareness are merged, attention is centered, ego is loosened. You know what to do. You feel the exhilaration of times of high crisis and decision.

The marginal state will also be frightening and overwhelming. You do not know how to manage and tame the cognitive restructuring it suggests and the feelings that accompany it. Rightly, you might be afraid. In transformation, decisionmaking, and making a commitment to a way of life, there is a period that is not tame. This period has the potential, as well, of letting you see what is whole and good and unified. From the point of view of what we ordinarily call rationality, this marginal period is irrational, contradictory, and unhealthy. The reports of most people during this period suggest that the quality of irrationality is persistent and cannot be dismissed. It seems to be intrinsic to these transformations. It is not only a psychological fact, but a logical fact as well. For the middle ground must mix the incommensurable Before and After, as we eventually label them. It must look inconsistent and incoherent.

How might we think of the logical structure of the world we experience? (See Figure 4.) We live in an ordinary, everyday world in which we know how to get along. For the most part we do not reflect on what

FIGURE 4

we are doing, even if what we are doing is philosophical reflection. We follow standard operating procedure. We rely most often on what is usually done, the appropriate reliable methods, even at times that seem to others, or to ourselves retrospectively, to require deliberate choice and commitment. If things do not work out, we have done our best. We have been careful, have followed due process, have not committed malpractice. And if things work out, we receive our due reward.

But, alternatively, you can be authentically responsible for your choices. While you acknowledge that there are standard operating procedures, you also acknowledge that it is up to you to select a particular way of living or proceeding rather than another way. Even if you were to choose to follow the standard procedure, still you have chosen it and you act as if you did.

Your choice, the way of proceeding you work out, is no longer the obvious, only, or necessary one, but one among other, perhaps mutually incomparable ways. Having chosen, you can take responsibility for what you have chosen, taking a past to your heart. Each of us repeats or enacts a way of proceeding, making it our own. We understand what we are up to because we have a sense about what we have been up to before. Heroes never venture in totally uncharted lands. They follow one of a number of heroic paths in the footsteps of others just like themselves. We could not recognize something entirely new.

When you are called to account for what you have done, you cannot use the defense that it is a standard procedure. You could have done otherwise. Even if your reasons for embarking on a path were the usual ones, you still invoked those reasons.

If a procedure fails, there is no way out for you. When you fail, others call you, not just your method, to account. But they cannot then treat you as diabolical or idiosyncratic. They realize that the method you used is probably one of the standard and well-justified methods, a method with a reasonable record of success. Their judgment of what you did must take into account that they could have chosen as you did. Still, you must stand on your own.

This position balances two extremes. At one pole is a methodism that views method and proper use of it as primary. At the other pole there is absolute individual responsibility for what you do. We may temper each pole by noting that you are always following a procedure you have selected. You are both prudent and idiosyncratic.

If you are buried under the weight of the standard way of doing things, how do you discover the possibility of being authentic? There are times when you cannot go on as you have been, times of decision, of epiphany, of almost dying. You can rationalize and normalize even these times. But not always. These are times that hint to you that there is something more. You feel especially alive; it is a moment of discovery. Perhaps you hear a call of conscience (as Heidegger puts it), of a possibility that is more than just going along as usual. At these peak moments you can feel anxious, distant from your ordinary involvements, standing before the world, watching it anew. It is a return from death. Momentarily freed from your entanglements, you see the possibility of choice, of being free, even to choose again what you were doing and to simply resume where you left off.

When we make a decision we can feel anxious; and anxiety makes it possible for us to make a decision authentically. The feelings are not only psychological, they are logical as well.

Let us continue our exploration of the middle or marginal state, returning to the moment of transgression (and to Figure 2). You have entered the marge where you are subject to anxiety. Ecstatic, you see the world as whole and coherent, even if you are unconnected with it. You cannot yet know how you shall emerge from your decision. Perhaps you do not emerge, and so you become a monster. Monsters are artifacts of the limited capacities of our rational apparatus, of our ability to make sense of what we do. You seem to others never to have returned to the ordinary state to resume one of the acceptable and cognitively recognizable roles. The transgression leads away in ways those in ordinary life cannot comprehend. So they call the extraordinary cases failures or monsters. And they are failures or monsters. You are (thought to be) crazy then, a permanent outcast rather than being in transition. The contradictions of the marginal state, the seeming logical incoherence of reports of transition periods and mystical experiences, do not cease when you are thought to have returned to the ordinary world. The ordinary world does not even tolerate marginal persons very well. (On the other hand, to the putative monster, the ordinary world may well seem truly monstrous, while for the monster the liminal community is the sane and healthy world. A liminal community, such as a monastery, may be the only place for you. History may show that the monsters of one time are the true precursors, and the central figures for the future.)

Of course you may be still in transition and others may not realize that. But since the ritual frame is determined not only by you, but is a social fact, your being out of place is enough to condemn you. Put differently, decisions are not only your own, but take place in a social, economic, and political matrix. Your experience in making a decision can be only part of the story. Everyone else, even though he or she is not the actor going through the ritual at this time, will have other roles to fulfill, from being spectators to actively guiding you through the process. They are watching you as they participate in it.

Your way of thinking of yourself as you transit the marginal period is mediated by what you have been taught to expect, by what others tell you about it, and by what you can understand of what the spectators say (through a gauze, since they exist in the ordinary world). So you may end up thinking of yourself as a monster, if they think of you that way. An acceptable crazy person agrees with others' judgments of himself. If it seems to you that you are either still in transition, or that your state is an ordinary one, even if most others do not realize that, you must find support the best you can. Perhaps your accompaniment will be the furies. Perhaps it will be a liminal community that will take you in.

During the process of decision and commitment you may be anxious, as I have suggested already. The feelings you experience in anxiety show you how disastrous the outcome can be. You feel unconnected with the world, out of it, not part of the stream of life. You have abandoned any possible way of living. The world is just there for you. You watch what is going on, it is a return from death. Will you emerge from the middle ground, whole and well and alive? Will you never emerge? Anxiety also reminds you that choice is possible. The standard operating procedure need not determine the world. It does not do so now, nothing does. You can choose to begin again.

Anxiety is a sign to you that you can become disconnected from the world and be monstrous for others. And your experience coincides with their opinion. At the same time, it is a sign that you can be free for an authentic choice, you are not stuck. And your experience confirms this too.

Highly ritualized transformations tend to be more reliable, and anxiety is less of an issue in them. You are likely to emerge ordinarily, less likely to become monstrous. Better guidance is available, expectations are modest, deviations are handled with greater finesse. Not surprisingly, this set of prescriptions also characterizes decisionmaking that is patterned and standardized.

Rather than becoming monstrous, usually you are *saved*, returned, brought back into the ordinary world from the abyss-filled marginal one. The risks you took now make sense in terms of how the situation works out. You find that you and others can account for your decision, just as Abraham accounted for his willingness to sacrifice Isaac, and not see yourself as a murderer or imprudent revolutionary. Or you may fail in your effort. There is no heaven on earth and your project may not work out. But you can still understand why it did not work, how it might in the future, and appreciate the risks you have taken as part of a long-term strategy. Entrepreneurial innovators and social reformers must return to this tack again and again.

In any case, the transgression of the ordinary way of living is now healed and forgiven. In the middle of the transition you could not expect so much. So as you return you have that sense of *manna*, of a miraculous windfall. Some might want to argue that this sense is false and illusory, since it is in the nature of a ritual to come out all right, as it is in the nature of ritualized decisionmaking that it more or less works. That may be true. But for the person going through the transition, and even for those who participate with him, it seems much less sure. And sometimes things do fail, spectacularly.

Where do manna and salvation come from? Do they come only from your own self, or more modestly from "all of those who worked to make this a successful project"? Since you have gone through such a frightening time, you find it hard to believe that you did it all alone, so mundanely. Depending on your other beliefs, you may credit your success to God's grace, to careful method and good work, or to luck, as well as to astuteness, and so forth. Even if you know that you have every right to have succeeded based on your prudent efforts, you know you could have failed. And others suspect that too, or at least they are only too willing to give you supernatural credit, calling you a genius or a hero.

Having made a decision, having interrupted the course of events (even when that interruption is only a thought-experiment), and having returned to the ordinary life, you cannot avoid the fact of your having transgressed. You took your life in your own hands. You are now marked, you are *stigmatized*. You are no longer the same as before, even if you have returned to your original role and way of being.

Imagine if you treated your whole life in this way, if you always saw yourself as stigmatized and graced. Imagine if you thought that your plans and designs mattered and were not just well-done, methodical jobs. It is very hard to do such imagining, for it is the nature of living an ordinary life that it is not marked, but just goes on.

Were I a director of a large enterprise I would want my staff to think of themselves in this way, as I would if I were a minister concerned with his parishioners. But decisionmaking is not a matter of needless risk, gambling, or anxiety-filled confrontations with yourself. Rather, it is a matter of your attitude toward yourself and your ordinary activities. Are your actions marked and significant; are you an actual actor rather than a functionary; do you have purposes whose meanings you appreciate; do you realize that failure may be unavoidable yet you must still go on?

Making a decision is a transformation that has moral, logical, and experiential qualities, which this model tries to capture. The model does not preclude any method of decisionmaking. Rather, it gives a context for applying a method, and it suggests limits concerning the self-sufficiency of any method, for every method will be subject to anxiety, ecstasy, and grace.

The distinctive features of this picture of making a decision are most apparent when we make crucial choices or dramatic changes in our lives, or strong recommitments to what we are doing already. Less momentous situations will pass unnoticed; you have a sense of acting as if you are following standard operating procedure. But if this model is viewed as fundamental, then it is a model for how even less momentous choices should be seen. It is a way of thinking about the problems you get into when you violate the ordinary ways you are used to. And even if you can be methodical and ignore your own complicity in a decision, the model suggests why you will be affected by an appeal that emphasizes that method is not something given from nowhere, but a re-creation by and from yourself. You follow a method, or a cookbook, or cost-benefit analysis, or PERT, because you know how to be a human being, and follow instructions, and not do irrelevant things. And if you do something strange you know you ought to account for yourself.

BART's entrepreneurial and professional designers are responsible for the errors they made in assessing its future patronage. The adoption of a particular method of transport planning is not automatic, even if it is customary and the currently acknowledged best we have. But if we lay particular responsibility on the designers and planners, one they even accept and concur in, then we cannot conclude they ought to be banished for their error. Forgiveness is part of the process of healing. And in time, our conception of a project and what we are up to are transformed. Bondholders are paid off, and economy and private property need no longer be the regime of evaluation in the second life of the project. And so we can be forgiving. But that forgiveness requires humility on the part of the designers, their acknowledging that we give them authority. It is a change in the style of professional practice that may be incongenial with the public's tendency to give professionals too much respect or, in reaction, too little.

The stigma of the past should remind us that there are nether regions. Our methods will fail us. And failure and forgiveness must be part of how we think about a method. The failures are not simply matters of error, but of errors we make and we must cure.

One mode of cure is through sacrifice. The model of decisionmaking based on the ritual of rites of passage suggests why our commitments may require what seem like irrational sacrifices of what we possess. A sacrifice is a total loss that, when viewed from a larger perspective, seems rational and a gain. Why else would Abraham think of killing Isaac if not for a sacrifice to God? A sacrifice fly benefits the team even though the individual player is out. But when we consider the analogy in terms of a secular complex society, the measures and the beneficiaries of the gain are much less clear than in religion or baseball.

Sacrifices are performed during rituals as a way of restoring the natural order, of propitiating the gods, of clearing the air. They take the accumulated defects in the world and concentrate them onto the sacrificial victim, who if he believes in the ritual may well assent to being sacrificed. When that victim is destroyed, the society can begin anew. The non-rational parts of the world, the errors, the mistakes, the parts that do not fit in with what we want must be gotten rid of, completely and justifiably and ceremonially. In the story of B A R T, we shall have to describe the sacrifice of the horse, the interurbans, and then the automobile, each to its successor and ultimately to B A R T. The victim absorbs all the costs of a transformation, and hence we can maintain a notion that the system is otherwise continuous and rational and economical. (Note that we use the term rationalization when we refer to making things more efficient by eliminating duplication and so forth, which is another form of sacrifice.)

Sacrifice in economic transformation makes rational the waste and ravaging of market capitalism. It becomes a natural process to dump vast capital resources when more efficient means of production come to the scene. Schumpeter was right in pointing out how we would have little stomach for that now, in capitalism's triumph. At least we are less than willing to sacrifice those who belong to the most powerful groups, such as men or large corporations.

Sacrifice makes up for the defects in the economy by periodically wiping them out. A side benefit of this erasure is that the economic rationale provided by the neoclassical synthesis, which views changes as smooth and commensurable rather than sacrificial, seems to be in good shape. The sacrifices are ignored. But, of course, the systemic production of defective material, such as inefficient producers and unemployable workers, needs to be concentrated onto certain sacrificial victims. As the economic system's problems become more profound, the victims might become white men and large corporate entities. Then we have a "crisis" of capitalism. When it is women and shopkeepers, it is the way nature works. In either case, as we try to buy off the victims in order to retain our putative legitimacy, we seem to generate further instabilities.

If B A R T is to succeed it may have to kill the automobile, and so sacrifice a very large capital investment. Rapidly rising fuel prices might effectively perform this auto-sacrifice, B A R T being a passive onlooker comparatively less affected by fuel costs. The sacrifice will be a repetition of the sacrifice of the interurban tramway systems. Whether, in fact, the systems were falling apart on their own, or whether the automobile manufacturers made poor investments in those systems, which they then abandoned, or whether people "naturally" preferred the auto, or whether the system of technological economies was changing, may be open to argument. We must think about such transformations realizing that the economics of a particular set of alternatives is not natural in any way. It depends on the structural factors and hidden subsidies, as well as, in the case of large capital reallocations, the possibility of using depression and bankruptcy to deflate old costs, discrediting bondholders, and the possibility of a boom to provide capital for the new investment. And inventions, which are not random but are a product of the structural factors and hidden subsidies, may introduce what seem like manifestly desirable, low-cost innovations.

If this is the kind of transformation involved in some of our choices, then we cannot understand them by comparing costs or payoffs. We must include sacrifices, how they are rationalized, and how they may even come to be seen as good. The rites-of-passage model does exactly this, developing a rationale for the connection of what seem like incommensurable states. The middle ground of marginality permits the connection to be made, yet we need not assume we shall know ahead of time how the choice will work out. What we do know is that the connection will require a fairly complete story that appeals to both Before and After, and to the sacrificial victims and their successors. It will be, manifestly, a transcendent story. The connection will require an emergent invention, a new truth, a different economy. Afterwards, of course, we may see the invention as a member of a sequence of such inventions; so it is rational, mundane, and commensurable after all.

We need not be wanton or careless, or be committed to wasteful or hurtful transformations when we use this model. It does not justify them. It does not say who or what should be sacrificed. It says that decisions, even small ones, involve incommensurable changes, changes that are not smooth, changes that transform what we think is important. We have ways of giving an account of the incommensurable, making it subject to a special kind of rationality. It is not the usual one used in theories of planning and design. But I believe it is the actual operative one. And the account is not only historical but experiential, about how we feel during a transformation. The logic we use to structure the history is effective for thinking about the experience of making a decision.

Evaluating, planning, and decisionmaking are central activities in the public arena, in private enterprises, and in our personal lives. They have much in common with criticism of literature and art, with the logic of visionary political and social thought, and with the way we commit ourselves to great ideals and values. Like humanistic studies, the practices of evaluators, planners and designers, and decisionmakers refer to a perfect whole world. Yet that does not imply that they are totalitarian or illiberal. That perfect world is a generous ideal that gives us hope and sets a standard for what we do.

The constellation of ways of being around our works of art provides a good model for what we do in the rest of our lives. The world of art is part of a godly world, one that is whole, all-there, available to us. Yet we can fall into a state of anxiety, where we cannot make connection with the world. From anxiety, a central feature of decisionmaking, we usually return cured and stigmatized to our ordinary world, but there is a chance of monsterdom, of never returning.

Scientific research and theorizing share many of the features of these humanistic models. Scientists judge other scientists' work and they convert to new theories. A certain kind of truth is the ideal in science, and it works in the same way that other ideals do.

I have described a way of thinking that can help us make fairer claims about the power of our means of inquiry for deciding what to do. Our ideas about the foundations of policies and plans determine what we think is necessary and proper about them. If we understand the origins of those foundations, we are not so likely to be trapped by idols.

The models treat us as richly endowed human beings. They emphasize our capacity to be responsible and methodical. They allow for our being both evil and loving toward each other. They make what we do as public actors continuous with what we do in the rest of our lives.

APPENDIX: HEGEL'S SCIENTIFIC QUEST

Confession literature is not restricted to religion or to social and political transformation. Changes in scientific theory exhibit similar formal characteristics, although a final perfect world is sometimes not so overtly thematic there. Scientists sound more tentative; at least that is a common claim. But for a scientist, truth functions in much the same way that God does. It is the sign of perfection, wholeness, and coherence. This has substantive consequences for what we expect the truth to look like. For example, most physicists expect that the truth about elementary particles will be expressible in terms of simple symmetry principles, such symmetries having had a long association with perfection and order. And, of course, those principles have been extraordinarily powerful in understanding the world.

The processes of invention, discovery, and consequent justification found in natural science, in metaphysics, and in policymaking, are remarkably similar. Examining an unlikely example will make this similarity more clear.

Scientific explanation need not encompass only inanimate nature; it can also include history, human nature and its development, and even the history of our modes of knowledge and of science itself. Imagine a systematic description of what is true knowledge, of our modes of ascertaining it and how they have developed, of our own individual consciousness and how we have articulated it, of what there is in the world, and of history. Imagine that the description used a single organizing principle and that it applied that principle to a very large array of cases. Imagine, as well, that the description included a rough description of its own processes, indicating their own limitations, putting them in historical and logical perspective, and that it displayed the limitations of previous modes of describing what there is. And perhaps all of this were in a comprehensive, dramatically and rhetorically effective whole. Imagine, finally, that the conceptual structure of the description was a mirror of the world's structure. They were of the same form. Hence we might claim, naturally, that the limitations of the conceptual structure, at any time, would indicate where the next development in the world could occur.

Now imagine discovering such a grand explanation and description while in your early thirties, an explanation that was a powerful critique of the current mode of thought, one that captured the exact limitations and errors enforced by your contemporaries on themselves, one that led you out of your own limitations. So not only is the way to the truth finally discovered or revealed, but you too, as well, are liberated. The midwife (Moses, Socrates, Jesus, Mohammed) is reborn at the moment of birth. That would be a moment of conversion, a moment of the discovery of perfection, truth, and science, and of a reasonable road to transcendence. The logical structure of the world, its history, and your personal development have met at this crucial moment in our thought, and in our time and in your own time. No wonder Hegel must have been elated when he wrote *The Phenomenology of Mind*. He had found a way to pull everything together. He was out of the morass. He had at least a foothold that would make it more difficult to slip back in. Imagine solving such a problem. You can go home to eat dinner. (Better known to us is Watson's discussion of the discovery of the structure of DNA. But the story is the same, as it is for visionary designs and plans.)

Hegel's basic principle might be called the sin of pride. Societies, institutions, and persons will at a time act and believe that they are all-powerful, that they are in control and command, and that they understand everything. In each case the limitations of that overwhelming assumption lead to their defeat and the eventual succession of a more comprehensive whole. An historical account describes these penultimate situations and how the society destroys itself.

Hegel's theory is explicitly not predictive, since for him a scientific theory cannot substantively predict what will be beyond it. To be scientific is to be systematic and to have a notion of beyond.

There is a loophole that permits Hegel to account for everything yet not manifestly commit the sin of pride himself (although he must). The application of the model principle explicitly allows for the fact that new events will cause us to recast our scientific understanding. The principle is a formal principle whose substantive, specific realization depends on what happens. Logically it gives Hegel enough space to do his work. He does not trap himself by believing that the truth is substantive. For Hegel, truth is formal, and form or the basic principle has its meaning in its substantive realization, the actual history and logic of the world, as we describe it. Analogously, a planner might have a sense that B A R T was the answer, but not know exactly how it would be the answer until it was built and used. The answer would be judged in terms of how well it did encompass our world. Would B A R T become a plaything or a central feature of the Bay Area?

Our contemporary scientific theories claim to predict what will smoothly happen. Emergent phenomena are acknowledgedly beyond their systematic predictions. Still, we may have a good guess of the shape of an emergent object and test it out using the theory, or the theory may account, after the fact, for something that emerges. Hegel's equivalent to our contemporary predictive claim is to say that his theory will be able to explain and account for what happens after it happens. But he is not so concerned, as are scientists today, with smooth future changes.

The true meaning of Hegel's work itself was not available to him, and perhaps not even to his own method. It will only be available when we have complete Godlike knowledge, something we cannot have in our time on earth even if we are After. Like many scientists at moments of discovery, Hegel has the sense that he really is on to something. It feels so right. The moment is marked. But elation is not enough, and the pro knows that. Hegel's systematic explanation is so amazing to him because it is self-consistent and able to acknowledge its limits and not fall apart. He can write coherent history and logic.

Today's natural or social scientist seems more modest. Usually he does not try to explain the historical, the personal, and the natural at the same time. But perfection and ideal models, an urge for a true and simple understanding, influence his mode of explanation.

Our response to our own discovery can be fanatical, insisting on our own way, or more liberal and accepting of the political discussion and dissent that we shall surely encounter. If we look at most converts, people who have discovered the truth, they are not so liberal, at least at first. They are impressed by the effectiveness of their discovery or plan or design. So a confession or theory written soon after discovery tends to be more dogmatic and sure than one written later. The later one is perhaps more measured, although it can also be more polished, covering over lacunae and errors.

Hegel believed that comprehensive explanations were the only kind that could be true. They would not leave anything out. There would be no artificial boundary that said that *this* was worthy of scientific explanation and *that* was somehow casual or unimportant. The historical is universal and, at any time, the universal has a concrete historical realization. He claimed, as do all scientists, that some data were crucial and some much less important, that some events were the significant ones and other aspects of history were less significant. While we might think his belief in comprehensiveness would be overwhelming, it does not turn out that way.

A commitment to perfection and truth, even in the most architectonic and comprehensive of thinkers, can go along with a generous attitude and a feeling for the specific and the mundane. We may think of planning, design, and scientific theorizing in terms of invention in the light of perfection, what we must do when we try to create systematic visions of the world that guide our action and understanding.

# ✒ Planning in Time

*"Planning in Time" is somewhat more difficult and technical than the other essays. I review the ideas presented in "Criticism, Conversion, and Confession," paying attention to how the thinkers express what they say. The main substantive issue is our search for absoluteness, timelessness, universality, and certainty in the plans we make. We are always up to something, subject to interruption. We are always engaged in plans. And plans are means of controlling time. I will argue, however, that we do well enough without absolute control. Plans control time through narratives and stories, as well as through personality and the soul, and so we return to the central ideas of "Advice."*

*The essay's recurrent theme is the same and the different, the nature of repetition and recurrence. These are ways of describing how time plays itself out. I shall discuss several of them in detail.*

*Hegel uses a universal principle of the dialectic to obtain universality. The principle recurs in all manifestations of the world, and he shows how that happens. Nietzsche sees us as condemned to a universal principle of genealogy, of inevitable repetition of our inheritance and endowment. How can we be in this condemned world, realizing our damnation, and at the same time be critical of it—knowing that we are not to escape that damnation? How can we be "in" time and "out" of it? How can we be the same, but be ready to be different?*

*Hegel and Nietzsche obtain universality through history and narrative, while Kant tries to find universal logical laws. In Kant we explore the difficulties of applying a general law that would command the world. The interesting problem is how our common sense and our understanding of taken-for-granted particulars make it possible for us to apply universal rules and give them meaning. Plans that are logical in form depend on particulars in such a way that they cannot be simply universal.*

*The last section of the essay is on personality as a way of being timeless and universal. The soul is the locus of endurance and universality, and we end up with the problem of the relationship of the evanescent, called the body, and the transcendent, called the soul. This separation of body and soul must be accounted for, either by means of a reconciliation or by an account of how we performed such a separation, such a cognitive abstraction. Finally, we return to the original problem of planning in time by discussing memory and narrative, the relationship of the embodied soul to the community's history of itself. More than the other sections, this section is a demonstration of a way of thinking about the same and the different.*

> *Now does my project gather to a head*
> *My charms crack not, my spirits obey, and Time*
> *Goes upright with his carriage . . . .*
> Prospero, *The Tempest* (V.1)

TIME

Because we are always up to something, done with others, and have more in prospect, succession and sequence can be *time*, a time in which our projects are worked out. Since we can review what has gone on and think about where we are going, we might command time by reflectively using time, that succession and sequence, to understand what we are like and how we might fulfill that more effectively. We'll call this *planning.*

I use time to mean the possibility of a genuine narrative structure in our lives, not something, also called time, that comes afterwards, given to us by a clock or a physicist, a clock-and-bell story. The genuine narrative is one we might offer to others like us as an account of what we are doing. When we plan we write a narrative that says how things could be otherwise than is given by the usual account. A plan, a narrative that controls time, is a reworking of everyday narratives to find a potentially truer, more comprehensive one that will be more satisfactory as we encompass larger numbers of projects. Planning commands time by taking the narratives we have in hand and re-fashioning them.

Narratives go together with our actual projects, and so planning is never simply a manipulation of words. Only some narratives will be adequate, and if they are good enough the projects will be transformed. The projects will have different meanings, how we think of ourselves is altered, and what we do next may change.

So far I have said that our lives develop as exfoliating projects rather than as sequences of discrete events. Time peels off in the fulfillment of a project and to some extent we can control time, the way the projects go, by thinking about what we are doing. Thinking is part of a project too. Narratives are the way we tell about our projects. We can write different narratives to encompass a project; no single narrative is the only one. And for any plan, we have to give reasons why we make an investment that might not be in accord with the plan, just as we have to explain strange usages of a word if a dictionary is taken as fiducial.

Treating time as I have is not so strange when we look at what we actually do when we are thinking about our projects. Surely there are time constraints and interest rates. But time constraints are demands that we coordinate what we do with another narrative or project. Interest rates are requirements that our project be interesting enough to hold a bank's attention for the while.

Good planners and novelists know that things do not just happen. There is no bare or innocent set of projects or plots standing imperially outside of time. They are always enmeshed in some larger narrative that may not go the way you wish. The trick is to make your narrative the most captivating of all. Then others will be part of it and the plan may be deemed successful. It is successful not because some particular event happens, it might have anyway, but because others acknowledge as necessary the net of requirements you have set up if their project is to be meaningful and viable.

Modes of universal explanation, such as religion or natural science, have been effective ways of controlling time. These modes specify how a narrative ought to look, the nature of its sequences, what it means to be causal, and which details are relevant. Being universal, they exclude everything else. In a religion that has a final conversionary moment, time is fulfilled then and there is no more to narrate. There are no more projects, at least ones that we can say anything about now. Utopian plans often share this inarticulateness, describing a static world that can no longer develop. Ahead of time, we do not know how to talk of development after the moment of conversion. We do not know what to say about heaven. If a plan allows for only a partial conversion, a first but not yet a final coming, its moral force and universality is much harder to maintain. It is still mundane. But at least we can say something about the future.

Common sense controls time by taking the narratives that "everybody knows" as the only ones. It works well enough as long as no universal mode, say a scientific revolution, comes along claiming to supersede and incorporate previous common sense, and as long as there are no big changes, such as political or ecological upheaval. A religion can stigmatize common sense narratives as being mundane or barely adequate. For example, Luther spoke of natural and presumptive reason versus regenerate reason.

When there are big changes, religion and science may not be the best modes of planning, because they control time in systematically entrenched ways. Unless we have a new theory that incorporates the old one, they are likely to incorporate countervailing or contradictory evidence the best they can, rather than change their mode of organization. Technology is a label used for one kind of big change, and time is out of control in technology. The natural sequences of typical narratives in the universal modes of organizing our lives are constantly displaced by this exogenous source of indigestible shocks that we sometimes call invention. European history is often written as if it were motivated by invasions of the Mongolian hordes, that is, by essentially unmotivated exogenous shocks. Similarly, bourgeois secular political economy, the synthesis of Adam Smith and Alfred Marshall, seems purposeless, constantly consuming itself under new regimes presented by what look like random opportunities for profit. The invisible hand draws no beautiful pattern as it smoothes things over, even if we, latterly, discern such a pattern. Time is out of control in both cases, since technology and economy offer no large-scale internal accounting for their development. Technology and economy claim as well that it is in the small, in invention and market behavior, that the true story lies. That is why planning is always posed as alternative to them.

But, of course, the exogenous inventions and opportunities are not inadvertent. They are planned. They are seen by their entrepreneurs as part of an ongoing narrative. But the entrepreneurs' plans are much less presumptuous than those of religion or science. The inventions only turn out to be big changes. The original plans underestimate what the inventions are actually about, what their consequences are. Entrepreneurial plans rarely have an imprimatur of universality, and entrepreneurs cannot be so sure that the projects will work out, as if one could ever be. An in and out stance, practicing technology as invention and creation, but stepping away from it in order to plan, permits plans to be gentle but not absolute guides.

## THE SAME AND THE DIFFERENT

Big changes are controlled, and come more comfortably under time and its narrative net, if they are repetitions of other projects. But they are big changes, so they are not identical to another, the same in almost every way. It is hard to see them as repetitions. Yet in order for them to be under time's command we identify them provisionally with other projects, and we can then begin to make sense of what is going on. Even calling a change big, as such, may be enough so that we can get a purchase on it.

We use this strategy of provisional identification more generally. What we are up to is always the same as something before, as well as different. Distinctively, it is what we are up to now. But there are differences that we then may treat as the same. The narrative turns out to be in a genre inflected by distinctive features that we eventually recognize as a style. The style is then violated, yet we discover something we might call violated style, and so forth. Each identification has impure elements that infect it in such a way that a new identification may eventually be called for. Infection is natural. Narrative guts are rhetorical and filled with bacteria and virus that digest one story to yield another.

Plans must be familiar if we are to recognize ourselves in them, but not too familiar. They must control time sufficiently for us to fit in. But if that control is too great, big changes will completely elude the narrative. The plan will not be able to fruitfully acknowledge a change we intuitively recognize.

For example, in a particular ritual not everything that happens is the same as in previous enactments of it. At the least, it is my own repetition of that ritual. Repetitions of childhood experiences when we are adults are not the same as the first times. Textual interpretation is a repetition that does not deliver the text back to you untouched. Repetition is the assertion of the notion of the same, not a reassertion of the same. It requires rededication and reacceptance of the ritual form, but these are not acts of merely following the form. They are re-enactments. Planning as repetition is a statement of responsibility: This situation is different, and it is the same, and it could be otherwise. Each repetition or account of a project is not automatic. How we do it is our responsibility, for which we have to answer.

Planning controls time through a narrative. Repetition is a mode of control that takes a narrative and collapses its time back on to other times. Planning and repetition are techniques of control that depend on our assertion: It is the same and different. Our problem becomes one of developing a notion of rational command, a way of arranging plans and narratives and of saying just how something is a repetition, a command that is not rigid, one that is open to our own possibilities yet overarching enough for us.

HISTORY

We say "It is the same" by writing a history. We give the world back to ourselves. We repeat it in a structured way. We gain control of time by having the narrative tell a story that has not only a plot and characters, but also a homiletic lesson. If plans are histories and their lessons, then we can see where those lessons come from and the lessons will have no absolute command over us.

Let us recall Hegel's repetition of the world, one of the most comprehensive and systematic.* He controls time by using a universal formal principle to account for everything. All succcssion is defined in terms of the principle, and the meaning of what we do is derived from our realization and appreciation of the principle's all-pervasiveness. When time is fulfilled, that is, when the principle is fully realized, then time is controlled and it is over.

Hegel's formal principle is that at any particular moment of time we overreach. We believe and act as if time is over, that there is no more, that we have all of it and we are universal—a sin of pride. But of course we do not have all of it. There are nearby, unconscious, subversive, "feminine" parts of the world not under our control and understanding. Time is not up. The moment of time is merely an aspect, an abstract isolation of a particular perspective. And so, by our presumption, we are forced to face the limitations of our positions and we are thrown back on to ourselves. The parts that we repressed, that we thought we understood but actually did not, come back, like the furies of the Greeks, to destroy us. Our conceptual power gone wild, we think we command the world. But we depend on what we command for our sense of power and so we are vulnerable. The world is not all ours.

Hegel uses this principle in three pervasive ways. First, he can develop hierarchical classifications of natural phenomena, logical categories, social or political events, just about anything, based on the principle. In each case higher levels incorporate the defects of lower levels and make sense of them, so that there is a complete understanding of what there is. Second, he can write a world history that goes up the hierarchy to account for succession, what we ordinarily call developments in time. Finally, in that history he can also account for our gradual appreciation of the basic principle, and hence his own discovery of it. So we see how truth, history, and consciousness are the same, both in form and in how they are realized and made actual.

---

*I take the liberty of reviewing some of the Appendix to the previous essay.

A Hegelian plan would be written using a formal principle, perhaps like the one I have just described. It is a plan that would be self-consistent and so necessary. It would incorporate everything. There is nothing else. What might be other is false. The plan is necessary because in its self-consistency it includes all of us and how we shall come to understand it. It would be the most powerful plan we might rationally imagine, even if here on earth, now, we know the plan we draw must be incomplete and false. The Hegelian plan sets a standard for any plan concerned with development. It includes the persons who are involved in the plan. How they think, how they will discover the plan to be true, must be part of the plan.

Hegel was a visionary but he looked backward (to Greece). He never claimed to be able to know substantively what would happen. He understood only the form of its appearance, and he could only write about it after it took place. He was an historian. Even if his method were true, he could only know what it meant through its concrete development. As a method, alone, it was abstract and empty. Hegel's procedure might be a model for a plan because it does not claim to plan everything, yet does not leave out anything that is crucial, including the planners. Still, this is too demanding were we to cover every detail. But we only need touch the bases when we aim for a home run. The plan is at the same time visionary and hopeful and profoundly rational. It says our lives do make sense, and then says we might conceive of a better life.

But what about Hegel and his sin of pride, thinking he finally has the true principle? It seems that he is that most dangerous kind of planner, a true believer. But that is not Hegel. He had a rational mode of accounting for everything, perhaps, but he kept testing it, working out its ramifications in history, religion, nature, and psychology. Since the formal principle had meaning only as these ramifications, the principle is not half so presumptuous or final as it might seem. Hegel's principle may well have been superseded in the last 150 years, but we can know that only when we have decided that a second or third coming, a different kind of principle, is here. For he never claimed to be out of time, only to have controlled it through understanding and reason. How his formal principle is to be applied remains open, even if the system itself is complete. Plans are similarly open for interpretation. Criteria of rationality and adequate evidence assure that not all applications of the principle are equally good, nor will any one application be able to claim absolute dominance over others, at least in this world.

Nietzsche was a professional philologist at philology's greatest moment, when historical philology began to be systematically understood. But he could not adhere to a system. Christian belief could never function for him, as it did for Hegel, as a model that modulated and completed Greece. Still, the regularities of words seemed to reflect the most powerful of laws. History had to be the model, and the recurrence of forms is a basic possibility for understanding history. That is how time is controlled. In Nietzsche we are condemned to the forms as we are condemned to the furies, and genealogical forces are pervasive. To believe otherwise, to control time arbitrarily, is to speak nonsense as if our words could exist without their roots. So we repeat ourselves everywhere unavoidably. When we try to do otherwise, be original for example, we only control time compulsively, creating gibberish. We are actually out of control. Hegel's progressive hierarchical system is alien to the aleatory but regular changes characteristic of philology, ones that may even return back to themselves.

Our genealogy is the forms we are endowed with and condemned to. They are the forms of living, of expression, of inquiry, of truth, of love. Genealogy is the fact that there are such forms, that we find ourselves repeating them, that they are enough, yet not quite and too much. And they are our forms, which if we think they come from someplace else such as God or Truth, come from those places only because we have endowed those places with our own endowments.

Genealogy, unlike Hegel's principle, offers no compensation in the form of salvation or truth treated as other than ourselves. There is no authentic meaning, no repose, no finitude. Genealogy just is, and is unavoidable. To be the same has no positive implication of hope; it is merely the debt that is sinfulness. We ask for hope or salvation when there is none, at least other than our own. We cannot control time, it just is. Our projects offer us no hegemony over it; they are the only way to be. There is no eschatology except recurrence. And recurrence is always almost the same; it is never circular.

We can conceive of a world other than what we have, but only as other, as not-a-repetition of this genealogy. That is all we can say. Completely other, such a world would not make sense to us now. The best we might do is to set up the formal conditions for being ready for its arrival or recognition, and the conditions for avoiding the deception that we can escape genealogy. For the completely other will still perhaps be a genealogy, still the repetition of forms. What would be a genealogy that was not a reaction to, and so a form derived from, the present genealogy? An identical genealogy to the one we have already; or one we could not recognize; or a mixed case? This next world does not signify the end. At best, that is never a question. So origin and repetition may no longer be an issue.

Genealogy's power over us is that we act as if we could be outside of its power, as if we might be beyond it. We are crushed by our presumption. A genealogy is a mode of articulating our lives, and we always need one. It provides us with the forms of expression we exercise. What we eventually call the next genealogy could be the same as this one, but then we would no longer treat it as other than us, as if we wore it and so could undress. It is not something we must be freed from.

Nietzsche argued that metaphysics, our current genealogy, could not be the next one, since into its structure it builds reaction, alienation, and the thought that we might escape genealogy. Rationality in planning and design, as a way to control time, is one version of the problem of metaphysics. So Hegel's rational utopian plan must prove to be a cruel deception, for there is no ending or even progress.

Rather than rationally controlling time, we might be *in* time or be *out* of it, not at time's end or beginning. To recall, time is that purposeful, meaningful, series of projects we are involved in. The projects do not each stand separately, only needing to be attached to each other, hooked together like Velcro. They are already hooked. We live in time. Projects and their meanings and events are abstractions from our lives we use for telling people what we are doing when we stop doing what we are up to, or when what we are up to does not work out quite right. When we are in time we are in a genealogy, with no way out.

Being in time, what we are up to and our purposes articulate a genealogy into a particular realization that is ours. So we can take responsibility for time not because it is rational or because we can do with it as we will, but what we do with it we will to be ours—not someone else's. Such a genealogy, which we do not treat as necessary, is other (than metaphysics). And it is our freedom. Yet it might turn out to be the same complex of forms we have already. It is a "beyond" metaphysics, which is not a matter of knowing whether we are beyond.

Planning, which reflectively uses time to understand what we are like and how we might fulfill that more effectively, might be *in* time and so be responsible. What does it mean to have such an attitude toward ourselves and what we have been given? Planning is a continuing selection from what we have been given to accord with what we want to do. It can be what we call decisionmaking when we abstract away from planning as choosing and according with what we are up to, and view what we are doing in terms of isolated events. Perhaps we can isolate a significant moment when we decided, or so we say. But, for the most part, planning is a matter of taking issue with what we have been given and we have taken issue with before. We treat ourselves as if we always have that potential to take issue. No technique or planning method relieves us of responsibility for reaffirming or denying our plans. Planning is a matter of repetition, retaking what we already have taken, reaffirming what we have affirmed, and acting as if that possibility were always the case. Repetition does not mean that we are constantly thrashing, breast-beating, turning pages back and forth to check out where we are. It is just that we might have done otherwise, and we can be called to account for that.

Now, when we are in time, retaking and repeating in a way conscious of our selves, so that a genealogy is ours and not something outside of us, we may have an experience of being *out* of time. There is no end or beginning. Our model of aging, our bodily selves, is left behind. There is then ecstatic experience, when we are timeless, unselfconscious, fully present to ourselves but not alienated. We are not anxious, but calm and whole and collected. How are we both in and out of time, engaged in our projects yet outside of them? Since we are in time, and so not in the adversarial relationship to time implied by a notion of controlling time, we can give up control and give in to time. We are aware, but there is no place else to be, so we are not selfconscious, not monitoring ourselves. Yet we are able to watch ourselves as a whole, and so we must interpret ecstasy as an out-of-the-body experience. How else could we watch ourselves? Not narcissistically, where we need the world as our mirror image, where we never see ourselves but only the world as ourselves. We interpret being out of time as a worldly transcendence because we are no longer bound to mundane genealogical demands, even if we fulfill them.

Ecstatic experience is a touchstone that marks being in but not controlling time. We are timeless (for the moment) because we are part of change, in touch, fully here. We are at home. The experience may not continue for long, and we return to our everyday lives in touch, but no longer watching ourselves.

One might misinterpret this description, attributing its content to subjective factors or to an uncritical irrationalism. But when we are in time we are the most critical and fully responsible. We do not rely on apparatus, including technologies such as economics or physics, to the extent that the plan is no longer ours. It is hard for us in our present genealogy to understand how we might be critical and responsible, yet not be alienated. It is hard for us to understand how subjective experience need not be arbitrary. We might recall, however, that despite changes in fashion, despite rediscoveries and condemnations, there has been substantial continuity in educated connoisseurs' sub-jective experiences and judgments of artists and paintings—especially the greatest of these—as well as of food, mountains, drugs, and religions.

A notion of gifts and grace is needed if we are to understand deci-sionmaking, how we take what we have been given. Gifts and grace, like manna, come not by your choice, but you can be ready and pre-pared for them. Having set aside the time and place, having made room, you can be at home and receiving. You can recognize the appro-priate ideas, the right ways, the good plans, and if you are wrong you'll be able to recognize that too. Still, nothing may happen. We do not work for grace, but prepare for it. The expectations we might have for a planning scheme would be fulfilled somehow, but just how we do not know ahead of time. There may well be waste and you may not get what you pay for. On the one hand, gifts and grace are not earned, even if they are deserved, and there is no accounting, no adding up, no conservation, no long-run average that lets us gain a stochastic pur-chase on them. On the other hand, they have proved as sensible as any rationality in the stories they tell. Pastoral work under a regime of grace and miracles is effective; it does guide us to living good lives. What we call miracles are signs of meaning and fulfillment, as are bet-ting payoffs and confirming experiments.

Under a genealogy, plans guide us in roughly the same way they do under conventional rationality. But what we expect from plans is dif-ferent. A plan is good if it works, but working involves purposes and meanings, and rich and effective modes of thinking and acting about ourselves in terms of our projects—all of which we create and stand for by our selves. Being in time, in a genealogy, we are responsible for our plans. They are ours. Even though the furies are still present, we are no longer ruled by them. They are just there. We are in accord with time.

Hegel and Nietzsche have different ways of bringing us back to our own resources without making us victims of our own presumption. We can gain command of time without killing it. Rationality's origi-nal purpose, to see an order in the world, is vital. But rationality need no longer be construed in terms of surety and necessity.

The forms of repetition described by Hegel and Nietzsche are the-ological in structure but mundane in intent. Timelessness is death, and they are necrophiliacs. No wonder they are strange in an age that isolates the dead and the dying. Planning is about death, about being *out* of time and being sure, and about being *in* time and eternal.

Hence we need to be necrophiliacs to be true to the activity. Otherwise planning is propped up, made to look alive.

## LOGIC

A universal formal logic is an alternative to history as a mode of repetition. The logic shows everything is the same because everything is derived from a set of general principles. The logic must be universal and formal so that it applies everywhere, with no specific exceptions that deny its truth, although some cases will happen not to fulfill the basic assumptions. Then it might be timeless and true. Unlike Hegel's, most history acknowledges only a residual obligation to show that it is based on some general principles, but a logic depends on those principles. A logic will also have to show that it can be applied sufficiently widely. Even if a logic looks universal, filled with $x$'s and $y$'s and general ideas, it may not have any realizations in life.

Kant tried to develop a logic that encompassed a domain, but was also universal and formal. The problems he faced exemplify those of any logical mode of controlling time.

In *The Critique of Judgment*, Kant gives an account of beauty in terms of an account of how we judge something to be beautiful. His argument is complex, but the following summary will do for our purposes. Judgments of beauty are a model for judgment in general. Such judgments are disinterested, universal, formal (not dependent on content), and necessary, he argues. They do not depend directly on any particular features of a work, although these features will be pointed out when we try to convince others of our judgments. Still, no collection of features could force us to decide that a work is beautiful. There will always be works with those features that fail. Nor will the reasons we give force compulsory assent. Yet Kant finds that we demand that others agree with our judgments. He suggests that members of our community, persons like us whom we might try to convince, share a common sense with us. We know about this quality of our faculties from the fact that we have a shared and agreed-upon objective knowledge of the world, and such knowledge must refer back to a common sense we all have. When that common sense is excited in a pure non-objective way, judgments of beauty are made. He can then show how the harmony of our common sense is disinterested, universal, formal, and necessary. The beautiful is what is in harmony with the sense of reason. So if we can agree on our knowledge of objects, we shall agree as well on beauty. But no marks or features of a painting will determine that we should agree.

A Kantian critique first describes how a particular activity, such as science or morality or beauty, appears to us in the world, that is, its phenomenal structure, and then gives fundamental principles of our nature that show why the structure makes sense, and why it is necessary to do things in the manner we do them. Kant asks, How are judgments of beauty possible? At the least, we must be able to have knowledge of the world and to appreciate the lawlikeness of (moral) judgments. But unlike for science and truth, knowledge of an object does not determine whether it is judged beautiful, and, unlike for morality, there is no law we can give for lawlike aesthetic judgments. Without objects or laws, what is to make our judgments universal? Kant's answer is that we have a common sense, a sense we all share, whose operation is in accord with and grounds these judgments.

Common sense provides Kant with a universal notion, and hence the possibility of universal judgment. He must use it in such a way that the universality is not lost. He cannot specify the contents of common sense; they would be particular. Rather, the notion of common sense must be used formally. It is a source or logical foundation for agreement. Kant cannot depend on a fixed set of specific features of the objects we judge, or on a set of specific reasons we give to others. If they are too specific, they are likely to be changing. Even if they are more general, just what they mean will change with instantiations of them. Kant's account of judgment will be good if judgments and evaluations comfortably fit the forms he gives for them.

Put in logical terms, we seem to need an interpretation of his formal rules and preconditions for judgment, and rules for doing that interpretation, if we are to know if his formal description is correct. This is a problem in any theory. As we shall see, we can never explicitly give all of those rules for interpretation. We depend on our shared common sense about how to get around in the world to provide a foundation for those rules.

Say we examined a set of judgments to see if they are adequately described by Kant's framework. We would find that the pure formal description of judgment he provides is inadequate. It needs to be interpreted, given a concrete realization in terms of referents to our particular situation, as Kant was aware. The interpretation is not always straightforward. When are the formal preconditions fulfilled for a judgment to be an aesthetic one? Is it possible to be truly disinterested? How little interest may be ignored? The boundary that delineates material that is irrelevant to a judgment will have to be specified in particular, not only as the formal fact that there is such a boundary. Should the frame count in judging a painting? It all depends on the particular form of art or the situation, although it seems that some notions of irrelevance have near universal applicability.

We might hope that many of these matters of interpretation and boundary definition would be more or less straightforward. Most members of the community would know, perhaps only implicitly, what is relevant and what is not. What "everybody knows" defines a community. It also defines the kinds of arguments that are likely to take place in a community when people are not sure about what belongs or how to interpret a formal rule.

Common sense becomes the umbrella for all that is particular, for all the detailed ways in which we know that a person is or could be part of our community, for how that person knows himself to be part of the community. Common sense expresses our common understanding of what we are up to and how we interpret what we say. The formal universality of a logic depends on its interpretation being detailed and particular, on our shared conventions in our community about how to understand it. Historically, what we call common sense has been richly embellished and given meaning by our political and social situation. Pure Kantian judgments are pure only by a sleight of hand. Surely they are formally pure, independent of details. Common sense is stripped of its manifest political and social meanings. Yet it retains, even in their absence, an implicit notion of a polity and a community.

Common sense is the location of prejudice. If we do have a rational Kantian argument about beauty, it is based as much in history as in formal logic. One might then argue, as Hegel did, that history is logical and formal, and that prejudice is not in any sense arbitrary. The particulars may not be manifestly universal, but they are universal. But even Hegel cannot be specific about what the particulars will be until they appear.

Even if universal formal logic as a model of repetition stands on a base of history, and even if the history we tell and write is not predictive and can only come after what happens, the organizing power of a formal logic should not be undervalued. A formal specification controls and orders a plan, gives it conventional form and an initial purchase on making sense. But the form is not up to its own pretense of being independent of time or universal or true. As in Hegel and Nietzsche, the best we can do is be in time. Necessity, that you ought agree with me, comes from the fact that we are in the same boat, now, together, not that the boat is fixed on land or in a rotting dry dock.

Kant's formal description of judgment in *The Critique* is one of the most generous and realistic we could imagine. He does not depend on a symbolic logic, he does not demand deductive certainty, he takes a radically subjective position. Surely his description is a product of its historical time, and that may lead us to prefer styles of art or policies that are more straightforwardly in accord with the description's parochial implications. But the description is still quite open in its interpretation, and it can accommodate a wide variety of styles and endeavors. To apply his formal description requires a powerful particular interpretation of how it describes what we do. We want to say how the formal description is the same as the situation we are concerned with. But for each case the same is always different. Different kinds of rules of interpretation will be important in different cases, although there will be classes of cases where a single set of rules will be generally applicable. We might tighten up these rules and make them explicit, at least for a few cases, and then we get some seemingly universal rules for judgment. They apply in a large but not universal arena.

I have described Kant's form of repetition because it is so generous as a formal logic. Kantian evaluation and judgment is universal and subjective, but not arbitrary. In common sense, Kant acknowledges time as he attempts to control it. He stuffs all the interesting tough problems into common sense.

The formal character of a plan, whether it be mathematical or aesthetic form, only belies the plan's dependency on what is common and particular among us. As we shall see in the last two essays, politics is the mode we use to exploit the common.

PERSONALITY

Besides history and logic, personality is another mode of timelessness. A person has coherent and enduring modes of being with and interacting with others. I know roughly what you will do when I meet you, hug you, and begin a conversation. I can recognize you. And you do the same for me.

In most situations I know roughly what you will do. Every once in a while I find I am surprised, and this is just because my expectations are generally reliable. Being different is also possible, again just because we are the same most of the time. I might ascribe enduring features to you that epitomize how I understand you and that you, too, might recognize as characteristic of yourself, even if you reserve the right to violate your epitome. If I can do that to you, then it can be done for me too. I might then come to believe that a personality is a unified incorporation of those features. But of course we encounter each other as persons first, and then we abstract features from our interaction.

tion (in order that it be absolute and universal) will still in the end depend on our particular situation. The historian will show how particular and culture-based it is. Its pride of universality will be undermined by the facts of life. But this pride is our human condition. Alternatively, we realize that we can have absoluteness, at least as much of it as we can hope for, even though what we claim to be true is a matter of our relationships. Unbound by culture and biology, we would have nothing meaningful to say.

A soul gives a name to the enduring regular quality of our lives, and to the tameness and recognizability of life's surprises. But how can we be timeless yet live in this world as well? This is the question of body and soul. The answer must finesse the original division of the evanescent mundane and the timeless eternal. The answer need not be any more clear about how it transcends the apparent rift between the mundane and the eternal than we are about the source of the rift. Radically, we might get rid of the soul, say we have just a body, and call the body's enduring features a soul, as I have suggested. Then there is no question about reconciliation. We merely have to describe how we get around in the world and what might be called the regular strategies of life, and we have done the work the notion of the soul does.

How do we play out our personalities? If we have eternal or unchanging qualities, the soul of our person, then personality is the realization of those qualities in particular cases. If, on the other hand, we have enduring roles or modes of being with others, whether they be cognitive, behavioral, or cultural, then we might speak of enacting a role or a personality. Realization and enactment seem to require a list or script that we play out. Where these scripts are located and just what are the rules of play might be called rift problems. They make sense as questions as long as we separate our selves from our ways of being in the world. But our selves are known to us through our ways of being. The list or script is an artifact of our thinking about ourselves. Now we must think about ourselves, or so it seems, and it is positively helpful to do so if things go awry, as in advice. So the separation between an absolute self or soul and its ways of being in this world, while it is an artifact of how we act and think in this world, is an unavoidable artifact. The rift problems we then inherit, such as where the scripts come from, or how to combine theory and practice, are problems of application. We will not have to describe application if the soul is treated as an artifact of our attempt to find something enduring. For then the rift problem is an artifact of inquiry, not a true problem. But then we shall have to say something about the nature of cognitive abstraction, how we find "the soul."

We take it as a sign of the soul's existence that we are resistant to some of the world's entreaties and demands. We do not do everything we might. But why should we expect that we ever would do everything? Only if we believed we had an arbitrary body, with infinite possibility harbored in the body. Then we would need a controlling soul. Then we would go wild without our souls, committing mayhem and evil in arbitrary quantities.

But we do not. The soul might be the fact that generally we are decent with each other. Appeals that we treat others with respect can be effective, and we have self-respect. We allow that other persons have enduring aspects called souls, and that they are like us. Each enactment of personality is a re-enactment, a repetition, of what we have done before. There is no script, only actual enactments, but we do reasonably well each time. The timelessness of personality is not absolute, but it is good enough for getting along in the world.

The locus of endurance is also that of memory. So the soul is what makes it possible to call us to account for what we have done. If we have a memory, then we might produce narrative accounts of what we have been up to. We can say how and why we did or will do something, and so we can be responsible for what we do. The past becomes ours and we join it with future prospects, the soul being the source of coherent human intention and purpose, and so we can plan.

How we understand the soul's eternity determines the kind of memory we have. If the soul is eternal because we can continually recognize ourselves, then memory is about recurrent forms of history, different but the same. Each rewriting makes it possible for us to be responsible for what we are doing. It forces us to re-recognize ourselves. Recognition is basic to self-consciousness and to treating ourselves as persons. In each case we gain a purchase on our selves. If the soul is eternal because it has eternal qualities, then memory is about the reappearance of those qualities. Were those forms or qualities absolute, independent of us, then our memory would not be ours, as such. Calling to account would not call us at all. Without memory we could not be called to account, but only with memory, which is our own recalling, will accounting be an effective way of making our actions meaningful and better. Even formal moral laws, such as the golden rule, can make sense to us only when they are filled in by the particulars of a situation. Our formal assent to them will not be effective unless their substantial detailed instances involve us logically and personally. The laws must be pastoral, and show why we should do or should have done a certain act. We have to show how the formal principles apply and why they are cogent in this particular case.

## CONTROLLING TIME

Personality returns us to the question of timelessness in history and logic. What we mean by controlling time in plans is the same as what we mean by having control over ourselves. The logical structure of narrative and repetition manifests itself in each case.

Control is not absolute. It is not a pure command over the world or our persons, not without impure polluting elements of chance, others' intentions, and confusions about our own. If we think it is pure, then we set up conditions for a pathology, the putatively pure constantly to be invaded and reinvaded by the pollutants. The dynamics of this process are quite general. The polluted, wrenched from its natural home among the pure and sent off to the backstage parts of the world, comes back later—more powerful and more insidious. If rationality, or decisionmaking, or formal logic are treated as pure and fully determinate, then funky details and particularities, as pollutions, reinvade the now sundered true unity of life to destroy those pretensions of purity. And in time the invaders become the pure. The thrust and counter-thrust will continue; the curse is eternal.

We need not control everything to be in control of time or of ourselves. Most of the time a little dirt never hurts anybody. It is always present anyway. By not spending too much time cleaning up, we can be more successful in what we try to do. We need not feel remorseful if infection sets in, either. We just try to avoid plague and recurrent disease. Repetition need not be compulsive, it can be just what we do. Under a regime of health we worry less about purity, and more about responsibility. We shift from polarities of death and life, rationality and silence, universality and particularity, or soul and insanity, to problems of making our life our own. No method will do that for us. The pathological argument about which is the best of the pathogen-infested methods for planning must leave us with no choice. A variety of approaches will do. It is a matter of what we expect from them. Timelessness is a matter, not of stopping time, but of being in time. We make our lives ours in time when we treat plans, which anyone could have, as our own. Then we can pursue or reject them for good reason.

**III**

There is always the very great temptation to describe the world—just the way it is. But there is no way to do so, for we are likely to bring in all sorts of not quite right stuff along with our description. And of course any olympian position that tries to describe the world is unlikely to be adequately perspicuous about its own position. Still, the temptation is a powerful one.

# ❧ What We Are Up To

*"What We Are Up To" continues the exploration of the themes of the same and the different, of reconciliation and diremption. Its subject is the limitations in what we can do to make a better world, and how we use limitations to justify creating and maintaining racism.*

*We conduct politics nowadays in an economy, in which conflict is expressed as a matter of resources and their limits. How do we convince ourselves that this is our real world, and so convert discussions of limitation into technical statements about what is necessary, rather than discussions about the good world? And how does our conduct express the world's actual roominess and flexibility, even if we tend to think about the world in more rigid and agonistic terms? The description of the shape of the world and how we manage in it, in the first half of the essay, is meant to answer these questions. Arguments that we must do something because that is the only way we can survive must be understood as a form of rhetoric about the cycles of sin and redemption. Similarly, our views of goodness tend to be either exclusive, rejecting alternatives, or residual, goodness being what is left after defining the bad. Can we say something about survival or goodness— for example, about the necessity of the family—that will justify our conventional lives, and that will, as well, not oppress those who are less conventional, and perhaps liberate those who are conventional to think of alternatives? I believe we can, once we realize that the necessity of the family is not something we prove, but is a topic for discussion that allows us to take ourselves seriously. We make sensible choices in our lives, without having to follow absolute rules.*

*Racism is how we express exclusivity and residuality, treating what is left over as other and alien from us. "We" and "they" is a fiction that temporarily allows us to work on them, whether they like it or not. But separating we and they is like trying to separate a treatment's therapeutic effects from its side effects. They are often intimately related. I try to sketch a mode of reconciliation, and then explore its implications for politics and community. We can have a fairer world. Recon-*

*ciliation depends on our realizing that we can get along quite nicely without patching up the world completely. I work this out in a story about desert wandering.*

*Throughout the book I have deliberately described the world, rather than argued against alternative conceptions or for my own conception of it. Of course, any description is always given against a background of the usual conventions, and we pay most attention to where we differ from the conventions. So no description is pure, all are influenced by agonistic and rhetorical intents. But I hope my description is persuasive because it is familiar and fits what we already know, rather than because it explains esoteric phenomena. The style of this essay, and the others, is intended to reinforce its descriptive purposes.*

## I (BEGINNING)

[There is a fruitful conflict of the ideal and practical worlds. They keep each other from being stuck in place. We understand each in terms of the other. And there is only one world, the one we live in.]

Around us there is multiplicity, variety, and difference. We grasp that with concepts and talk, and so we can command our surroundings. The unity of the Edenic world is broken. The dilemmas and arguments that make up human life become manifest. The accounts we give about what we're up to hint at a better, more perfect, other world. There, authority coincides with necessity, goodness, and freedom. Made immanent for us, that world might be totalitarian. So even if we act as if that ideal were ours, we know we are not in that world. We never expect our arguments about authority and the nature of the better world to stop, even if there are periods when we agree for the most part. Without claiming that here and now or at some time we shall be able to say what is good, believing that we could know and say what is good lets us have serious arguments about it. And perhaps we do know what is good. Of course, agreement is not a sure sign of perfection. Poetry and politics, for example, are rich activities because we allow ourselves to play in the space between this world and that hinted-at other, but we are only in this world (and that hinted-at other world is in this world, too). So poems are filled with surprises as they deftly fulfill all sorts of metrical requirements, and remarkable human products arise out of the mundane conflicts of politics.

What is so distinctive about us is that we can be quite comfortable living close to the possibility of living all sorts of other lives, better or monstrous, yet we need not pursue them all. We have good conduct. Temptation, what we do not give in to, is one way we express that. Yet, of course, we can give in to temptation without falling apart.

We do not actualize every possibility we can conceive of, at least if human nature is to remain human and decent. The wilder parts of the range of choices are not possible, because other things are thought to be necessary. That is, necessity manages the wilder parts by treating them as incompatible with what is necessary. Food, clothing, and a next generation are requirements that eliminate some possibilities. Taboos, often related to subsistence necessities, eliminate others. The ecology of the more ordinary or central choices is influenced as well by these boundary-setting necessities. In a determinate system such as classical mechanics, it is not easy to differentiate the boundary condition at infinity (necessity), a set of conservation laws (taboos), and a specification of the boundary. In each case, the effect of the givens, whether they be necessity, taboo, or boundary specification, is to determine the contents of the enclosed space. Actual necessity and taboos seem not to be fully determinate of all the features of a culture. The world is still of our making, and although we must make it out of these necessities we are free to choose our necessities. We are responsible for the world, since we choose the way we live our lives. And choice is the possibility of being responsible for what we do.

We act as if we know all of this. But we do forget. Sometimes we try to eliminate rather than live with the other, seemingly wilder, possibilities. War and racism are varieties of this temptation toward perfection.

## I.I (BEGINNING, RHETORIC AND OTHERNESS)

[The manifest world is not alien to us and most of the time it is all we need. There is a kinesthetic ontology in which we feel the way the world is.]

We always understand what we're up to. Sensible persons, we feel that understanding—literally—as part of what we're doing. What we say about it, the stories and arguments and whatnot, are kinesthetically comfortable gestures of our embodied selves. Talk, which often expresses understanding, comes from the same place as the rest of what we do. What we do does not come from anyplace else (but ourselves). We can talk about part of or an aspect of what we are doing, or about being kinesthetically comfortable, because we can be distant to or other from ourselves, resistant to where we are right now.

Of course, we always misunderstand what we're up to, too. But usually we do have a provisional understanding that is good enough, at least for now.

What I have just said is a report on some of the facts of life.

## 2 (RHETORIC)

[Policy arguments and literary forms share a set of rhetorical structures. Both are about how we should live. The structures, such as tragedy or romance, are flexible enough to accommodate most of the arguments we want to make.]

Rhetoric is the way we express resistance to where we are right now. So it is persuasionary, since its purpose is to replace our immediate commitments with others. Otherness is expressed in a small number of reuseable forms of replacement called tropes, such as metaphor and synecdoche. They shift us away from what was obvious and make us think again about what could be a natural association. Larger forms, such as lyric poems, tragedies, scientific papers, novels, and legal briefs, are tropes (modes of attraction) that are themselves composed of tropes. No wonder we call them moving. They never let us believe we have it all down pat.

Why are there just a small number of tropes? It could be that rhetoric itself is rhetorical, it is the trope of finiteness: what we call a systematic body of knowledge. Or, polemically, we might say that because we are biological we may understand only a small number of tropes. The body and biology are then about a kind of graceful limitation on the monstrous, the wild, the multiple, and the eternal.

Perhaps there is only a small number of tropes, but what does that mean? The claim is seemingly not tropological, it is just a statement of what is so. But that is the most powerful replacement strategy— self-evidence or science—denying space for all the others.

Almost anything may be expressed in any form. The form itself does not determine what you can say using it, but it provides a set of terms so you can say something at all. One way to organize the forms is by season, so tragedy is for winter and romance is for spring. Whatever the season, the whole year's activities are possible during any one of them. A snowball fight in summer, especially if we have a high technology called the snow maker and the refrigerator, can go on for a while. Tragic form might be adequate for a scientific paper. But a mistake we then make is to conclude that the snowball fight could go on forever, that the tragic form is ideal for the scientific paper. Even that is not quite a mistake, since winter eventually does come and makes our snowball fight natural again; tragedy may turn out to be the right form for the scientific paper.

Methodic procedures were developed to control the wiles of rhetoric. Method was not supposed to be rhetorical, its purpose was just to organize and set forth what was true. It would be automatic, reliable, passionless. Like modern managerial economy, it would smooth over the extremes of life. But method is a rhetoric, too, but of a form that has forgotten that there are seasons. It aims for an equatorial life, and insofar as it achieves its aim it will account for less about the earth and what we do on it.

## 2.1 (RHETORIC, SYSTEMS AND ECONOMY)

[In a fetishized economy of commodities and prices, resistance becomes reduced to an algebra of exchangeable objects. These objects have no essence outside of their exchange values, and in transformation they can lose their value.]

The resistance we exhibit is a sign of our being human and alive. However, we might take it as identical to being itself, and we might see the overcoming of a particular resistant complex as a complete replacement of our being by another. What was essential, beyond mundane consideration, is now subject to a market economy, replaceable by an exchange of goods. Interactions are mediated, not by objects, but by their properties, such as mass or price. So inertia becomes the property, mass. If we are concerned about gravitational interactions, it is most of what we need to know. But does the property of mass say enough about how we live with objects? Probably not. Similarly, economy converts resistance and its overcoming into exchange values or prices, and systems analysis understands relationships in terms of the exchange of messages. In each case we have a powerful calculus that captures many of the crucial aspects of our resistance to the world, but, it seems, not all of them.

We control the resistant world by managing the economy of its properties: pushing harder, paying more, or creating extra signal pathways. These transactions may transform the world and its persons, who are now considered as objects possessing properties. In the exchange of properties, our intrinsic nature will change. What was absolute and fundamental about us no longer is so. And the resistance we exhibited may have lost its value, or weight (or even its mass) for the technical features of the economy have changed. (So coal has had a history of different values.) Perhaps we have become worthless as a product of the transformations. Now a different kind of resistance is in order. Different properties have high value. This is called the non-conservation of quantum numbers, economic transformation, or cultural change. While *I* might now be residual, others may now be able to pull their weight, pay their bills, express their messages, and so be brought back to life from the obscurity of a value-less state.

Nothing is intrinsic under this regime of Real Estate. Cities and neighborhoods fall, and rise, and fall again. Strange properties will be linked together in the unnatural acts that make a good deal, and they sometimes will even fly. These new arrangements and inventions, such as lease-back or condominiums or programming languages or airplanes, are fragile to be sure, but we have complex social arrangements to support them and take care if they fall out of the sky. The traditional problem of any political economy is to control these exchanges and transformations so they are fair. The political world makes up for short-term bankruptcies, picks up the pieces when there is depression, and says "stop" when the deals become too monstrous.

The rhetoric of systems or economy replaces everything by simile form. Even if all resistance might be expressed in this rhetoric of economy and simile, we may not find it adequate for expressing the intrinsic enduring aspect of ourselves. Other tropes imply there is something residual or symbolized, not completely captured by metaphor or metonymy. The soul or personality may not be only a matter of exchange value or messages. The resistance may be a sign, a sign of something, and we need a more full expression of our being to appreciate what the sign points to.

2.2 (RHETORIC, WORLDS)

[What the world is like.]

We act as if the world is whole, yet we discover and make changes in the soft and malleable places: something like a Claes Oldenburg soft sculpture of an octagon plug, floating in a blue felt sea. If we push in or remake one place, others pop out or become accessible to us.* So we keep on fixing up the world, although we cannot be sure we shall be able to get at every part of it, nor do we feel we must to resew every seam. We need to tend and mend the sculpture, and that need is evidence of those malleable places. But the need is not universal, or an

---

* This is a bit like Neurath's ship at sea. As Quine (p. 3) puts it, "Neurath has likened science to a boat which, if we are to rebuild it, we must rebuild plank by plank while staying afloat in it." But that ship is of rigid wood; it somehow gets more substantial as time goes on; and we believe we know what it looks like. The relationship between these two analogies of how we change our world is the same, I suspect, as the relationship between a ship and an Oldenburg version of it. The Oldenburg ship never looks quite seaworthy. Oldenburg generously allows the existence of many ships, not one, all of them different, each one a bit soggy, but never in danger of completely sinking.

uncontrollable desire. We might be satisfied not to fuss over the sculpture for a while, as we are satisfied after dinner. We do not immediately remake every place: we recognize, more or less, what is whole and good, and what is maybe only adequate and decent. We always try to do the best we can, but each repair engenders the next, so there is no final fix. Needle and thread are part of ourselves.

As we grow up and mature we discover and learn better what is whole and good. For the most part we have encountered and been brought up by reasonable people and decent citizens, so that is not surprising. What is surprising is that the exceptions have had so little effect. Surely we can be suspicious, violent, and even self-destructive. But still we have remarkable agreement and good sense about what is whole and good. We bear life's problematic qualities comfortably, fixing things up as we encounter them. We are sufficiently acquainted with the world to know which possibilities we might actually achieve. The strange and monstrous are not so appealing, no matter what anyone tells us. And none of this prevents us from initiating large changes and even revolutions once in a while.

There is no other perfect world. There is this one and within it we can aim for immortality among ourselves. Nostalgia for the whole, somehow outside of this world, is the dangerous polar leitmotif.

## 2.21 (RHETORIC, WORLDS, HOW-TO)

[What we do when things go wrong.]

Most of the time we know what to do, and when something goes wrong we can handle it. It's happened before. We attend to problems because we care for ourselves. We might forget or ignore what is in our own interest, and then others will remind us of what we already know and recall to us who we really are. Each of us can be a coach, pointing out tricks of the trade that another person will recognize, feel comfortable with, and so do better.

When we fail in what we try to do, when we fail in taking care of ourselves, the questions we then ask ourselves will suggest what we shall have to do otherwise, and determine whether we understood what we were doing. There is no more perfect person or more general true principle to ask us questions, to remind us of what is important. There is just ourselves.

## 2.22 (RHETORIC, WORLDS, AS-IF)

We act as if there are effective limitations on our capacities, as if there is a good, and as if there is freedom, but these cannot be said to be specifically *this*, or *this*, or *this*. We are limited; there is a good; we can be responsible for what we do. As for limitation, in any particular situation some ways of being are not possible for us, although they may be for others. For goodness, there are better ways to be and act, although they may be less preferable in other situations. And for freedom, our ability to act in a situation depends on how we see ourselves being responsible for it.

Natural resources might be said to be limited. But new mining technologies will change their accessibility or purity, and new processes and catalysts may make impossible transformations merely expensive or difficult or, miraculously, sometimes even cheap.

In a wide range of situations we may find that there are some things we cannot do, and we might then reasonably conclude that they are absolute limits. But we might not want to claim that, that some way of being is impossible. In another way of life, just as comfortable for us as this one, we might exceed what we once thought were absolute limits, effectively choosing a whole new world. That is what the New World was about. I do not believe we can ever have an idea of all the ways that we can be comfortable.

But this argument does not permit us to conclude that we do not have limitations. We live in this world, not all of them, and not everything is possible for us here, at least now. We're not protean. But saying that we live in this world is not enough to warrant a very specific claim about our being limited. We can usually get around that, perhaps at high cost. Or we may choose to live in the margin, giving up some of what everyone else takes to be necessary so as to decrease our limitations.

We need a notion of limitation that captures the idea of impossibility, but does not let us conclude that what is impossible is also necessarily impossible. It may be necessarily impossible in this situation, but small alterations in the situation may make it possible. It seems there are pockets of slack hidden all over, ready to pop out as we mend a seam or move one of the wall panels. The world may not smoothly change as we change its parameters.

If it were the case that impossibility implies (universal) necessity, then arguments describing our limitations and our limited resources could be used to deny the claims of the poor and the weak, they being the recipients of the consequences of being necessarily conserving under a regime of limitation. We might say: In order (for us, the men, the community) to survive, the poor or women must necessarily be sacrificed. However, if we could conceive of other possible worlds, other ways of living our lives, then we might move over to one in which this sacrifice is not required. Hence the sacrifice is necessary, but only in some conceptions of our world. Even if sacrificial victims believe in the original conception, and would at first be disoriented by being saved from sacrifice, they may prefer (and I think most of us would also prefer) in the end not to be sacrificed—perhaps even if sacrifice were the highest and most honorable act in the society—and to adjust to living with their disappointment.

The survival of this world cannot automatically justify limits or the lack of them, such as child labor, for there are other ways to survive. We might rearrange our social order, making unnecessary a sacrifice that was once needed to survive. Why stay with a social order that forces us to sacrifice those we love, especially if we have some doubt about whether the sacrifice is necessary? Abraham is remarkable and problematic because he had such doubts and he persisted. Imagine if God's will were merely a devilish intrusion.

Sacrifice might make sense, but only if there is no alternative. We need to ask what we want the good world to look like, then see what is limiting and what kind of limit that is, and then figure out how to organize our lives to achieve our world. And if we cannot be fair and just, perhaps we should not survive, and go down with dignity.

Of course, we are in this world. An alternative world or social order must always labor under start-up costs and historical precedent. We cannot change our situation that easily. But the conception of an alternative does let us question justifications for sacrifice. And, if necessary, we might rotate the poor and victimage roles among various groups.

## 2.221 (RHETORIC, WORLDS, AS-IF, LIMITS)

The most prevalent model of limitation we use is that of conservation of a limited resource. The limits we set depend on what we intend to do with the resource, the technologies we use to extract and recycle it, and the costs of those technologies. As I have pointed out for natural resources, changes in these factors will alter a limit.

If that which is limited is not extensive, material, or quantitative, then conservation of a limited resource is not an appropriate model of limitation. The limit might be essential, about the way something ought to be if it is still to be what it is. A person cannot randomly kill people if we are to consider him a person. Such behavior violates our notion of what it is to be a person, our notion of what a person does. He lacks the capacity for proper conduct. He seems to have no soul.

The soul, as an essential limit, is often associated with God, where God is the source of meaning, purpose, and design. God is a rhetorical source, since it pastorally guides us to a proper life. It is also a logical source, since the articulation of God (as a notion or through God's speech) justifies the world. God makes the world properly whole. The world might then be said to end, to stop developing, and to be perfect. Pridefully, we set up a notion of essential limitation based on our interpretation of God. But the world does not end. Varieties of proper fulfillment are possible. The good may be more completely realized. Even in perfection there is still room for development and for the interpretation of perfection.

What we have now, may or may not be justified by a notion of essential limitation. For example, some might say that a poor–rich separation must exist, reflecting an essential limitation. I might then argue, Why should these particular people be poor; why not rotate the role? Are there other ways of reflecting the limitation, other fairer social arrangements, than by this separation? Is this separation a reflection of other, less essential, principles that might be satisfied in a different fashion? The poor need no more be with us than many other facts of life. Our actual social order may or may not reflect any of its ultimate limitations.

A utopia is a counterclaim about the limits of our social order. It tells us about what we had never thought possible, how if we were only to move the fences around we might graze in virgin pasture. Only later, having made a utopia into an actual possibility, do we discover just why we held that social order to be utopian and impossible, and so held ourselves back. For example, a communal family will be impractical if most of us live in nuclear families. Social services are wrong, roles do not fit, tax laws are unfair. But later, having realized that utopia, we understand how entirely different services, roles, and laws could work, and how unnecessarily limited were our notions of the possible.

In any particular situation, we will be blind. There is no olympian location. We are always held back. But blindness, sublimation, and resistance are exploding bolts. They hold us firm, but when they fracture, they give way completely. And other bolts, just like them, take their place.

## 2.2211 (RHETORIC, WORLDS, AS-IF, LIMITS, REPETITION)

[The world has meaning for us only because it is the same as what has happened before. Yet we should not conclude that the evils of the past are necessary. New evils will come and we might distribute their harms more fairly.]

The world is limited but multifold in its possibilities, the same but different, fixed but changing. The hard problem is how we should think about what is enduring in it, the logic of the claims we might make about what is necessary in the world. Every cure, explanation, or solution of the world's fracture into diversity and difference is a repetition of one of the previous cures. There are no new miracles here. And the cures depend on the fractures. Reconciliation and forgiveness follow partition and error; each makes the other possible and gives it meaning. Otherwise, partition would be multiplicity, and error would be what we do. But there is more. Blindness hints at the spectrum of blindnesses, so what is other is never completely other to us. We always, in some way, recognize what we cannot see. Blindness allows for peeking.

If the world is sundered, it is sundered from a wholeness we find on occasion. The world becomes better and more whole for a while. When the world subsequently falls apart, it just does. It is not a matter of compensation, of the bad paying for the good. We are tempted by a tame picture of the ups and downs, which views them as a matter of sinusoidal continuity. What goes down must come up, and then fall again. The world becomes more whole because we have earned it. The linkage between wholeness and sunderedness is perhaps The Fall, but it is not a falling and a bouncing back that balance each other, or a frictionless conservation of energy, or payments accounting for debits. The Fall is a matter of guilt or sin, or economic waste versus efficiency. The cures depend on the fractures, but the dependence is narrative and theological.

Wholeness and sunderedness are not commensurable, they are not on a single continuous curve. The sundered world has its own integrity, even if it feels dissipated. Between are more frightening intermediate states, truly sexual, intercoursing with the whole and the sundered, outside the realm of perfection and failure.

Repetition of a cure is not a restoration of what has been before, except as representative of the narrative form we call restoration. Each restoration is a reenactment of the idea of wholeness or perfection or organizing form. We honor a form by treating it as a member of the pantheon of whole forms. But it is not the only one, and the members of the pantheon are not subject to each other's domination. There are many ways of being whole.

Imagine that each proof that something is false sets the stage for its being true in one of the next times around, although we do not know how it will be true. Or that each therapy or cure sets up the possibility for fracture. Every commitment we make to an endeavor would then surely implicate us in treachery, just because we are thoughtful, prudent, and responsible. We go on doing what we have got to do. Unavoidably. It works out.

## 2.222 (RHETORIC, WORLDS, AS-IF, FREEDOM)

We know what the atoms and molecules will do. That's physics. But we do not know which story we'll want to tell, this time around, about what we've been doing. That depends on what else we want to do, how we want to be remembered, and what others are saying. By selectively picking out and organizing what's important, a story creates room for action. Other stories will affect our story and what we do, and we treat other persons as if they were subject to our stories. We can give an account of ourselves and so be responsible for what we do.

Freedom is that accountable room for action.

## 2.223 (RHETORIC, WORLDS, AS-IF, GOODNESS)

[Justifying the goods of life, like families and work, in a generous fashion. The goods are rhetorical topics around which we justify how we live, and they are actual modalities for living our lives. None of this says just what the goods are, or which are the necessary topics and modalities, or if any are necessary.]

We assume that there is good. We argue about what it is and how it manifests itself in our lives. The argument need not be exclusionary, creating a good and then fighting off the rest as bad. Still, we must inquire whether what we usually call goods are representative of the good.

We assume that there are limits, goodness, or freedom, so that we can talk about them. But they are topics, not specific absolutes that immediately forbid or encourage what we abstractly want to do. They guide us only in the context of a particular concrete world. So we may find it hard to know how absolute their guidance is. Will small changes in context dramatically alter the specific guidance we reflectively deduce from a principle of limitation or goodness? Are there other more generous or very different interpretations of the principle?

Having ideas of limits, goodness, and freedom is a way of living in a world. More generally, it is human nature to take an articulated position on our human nature. Conceiving human nature (gestationally and notionally), we can be more fully human. But that does not mean that we can say just what human nature is, even if the acts of articulation, such as in politics or philosophy, are crucial to our self-definition. Any description will be formal, something like the second sentence of this paragraph, which we then will have to fill in.

For example, a useful start for an inquiry into human nature or goodness might be the statement, "It is our nature to have a sense of well-being and to know that we have that sense. We know when we are ill, and when we are growing and developing." But what more do we say? We can describe in much greater detail the feeling of well-being and how we cope with illness. There is no criterion that will surely say when we are well, but we do not need such a criterion. The acts of articulation, exfoliations that do not stop, are sufficiently definitive of well-being.

Can we be more specific? In each society there must be generic structures of human development such as family and work. Formally, they organize and give meaning to our everyday lives. The stories we tell use these structures as topics or categories. Our culture has been around for a while, and our topical vocabulary includes these structures as sedimentations of past history. They are achievements of the culture. They are, as well, the places where we look for changes in our culture, where changes can be expressed but also naturalized and brought home. Family and work are central to our society, but their specific forms have been changing. We do not need a defense of these structures. We're stuck with them, but not with their particular forms.

"Family" and "work" are topics around which we investigate what these structures do. The investigation is a serious one. No interesting set of functions seems to encompass any structure, nor is there an ideal family or form of work. The family$_{1970s}$ is a good example of a structure, but just how it is an example, which of its features are crucial and exemplary, remains open for investigation.

Describing what people usually take to be human nature will not tell us how to fill in the generic forms. It will not say what the family should look like or how we ought to work. We need to know more about the context provided by the social structure. And we need to understand the ways we forget or ignore how treacherous it is to make larger claims of necessity from our own limited situation, the ways we mistakenly insist on our conceptions as the only ones. Hence we study prejudice and pride.

Generic structures such as the family or work are often said to be necessary. We have always had them. How could we go on without them? But if we show that these necessary institutions are evil, as we are wont to do, then how could we go on with them? Necessity becomes the mother of re-invention. But when we examine how we have always had a family, then what is necessary or fundamental about that structure will not be so straightforward, and it will be less clear how it is a source of evil.

Perhaps our arguments will convince us that under our regime the family is necessary and evil. We decide that it must go. But what would be its successor? Only afterwards, with the successor in place, would we know why we cannot conceive (of) it now. Still, revolutionary arguments have to give us reason to believe we already know something about what comes next: the same, but very different from what we could conceive now.

### 2.224 (RHETORIC, WORLDS, AS-IF, FORMAL NECESSITY)

[Necessity does not prescribe how we should live, but it sets up the topics around which we argue about how we should live.]

Formal concepts, such as limits, goodness, or freedom, enable us to talk about what is necessary for our lives. They are the subject matter of politics. But because they are formal, they have no direct bludgeoning or hegemonic power over any particular realization of them. Argument might show that a particular realization of a family is a family, even though it does not look like one. Or, alternatively, a sham realization of a form may look proper and ordinary. But for a revolutionary, even the formal concepts are potentially false. They may guide us in systematically wrong ways. So the notion of a family is sometimes seen as dangerous. Prospectively, revolutionaries must argue that the family will have no meaning after the revolution, because it is so corrupt an idea. Afterwards, however, it never turns out that way. Under a new interpretation, family again has meaning, maybe even the old one. The revolutionary eventually appreciates how his before and after visions could be consistent.

### 2.225 (RHETORIC, WORLDS, AS-IF, CONSERVATISM)

[History and being in touch with what you are up to.]

Actual concrete reasonable persons are comfortable with imperfection in the world. They know that even if we treat the world as if it were whole, it is not finished or fully present to us. We keep discovering aspects of it. Nor is the imperfect world delicately balanced, likely to fall apart if we discover a new imperfection. It is robust and resilient. And there are persons quite other than us, and they do fit in.

The Burkean conservative argument about our world's wisdom is probably right. Experience has been a great teacher. But what is that wisdom and teaching? One need not conclude that the world will fall apart unless we make only small changes guided in a received way by historical precedent. It might fall apart if we did not make large changes, or if we did not choose to guide change by an entirely different set of precedents than the usual ones—if the world is going to fall apart at all. But how do things fall apart: one part randomly and intermittently failing as in a watch mechanism, or graceful degradation as in a defective or poorly focused lens? In the first case we fix a particular part and all is smooth once again. In the second we must adjust all the various parts, polish all the poorer surfaces, and slowly get everything into phase.

Whatever it is, history is a guide under our direction. Persons are usually sensible, and their actions, even disturbing ones, can be given an historical foundation. History seems to be available for much of the legitimating we need to do. When we forget the possibility of history's justifying something other than what we already have, conservatism becomes ideological.

Persons can be sensible if they are in touch with what they are doing. Its meaning and implications are then at their fingertips. But technology and economy often consider our actions over too short a term, such as for the invisible hand, with no immediately understandable larger meanings. Those meanings return to haunt us later. So we are out of touch in these realms, and hence they are subject to a traditional conservative attack.

The feeling of being in touch is subjective, but we are persons who are trained and socialized. Being in touch is a reflection of our cultural constitution. It is a good guide to what's up, but not a perfect one. Just as there is no guarantee that being historically grounded will guide us to a desirable world, your being sensible does not mean you are good. But if you are sensible, then arguments about the good may appeal to you. And if you are grounded, you are relatively stable, shocks do not destroy you, errors and falsehood need not migrate everywhere as insidious pollution and destructive contradiction. They just sit there and you tolerate them. You have a way of managing when things do not go quite right. For example, small errors do not destroy the legitimacy of scientific practice. It fails softly and graciously. But formal logics are more brittle, and will be destroyed by a single contradiction, or so it seems. But actually, there are ways of isolating the influence of those contradictions, or creating a more consistent alternative axiom.

## 2.226 (RHETORIC, WORLDS, AS-IF, SUMMARY)

Human freedom is based on our ability to be responsible for what we do. Since we can be responsible for what we do, the world is not alien to us, it can be ours. It is ours not because we made it, but because we can find a way to accept such a gift so it is sufficient for what we have to do. We find out what's there in the world as we make the space for our actions.

The space we make is adequate and excessive, available and resistant, enough but not quite and too much. That's how it feels. So we try to make a home for ourselves, appropriating what there is and arranging it, actually rearranging it, so we can do what we are up to as best as we can. To capitalize on what's available we change our plans accordingly. The situation is never just quite right, but we go on. We do not blame what goes wrong on what's missing. We take the credit and the blame.

We are always reappropriating what we have and what is around us as we alter what we are doing and what we are up to. Home decorating never stops. Making something your own, giving it a proper setting, means neither that you own it through purchases, nor that you want to. There is no private property, mediated by a market, that fixes everything in its place, because if there were you could be bought out or driven from the market. No, security lies not in the things you own, but in your homemaking capacity, in what you make your own, the ability to give meaning to your world as you reassert and enact it. Hence we do not control the world in the sense of setting all of it in place, but we do control what we can commandeer in our pickup truck and what gifts we can fit into our household.

Each time we redecorate or have a new plan we must start with what stuff, worn out and new, that we already have. We reupholster some things, bring in a few plants, turn the rug around, and somehow it begins to work. Heirlooms and junk, tradition and prejudice, are the foundation for each time around. Nothing's all new.

When we look around at our handiwork we can figure out what will work, what does not, and how we might do better. We may discern the forms of goodness, which are stable yet allow us to grow. We talk about what we are doing, how others might disagree with this arrangement, and figure out the best arrangement we can. And the discussion continues, since we never do come to final agreement. We differ. What we can hope for is that the development of our souls into their true full conceptions will be liberal and generous. Then the forms will be ours again and we can redecorate once more.

### 3 (OTHERNESS)

[How we manage among the intractable and resistant parts of the world.]

The world, like our food, is not fully digestible. We choose the food and make our dinner, but we cannot handle all of it. Some sticks in our throat, bones go right through us, corn barely gets touched. There are leftovers. No one else does much better. Still, we are well enough nourished. Even if we tried eating someone like ourselves, we would not succeed. There are bones there too. So we do not even try. Self-consistency, the logical virtue, is not to be ours. Instead, we agree that a proper meal will not be fully digestible.

The various kinds of purity and taboo, which are ways we pay attention to indigestibility, become a foundation for culture and a model for proper and improper action. We experiment with different diets, or even try some of the forbidden foods. Sometimes we find we can eat them and so we change some of the rules. But some rules remain resistant. Having been brought up in a Kosher household, a glass of milk with a steak is inconceivable to me. Cuisine converts what we can digest into a seemingly infinite variety of possibilities.

More abstractly: The world is not fully digestible. We never have a full grasp of it. It is ours. We give it the meanings it can have. But it is not all ours. We do not control it. And if the world is of our making, not all our desires can be made there. It is not possessed. The world has its own being. The world is just enough for what we want to do, or almost, or sometimes not at all. That is why I say the world is adequate and available, but it is excessive and resistant as well. Imagine a sculpture in a material that is a cross between mica and marble: natural structures always getting in your way but also providing nice surfaces and masses you work around.

We are members of a community, but we are, as well, other, incommensurable, indigestible, to each other and to ourselves: adequate and available, excessive and resistant. There is no absolute intimacy. We do things, make objects, talk to people, and our otherness and resistance is resolved and then made more profound. That's the way things are. Usually we do not think much about the rift between, say, availability and resistance, or about the world's being whole but not finished. At the rift we make and shape the world. We need a more practical description of how we work at the rift, more specific than the formal description I have given so far. How do we manage and cope when we are lost?

No description heals the rift. Understanding does not lead to total control. Each description shows what we might do. Following one description, we go on more or less in what we were up to before we stopped to think about the rift. The world is ours again. And we are still resistant, willing to alter it for the better or worse. Without a way of working at the rift, the world is not ours and we do not know where we are or how to orient ourselves. Then resistance has no meaning.

We're just thrashing about with no chance to resolve otherness, no possibility of being a member of the community. The realm of the diabolical. We slip into and out of anxiety and skepticism, somehow getting along much better than our experience of those liminal states would attest.

### 3.01 (OTHERNESS, RACISM)

[Racism depends on treating the intractable parts of the world abstractly, and as unrelated to the tractable, more familiar parts.]

If we are other to each other, we might divide the world into "we" and "they." But such a short division makes for hierarchy, since we can then easily treat we and they as good and bad. Rational long division can make for greater diversity, if we choose the numerator and denominator carefully. Otherwise, we get closely repeating groups ($\frac{1}{11} = 0.090909\ldots$) or terminating decimal representations ($\frac{1}{8} = 0.125$). We can prevent systematic racism only by paying attention to each place and the numeral that occupies it, each person in his own variety. A godly and transcendental world would be $\pi$. We are equal when nothing can take first place for very long and so be the good, when nothing is equal.

To be other is to be different, not alike and not assimilable. Being different may be understood as a set of differences, particular abstractions from the complexity of life. Racism depends on treating that set as summatory, as the actual properties of a person or thing, fixed and fully representative of him. Racism is a fetishism. We know that it cannot be quite true, for we are not so reductively treated, only they are. But we insist on its being true. We maintain that color, race, or gender could epitomize someone's (their) nature.

Racism also depends on the set of differences being small in number, say one. Then it should be easy to put "them" in a hierarchy with respect to "us." Even with two or three that is not too hard. But if we have many kinds of difference and all sorts of variation, it becomes more difficult to set up a hierarchy. We might even become less sure that any properties could epitomize a person or thing.

We and they, as a version of otherness, is the foundation of racism. But even when there is seeming diversity, we will be tempted to reduce it to an opposing pair. So we have to make that impossible. Rub our noses in variety.

Treating all of us as the same is not the foundation for equality. Differences do make a difference. If they are few, racism must follow. Only if there is no possibility of being simply the same will there be no chance to have racial characteristics. If we are the same but different there still can be community, but every difference can be significant and valuable. Then we can be equal.

Racism depends not only on reducing variety to a simple classification, but also on treating some aspects of ourselves as extra and eliminable, as forgettable. These non-white parts, these excreta, can be buried and we may ignore them. They have no relationship to us. They is the part of ourselves we do not pay attention to. But we and they depend on each other, and so what we treat as other returns as own. The return is more insidious because we are vulnerable, having thought we had gotten rid of it.

The repressed returns in the form of sin and guilt and takes over our lives. The modern history of racism will assume this form, a form which the Greeks, Augustine, and Freud also understood. It will not be about what we have done to them, but what we have done to ourselves. There can be a transcendent(al) resolution, like $\pi$, that stops the cycles of return so that we have a peace of multiplicity and perversion, but whether we can have it is less clear.

### 3.02 (OTHERNESS, TITRATABILITY)

[Racism is literally a disease, the side effects of which are thought insignificant. But side effects depend on the cure, and we may not be able to eliminate them gently. No measured amount of adjustment works, and we do not appreciate that the system may be unstable as a result of our trying to calm it down.]

They are side effects—what we would like to eliminate. But our existence (as we) depends on them. Our cures, actions in this world, are not perfect. Not everything fits. A simple picture will never encompass the whole story, if anything could, and so what is extra is called a side effect. It is a negative title in the aristocracy of miracle cures; a side effect never really gets known. We always investigate it as if it were a nuisance or residuum. It never has a life of its own. It is always seen as a pollutant of what is potentially pure.

Side effects, never quite known for themselves, return to poison us. We usually do not learn to live with them as a necessary part of the cure or the main event. So when "we" try to control only "them" we fail, since the cure also seems to dissipate. The side effects balance the cure, they go along with it. It is not a matter of we and they. The negative title we give to "them" makes us act in such a way that we cannot titrate our cure so that it works. We conclude that there cannot be a balance.

Sacks describes how Parkinson's disease patients may have some of their symptoms relieved by L-Dopa, but the cure's side effects are large as well. If a patient can integrate them into his life, then he might actually be well, although his life would not seem to be normal. Most patients cannot integrate and be well. There is no room for them in this world.

We might think of cure and side effect as unequally balanced on a see-saw that has a rotary spring at its fulcrum. A small improvement does not give too large side effects, but as we try to jiggle the system all sorts of rotational vibrations are set up. It is not a simple see-saw. The more we jiggle the less stable it looks. Fine tuning is impossible, it seems. Just when there is the most instability, we are most in touch with the authentic relationship of cure and side effect. They depend on each other, but their relationship is springy and even a bit dissipative. In the extreme moments we learn the most about the spring's characteristics.

### 3.03 (OTHERNESS, THE POSSIBILITY OF CURE)

[How cures work, and how we make our peace with side effects.]

Not all side effects need be disruptive. Most of the time we manage quite well. We can titrate and balance medical cures for the best effect. So otherness is not always an unstable problem. Simple categories, such as we and they, often work. So our usual ways of being may be founded on a convenient, even temporarily benign, racism. We are then tempted to believe that racism, rather than a transcendent multiplicity or perversion, is the true model of the world.

We need a way of thinking of a more peaceful reintegrative return of the repressed, in which we could reincorporate the stigmatized, what we have sent out as other. Is this reintegration possible, or is it just a pipe dream that avoids the necessities of our non-redemptive culture, which are perhaps to be avoided? Our closest model of integrity is our soulful bodies, each one whole even though we do much of our work together. For cures and side effects, reintegration is a matter of not separating off parts of the body as being where "those" problems are, whether "those" problems are what we wish to cure or the side effects that ensue when we apply a therapy.

A strategy of separation, a form of racism, sometimes does work. The problem may be sufficiently localized, or the cure specific and with few side effects, or the side effects may be sufficiently localized and specific. But we find ourselves insisting on separation when it is inappropriate as well. If the problems or side effects are large we must start off with the whole body. Only later can we select the right subsystems, if there are any and if we may speak in terms of a system with subparts, for separate treatment.

But we have already sent off parts of ourselves, for example the body (versus the mind) or the women (versus the men). We have created a repressed world, and so stigmatized the other as other and ourselves as not-other. Even if we were to formally insist on our integrity, say on the bodily location of all of it including the mind, whatever "it" is, we have still to say how we shall see ourselves whole again. The fracture of the world was noisy and compound and it is hard to imagine how it would just, somehow, smoothly heal. We know it does, we find ourselves whole again, complexities yield to overarching and simple pictures. The furies are able to make their peace with us. But it must be, it seems, on their terms. We do not even know what to ask for—until we have been given it. Only later can we see why a resolution is a resolution, how we can give up distinctions that are vital aspects of our being yet still be fully alive. The aspects we give up not only seem vital, they are vital, yet we can still be fully alive. All discussions of cure, love, or supermundane grace depend on this fact, that the repressed returns and can declare war on us but can as well declare peace, on its terms, and those terms can be benign and for our good, as we might eventually recognize. Anger, fury, and resentment can yield, flip-flop, to goodness and peace. And this grace can be mundane. Of course, not everything is cured, and some cures are temporary, the wounds to fester and become vital again.

Even after grace and cure, we still must reinterpret the miracles, what has happened to us, in the light of our new situation. Reinterpretation must account for the experience of disruption, and make the resolution be natural, smooth, and grounded in formerly less appreciated aspects of our original situation. So the transition and cure now makes sense. Had we only paid attention to the right signs, we could have known ahead of time.

A rite of passage is a model of cure and of transition to wholeness. There is an integration of what was once thought to be separate, a rediscovery of our bodies and social roles, and a dispersal of what we thought was vital. The myths of cure and transition account for what happens, saying, "It, before and after the transition, is the same but different." No rite of passage is smooth, but the account smoothes it over, even if it incorporates a tumultuous intermediate period.

We have some discretion as to whether we enter into a transition or rite, or whether we employ a cure. But once we take the medication or begin the ritual, it is somewhat less under our control. It just happens.

We do not completely control the resolution of our most profound crises. Our usual methods of guiding ourselves often do not work in these cases and may be positively misleading.

We are most bereft, most subject to anxiety, just when a new life could be possible for us—were we to accept it. What that new life will be and how it will incorporate side effects is exactly what we do not know and what we are rightly anxious about. It will not be 40 percent of the old and 60 percent something else, but 100 percent old and 100 percent else. It will be "compossible" (following Leibniz), a matter of ". . . how much we can summon one world, without summoning others, and of the strengths and resources which go with different worlds." (Sacks, p. 309.)

### 3.1 (OTHERNESS, POLITICS)

Politics is an expression of our otherness to each other. In that expression we may agree for a while, yet agreement guarantees its own dissipation into issue and argument. Whatever we are now doing together, we started off with different tasks and those are still with us. So having met in common purpose, our interpretations of what is happening may differ. We are up to different things. And we shall want to go in different directions before long.

In politics we argue about the legitimacy and authenticity of politics itself. For example, are the expressions of otherness and our then coming together genuine if they are not voluntary and responsible? Arguments about the possibility of politics are often about the kinds of liberty and freedom possible in what has been called political space. Space is the possibility of having separate objects (say, for Kant), and political space is, analogously, the possibility of having authentic others in the community. If our disagreements are genuine and of sufficient extent, and if we can be roughly equal in power, then politics seems quite possible. We are less sure we are authentically other to each other in a corporate world of widely disproportionate degrees of power.

### 3.11 (OTHERNESS, POLITICS, THE STATE)

Formally, we might think of the state as a mode of alienation and reconstitution—there was no original, first, constitution. For example, the political economy of the modern state requires that it aid in the accumulation of capital for production, and that it justify the lot of its citizens under such a regime, at least if it is to be viewed as legitimate by them. Accumulation tends to alienate the citizenry, while the processes of legitimation (in particular, paying off the have-nots) reconstitutes them as a community. The limited political and pecuniary resources are required for both accumulation and legitimation. We can imagine that there may not be enough for both purposes, and hence the political economy of the state may oscillate between two unstable poles and even fail.

But alienation and reconstitution are not only terms of economy; they are also terms of transformation and resolution, of different but the same, of resistance that becomes comfortable and then resistant again. The state rationalizes and organizes the production of the human world, and then, by its lights, justly distributes that produce. The state is an instrument of politics, a practical expression of our arguments about what is necessary and good. The state is an actual arrangement of people and bureaus and laws and modes of control. It is also a name and an idea around which those who are involved in these activities can rationalize and organize what they are doing.

Alienation and reconstitution is one way to describe a wrenching from ourselves and then a finding out how to make ourselves whole again. These terms recall that we are never comfortable with the state, for it is alienating, and still we make our constitution around the state.

### 3.12 (OTHERNESS, POLITICS, COMMUNITY)

In a community we can effectively talk together. Arguments might actually be persuasive, leading others to identify with a position. Rhetoric may work. Also, most of the time we know what is up for grabs, what is going on, what is at issue. Or, if we do not know, it is obvious to us that we are not sure, that we are confused and lost. The rhetorical topics (*topoi*) are actual places we can meet and join the issues. And then there are times when we are unclear about whether something is obvious or not, and we say, "Blockhead! Don't you see why you have to think twice about that." But usually the world will not go on unless we do what we must; and it makes sense why we ought to; and we know where we are; and we do it.

### 3.13 (OTHERNESS, POLITICS, PROFESSIONALS)

Someone who has seen lots of problems like the ones you seem to have can help you. But he may actually have no better grasp of your situation than you do, and you have to be sure you want to have his version of your life.

4 (AMELIORATION)

[A fable.]

Afterwards, when we have returned from our voyage into diremption, we can like what we have made because the new world is rich and growing. We can live in it. It is not better, just different. But we can make all sorts of particular comparisons between it and other worlds we know, in which one world will be better than another.

If what we have made did not turn out as we expected, we shall want to find out why. Still, we may have inadvertently done a good thing, we may like what we have, although the world we originally wanted might have been good too. We should find out why our inadvertence worked out well anyway, and why we believed that our failed intentions should have been achievable.

We continue to migrate in what seems like a desert, but actually it is densely polka-dotted with worldly oases, each good enough to support us for a while. While in the desert the heat rots our brains so it becomes hard to think about two oases at one time, although we can recall detailed aspects of all our encampments. Each one was exciting, some were especially good for the camels, others for the goats, and others for the people. Most oases were hospitable. No one starved, and since we depend on each other, we have to judge an oasis by how good it was for all of us. Because we could grow and develop as a community at each oasis, we had the possibility of making a good life at each of them.

Some oases did not have good water, or crispy plants, or pushbutton telephone service. But we got along pretty well. So we never can conclude that the world has to be a certain way if we are going to survive in it. When we leave one oasis and chuck its world, no particular or quantitative limits will tell us what the new oasis ought look like. It will look something like the old one, but we are not sure just how. What seemed necessary and certain there, might not even be relevant the next time.

But why do we leave an oasis? Most of the time we wander off hunting for a new telephone line or a wonderful succulent, but we forget about it after a while. We do not know quite why we are in the desert and, of course, sometimes we are scared. Eventually we find another oasis, which turns out to be just right. Just when we think we are more careful and vigilant so that we will not wander off again, something we never even thought of gets us off-track once more.

To boot, the "first" oasis we hit after we start counting time is almost always just right. Now we know that no one has a good compass, the stars are out of orbit, and most people are sand-blind. So it must be just right because we can make do in a good way with what we happen upon. Each oasis must be like a lock that can be opened by any key, but no picking will do, and when the lock is opened and the door swings free, what we see depends on the shape of our key. (If there is an actual "first" oasis, we either are blessed with a forgetfulness called God, or there is a zeroth and minus-first at least. There is no first oasis, except in our genesis stories.)

But we also leave the oasis deliberately. I have been too generous in describing oases, for some of them turn out to be disasters—at least for us. If nothing works at an oasis, if the world we can have there is not a good one, if what is good is impossible there, our affection for the oasis and our allegiance to it must decline. We know that impossibility has no meaning unless you are also quite specific about what you will not touch or alter in your oasis, what you take as fundamental and necessary. An oasis's contrariness to what you want to do is a sign that what was once most dear to you about it is now most dangerous. What we cannot touch, unless the oasis is to dry up and return to the desert, seems to be exactly what we have got to move around if the oasis is to survive. This contradictory situation, the necessities and impossibilities of life, might be what we are stuck with, but we should only believe that after we have visited a few more oases. The days we'll spend searching in the desert do not look promising or inviting, but they are a lot better than living in a necessarily not-good world. And we are not just searching. We are living in the desert as well.

This is our situation when we try to ameliorate the lot of the poor, the bad, or the inept. The civilization, the state, the community, or the culture will be destroyed, it is said, unless we respect civilization's necessities, including that some folks must be residual misfits in unhappy positions (as contrasted to the voluntary and contented misfits). For example, a fairer distribution of what we have might be less efficient in total productivity under a certain regime, so it is argued that processes like trickle-down are the only means for amelioration. Or, agreeing that we need a complex of institutions for a good life, we then conclude that we need to commit ourselves to the ones we have now. If the poor were not residual, but part of us, we would realize that our lives are not good unless we face the problems and residua that come with survival. If we let the camels drink the brackish water, even if they could handle it or they deserved it, we could not be comfortable drinking from the purer well. We have got to go to a different oasis. The oases are roughly alike, so civilization seems to come out well enough in the end.

If something good is called impossible in this world, then this world is no longer for us. Not anything is possible. Impossibility depends on our sticking with this world. If we abandon it, we have lots more room. For example, if a technology may only be introduced if it is available to all, then the possibility for innovation changes, but it does not become less rich.

### 4.1 (AMELIORATION, POSSIBILITY)

We make the best of what we have, but that does not say much. Chucking the world is frightening, but sometimes that is all we can do. It is good to know that the next world will be much like our own, only different and other.

Politics must be grounded in our capacities, and there are limits to what we can do. But we are not stuck with what we think of as the capacities or limits. Surely we are subject to natural law. We have got to make sure that no one can claim he knows exactly what it is.

# ⚬⋇ What Planners Do

*"What Planners Do" is an epitome of* Advice and Planning. *It makes sense in terms of the rest of the book, although parts will seem perfectly clear and obvious to readers who have come to similar positions on their own. Its statements are followed by scholia.*

*Advice and planning are human activities that make sense of the world by talking about it. The word, and its deliverers and hearers, play a primary role in our lives. When we give advice we tell stories, and when we plan we are figuring out what to do with others. So advice and planning naturally go together. Planning, even as speech and writing in presentations and documents, is a form of action, a stance in the world that puts the world in its place. It is a rhetorical activity. Even rationality is a rhetoric. Rhetoric is persuasionary and conversionary, and planning easily becomes a sacred activity. When planners become sacred advisors they inherit a priestly role whose dangers to others and to themselves are commensurate with the transcendence they acquire. Prophets—think of Teiresias or Moses or Jesus—have suffered these advantages and pains.*

*But we are not otherworldly figures. We are just human beings in this mundane world. We make mistakes. There is no way of avoiding error, and methods that claim to are doomed. At best, methods are something like cookbooks, which we are trained well enough to understand so we can use them. They depend on us.*

*All tracts are motivated by heathen positions. I believe rationality, method, and individual actors cannot be understood outside of transcendent circumstances, and plans and stories are not simply matters of thought and confection absent of an audience that they are supposed to move.*

1. Planners tell us highly structured, reasonable stories about ourselves, relating obligations and promises. The telling reveals what happens by saying what is significant and how it works.

   —The telling is in speech, which is a doing with others, and which, like much of traditional oral work, is complex, mythic, and highly structured.

—It is rhetorical and formulaic, intentionally appealing to its audience. It is specific to its time and place.

—The speaking is located: in a situation, and directed to certain purposes and an audience. It is warranted by knowledge, but that does not make it universal. It is subjective, but not arbitrary.

—It is not an abstracted, objective, argument, true for all time. But it is well supported.

—It is a prophetic speaking, revealing what is true and what is possible. The speech effectively makes the true and the possible, by saying it, but of course it is subject to actual circumstance and chance.

—Plans are about how things will turn out in terms of what we do now. They determine to some extent how our actions will turn out, and they develop the meaning we give to our actions and their consequences.

—The stories planners tell create the finite. They are the source of purpose, repose, grace, survival, and rebirth. Planning, like the astrologers' consideration, takes into account origins and outcomes in the largest spheres as well as in one's own role in the universe.

—What happens has no beginning or end, as such. We must make sense, that is, find purposive sequences among our successful and failed intentions and those of others. Religions have similar tasks and we can use processes common to religion to describe planning.

2. Planners act as advisors to others with whom they have a personal as well as a political relationship. Their advice is based on their knowledge of the world, and their personal and political understanding of others. The advice is fallible yet sacred.

—Sacredness means that a transcendent claim is being made. The advice goes beyond our knowledge, or a large-scale vision is being invoked. But sacredness does not prevent there being many such visions and mundane competition among them. Sacredness does not mean perfection, either. The warrant for a plan is that it is about us, it could work out, and it can be politically representative of us.

—Advisors become knowledgeable through their experience and that of others, through their reasoning and argument, and through their sacred connections with the proper forms. A priestly profession provides them with sacred connections.

—Scientific knowledge is only partly empirical. It also depends on effective modes of generalization and a good sense for how the world might work. That good sense is a transcendent one that depends on a larger vision. But even if it is transcendent, many of us might have it. It need not be a priestly province.

—How advisors are wrong depends on the kind of claims they make to being right. If they are professionals, they claim to give due care, and achieve malpractice; if they are gods, there is absolute truth, and tragic failure and forgiveness. Today, our god is the idea of clear scientific speech itself, the word delivered. But logic misleads us. And veridical reports are controlled by the imperatives of what we may say, such as grammar and coherence. And so eventually we go awry. The form of what we say abandons the truth of the world. This is the dialectic of science, the play between our visions and theories and the way the world is.

—Our theories have their own rhythms, and their music may not be that of the spheres, at least after a while. So our models will become outdated, perhaps only to return in some future time.

—When advisors such as planners speak, they must speak at times determined by others. They are sometimes wrong because of that. And like seers, they are forced to speak with their own survival and reputation at stake.

—Advisors must give their assessments of a situation well before the evidence is in. And like physicians, who are similarly constrained, they are held responsible for being wrong, even if with time they would surely have done better. Scientists, on the other hand, are comparatively free to take their time in figuring out what is so.

—The superordinate authority of professionals comes from the gods. But it is we who give that authority to the gods. We allow the gods' first-person claims to be sacred. ("I, the value of health, am of paramount importance.") The sacred gods may then renew and cleanse us. The advisor is the good physician.

— Some of our gods are health, justice, efficiency, and goodness. Nowadays professions administer those gods, gods we have created and we might deny. In the name of health a claim will be sacred. But we might deny health its godly place, or say that this professional claim is not countenanced by the god of health. But if the claim is justified, then we may sacrifice a great deal in its name, and have a new and clean world as a result.

—Advisors' authority is ours to deny. We say whether they know what's up. Yet we mystify ourselves, and see their authority as residing just in their selves or in their knowledge, and having nothing to do with us.

—But those who become advisors are of course not the gods or even their representatives, no matter what they might want to believe after a while. They are not up to the obligations of their situation. To avoid that ambivalent closeness to the tragic and the sacred, they then deny their selves. They say they are technocrats. This is not a Socratic denial, but a fearful one. Advisors see their speech incorrectly, as beyond persons and their failures, and its anxious but human possibilities for re-creation are anxiously avoided.

  —Advisors, such as planners and other professionals, are complicitous in our mystification, and they act as if their power resides beyond them, in techniques. It is a power they have miraculously come to possess and administer. So when things go wrong, they are as confused as we are.

3. Plans are accounts that tell how and why things are the way they are. The accounts produce and describe what there is. They are spoken or written indexes to what there is that point it out. They say or announce what must be reasonable for us. They say what is practical, by indicating the appropriate practice.

  —Plans are active documents and speech. So they show how to make happen what they will. They say what is important and point it out. They organize the world.

—Speech is magic, words that make things so, and plans are magic too. But speech is bewitched, leading us in ways we do not intend as we make things "clear." So plans, accounts in words and pictures, lead planners to a nether world they did not plan on.

  —Magic is effective words. But words may not be in harmony with the world. So magic may not produce what we expect. Further attempts at clearing the smokescreen in front of what we do may entrench us behind even more of our own detritus. (Of course, clarity can lead to better intentions and truer work.)

4. The anxious voyage to that unplanned nether world, a world like our own (for how else could we speak of it?), suggests that our rationality is a way of maintaining our community.

  —When we are buried under the detritus of rationality we can look up and examine it more closely. We note how it keeps us together, and it blindingly reinterprets the world so that there is nothing else worth knowing. Yet we know, in a strange way, choking on our own smoke, that there is something else. Transcendent experience and anxiety tell us this, but they can only do so in our common ordinary language. Somehow our ordinary language and planning models are sufficient to tell us about their own profound limitations.

—Rational plans are modes of indexing the world and putting it in place. The index is canonically ordered, and only in that sense is the plan justified. Rational plans are ways of avoiding untoward possibilities. They control the obstreperous, non-criterial aspects of what critics have called quality. Such plans are ways of avoiding the full power of what we say and our responsibility for it.

—Rationality is not self-certifying. It admittedly leaves out a lot that is important, often what makes for a good life of high quality. Stuff that does not fit in, or whose implications might overwhelm our control mechanisms, is put away and labeled beyond consideration. No straightforward criteria will delimit that stuff.

—But plans need not be so rational. They may be modes of listening, awaiting, and revaluing what there is. They may be ways of being in the quiet of an ecstatic, liminal, unified state, and so we renew our possible ways of being.

—In the nether world, behind the smokescreen, under the detritus, we might well be calm enough to see and hear other worlds of possibilities, worlds of irrational futures and plans, some good, some bad. Transcendent experience has this renewing and frightening potential. Plans are a way of making this potential actual in everyday life.

5. A plan is a search, a project, a mode of resolution, a way of being free. We pick out a possibility for life from the possibilities we already have, not from nothing. A plan is an anxious choice, potentially disconnecting us from the web of our lives, and it may violate what we take to be our laws and rules. A plan makes it possible for our actions to make sense; it connects them up. But since it may be a violation, without our having deliberately transgressed, our rational talk about it may be inadequate. We will not be able to be coherent and consistent. We are in another world.

—Plans are a means of re-commitment and choice, a way to be in the world. We might think of the plan in terms of how it breaks or follows the usual rules. But that is unhelpful. A plan that expresses in a project what we eventually come to see as a proper choice, will consequently in its course break some rules while reestablishing others. None of this says that we have a good plan. The rules are artifacts. But if we have misread our situation we shall be in practical trouble, and that is what counts.

—These moments of choice could be meaningless and irrational, yet they turn out not to be. We are always up to something, even when we are lost.

—Plans go awry, as do our lives. We get ourselves back together, redefine what we thought we were up to, and continue to make a life for ourselves. Of course, if we have just one set of criteria for a good life, or just one path toward achieving it, we are likely to fail. But we have many paths.

—Advisors listen to and dwell with what there is, seeing it anew, letting its qualities prevail. And so the possibilities of a situation are valued.

6. If we think of plans as modes of search and resolution, then they do work out all right most of the time. We make the best we can of the world. But there is no assurance that the plan is correct. Within our lives, no insurance is available. A search permits a person to fulfill the potentials of being a person, and permits a method to do what it can in negotiating the world.

—Methods never just work. When they work, they work only in part and in small areas, and then they claim universal hegemony. But in a search we claim no more than we actually do. Forging our way is more important than claiming dominance over the world. We are modest, we can be gracious, we can fail at low cost, we can be visionary without being totalitarian.

—Methods have an effective practical meaning when they are interpreted by us. They can make a claim on how we ought to go about things only insofar as we make them actual. Otherwise methods are abstract and dead. Persons invest methods with life, with their intentions, and with the difficulties they encounter in fulfilling their intentions methodically. Methods are a product of our work.

—Methods depend on our ability to use them. They permit us to be responsible persons when using them only if they are treated as dependent upon us and upon our interpretation of them.

7. A plan's claims about our lives are derived from what we resolve. Its authority lies in our being able to deny those claims, as well as affirm them. We can withdraw our support. The reasons we give for a plan are data that give us temporary courage that the search is still worth our while. And the reasons define a community of persons who find those reasons cogent.

—Reasons are rhetorical. They give us hope. By their form, what they appeal to logically, their particular content, the kind of life they describe, and the fact that the reasons do give us hope, they tell us about the kinds of persons we are.

8. A project or a search might be grounded by God or the State, and their Truth, if we could accept such absolutes. If not, there are our selves and sincerity, being true to ourselves, as a ground. Or if there is a community, we may be grounded in authenticity to a role and our condition.

—We like to have a point around which what we do is anchored, a source of meaning. The point is dimensionless and its own meaning. Of course, we have provided it with all its energy, its attractiveness, and its autonomy. But it keeps changing, and sometimes it seems to disappear.

—But what if there are none of these anchoring points? Say we treated ourselves as bare ahistorical individuals, abstract and not concretely enmeshed in the complex of life and in all of its connected relationships in the world. If we attribute rational values to such an individual, we generate modern political economy and rational planning. But where does the plan come from? What is the source of the project? There is no life to draw from. The plan's stories and pictures have no source, and so they are unpredictable and frightening for us. These artificial anchors are then treated as rational men whose plans are brought in by sleight of hand, men who have few rich human qualities, who are incapable of making genuine commitments or of having persistent projects.

—Plans so conceived are abstract: interesting, helpful, practical, but disturbingly wrong. The plan, and our project itself, cannot say how it fails. It has no theory of virtue or character, of sin or ignominy. All it can say is that its premises were wrong, or the calculus was defective, or the data were inadequate. All it can say is, "Men are not . . . ."

—We know we do depend on the anchoring point. Perhaps it is the idea of a point we need, and its particular name is important but not crucial to our well-being. We then try to construct our lives in the best way we can, never insisting that best is the same as the universal or the eternal.

9. Plans are cookbooks. Cookbooks are filled with projects or searches. But if you do not know how to be a person they cannot help you cook. The pictures, lists of ingredients, reminders, in-

structions, and general lore just won't help. They are addressed to persons who have had some experience in the world. You need to know what's up and what you are up to if the cookbook is to make sense to you.

—Cookbooks depend on our skills, on our knowing when the peaks are firm or the eggs are done. They provide methods that depend on our capacities to execute them. We must have a feeling for when essential ingredients have been left out, for when things taste about right, and for just what makes a meal and how we might get away with something else.

—A recipe is authoritative and methodical. It works and sometimes goes awry by respecting the cook and permitting the cook to find out how to make the food.

10. Plans are designs that are meaningful for us. They need be no more methodical than we require to figure out what to do.

—Plans depend on our ability, individually and as a community, to enact them.

11. We try to obtain assurance that plans will work by making them practical, rational, and embedded in the real world. But what is practical, rational, and real are conventions and constructions that we maintain in our community. Although they may not be easily changeable, they are not obvious or necessary either. In time they do change.

—There are no external assurances for plans. "It works" or "It is obvious" depends on us and how we conduct our lives. Our world could be different. So what we have is necessary, but no more necessary than some other, contrary, convention.

—We hide from ourselves that we are the source of convention and rationality and clarity. So we are bewitched by the process of making things clear. Plans, if they are thought to provide assurances, must fail.

—Actually, however, plans are searches. They give finiteness and grace to the world, and a chance to act responsibly within our world.

—It is not our epistemological eyes that ought concern us, but our ontological ears, which listen, hear, pay attention, and let the world prevail.

—So we make plans, not just to choose, but to find out what to do and to account for it.

## ✐§ Notes

### Acknowledgments

Personality may account for the kinds of projects one pursues, but the times, institutions, and seminal figures make it possible for personality to be concretely actual. My undergraduate education at Columbia was based in general education; my graduate education and training there was in a more disciplinary mold. Since then I have worked at research centers and professional schools, rather than in disciplinary departments. The academic residential research centers, including the Battelle Seattle Research Center, where Ronald Paul and Robert Fuller gave me my initial chance to work in this area, have been generous in letting me decide what was most important. They provide a congenial and homey environment, outside the university hierarchies, where the Fellows can support and help each other. The best professional schools of planning, architecture, and public affairs are quite heterodox, and there again, there is some freedom to work on what one thinks are the right problems. To boot, colleagues bring the world back to the study, and so even theoretically inclined thinkers are much better grounded than they otherwise might be. At the School of Public Affairs of the University of Minnesota (now the Hubert H. Humphrey Institute) I taught a diverse set of courses crucial to writing the second half of this book—reading Kant, Hegel, and Heidegger, for example—yet my enthusiastic colleagues only supported my efforts. (See Krieger, 1979.) My experience at Berkeley was similar. The large bureaucratic university offers some room in its interstices and margins for unacknowledged but known experiments.

Disciplines and professions support their members' inquiries as long as they follow the main line. But if inquiries are a mixture of lines then it is vital to know persons who are touchstones, who represent the possibility of living a life of inquiry, who provide a personal rather than a technical blessing. Chien-Shiung Wu, Abraham Maslow, Richard Meier, Hanna Pitkin, Albert Hofstadter, Chie Nakane, Robert Merton, John Hope Franklin, Stanley Cavell, Solomon Asch, and Caryl and Edna Haskins have done that for me, sometimes in only one meeting, and some over many years. These are not so much acknowledgments as further conditions for the possibility of doing a kind of work. Love, especially that of children, has also been a graceful blessing, and Jennifer and Joseph Sherinsky, and Jonathan and Benjamin Sousa have provided that in abundance.

# Advice

My approach is very much influenced by Heidegger, especially in *Being and Time*, and somewhat less directly by Wittgenstein, in the *Philosophical Investigations*. I also owe a great deal to Cavell's (1961) discussion of claims.

## INTRODUCTION

Rosenthal discusses the positive gains to professional practice of active client participation in personal injury cases in the law. Heidegger is helpful in thinking about the problem of adding-on personhood. C. S. Peirce's notion of conduct (see Bernstein) is also useful. See also Friedmann, *Retracking*, 1973, and Michael, and Krieger, 1974.

### Thinking about Advice

In the 1960s there was an East Coast and a West Coast. In the East they talked of a post-industrial, knowledge-oriented society, and in the West there was a growing human-potential movement concentrating on feelings and wholeness. I thought it was consistent that knowledge would encourage self-knowledge, that technocrats and scientists and scholars would be purchasing person-changing technologies and hot tubs. The War and the eventual decline of poverty programs contributed to a feeling of skepticism that rational knowledge could solve public problems. How could the Coasts meet? Perhaps part of the difficulty lay in the fact that we had forgotten that it is persons who work on problems in a community, and that knowledge is never disembodied or abstract.

I was impressed with how often good responsible guesses, risking at least the reputation of the persons who make them, are needed in the public and professional arenas. Experience (that is, having tried before) plays a central role that is difficult to analyze. It is hard to say what the experienced person knows. In practice this leads to overcompensation by professionals, to claims of competence beyond their capabilities, and to all-knowing attitudes toward clients. Physicians, for example, can be helpful in cases of disease, but are less informed about health. And their patients can decide that a therapy has not worked, is cruel, or is too risky.

I wanted to write a study that showed how self-based knowledge plays a central role in public affairs, even if it is not complete, well-tested, scientific, or the like. At various times I called it "synthetic knowledge" and "expert knowledge." However, my attempts to understand the role of some sort of personal knowledge were unsatisfactory until I realized that one did not just add on being a person to the usual pictures. Being a person was constitutive and fundamental to the logic of the enterprise of advice-giving. The difficulties I was facing in my argument were symptomatic of its lack of persons. Realizing this lack, I could not only describe a more coherent picture, but also indicate why the standard ones went awry.

"Advice" is not a study of how to give advice, or an exhortation that we must worry about people, or an explanation of what makes advice (and stories) good or bad, or an attempt to encourage that we give more advice and live a good life—although it indicates ways of thinking about some of these questions. It does not describe what makes a good person or even really describe advice. It does sketch the conditions for and relationships involved in advice-giving, in being knowledgeable in the world in a community of persons. It is an attempt to show why a set of human activities are the way they are in terms of what they are.

Nor is my purpose here to advocate or attack professionalism, planning, or expertise. They are necessary aspects of advice. This does not mean that their current institutional forms are good or coherent or necessary, nor that the way that we usually tend to think about them is effective in figuring out how to do better.

"Advice" is not a sociology or psychology of expertise. Also, I have spent comparatively little time on deception, lies, and the like in advice-giving. These problems have received the bulk of attention in the literature. I wanted to concentrate on the conditions that make advice possible at all.

*The Conceptual and Argumentational Structure*

I have tried to make the argument architectonic, transcendental, dialectical, and therapeutic.

The argument is conceptually organized by an architectonic, the details of which I will come to shortly. It is derived from an attempt to reconcile observations about the characteristics of advice, the social roles that embody it, and the ways in which it fails as an ideal.

There is a remarkable feeling, most beautifully illustrated in Kant, when one has such an explicit architectonic structure—that it is just right, necessary, a discovery of a fact about nature, about the nature of what one is studying. The architectonic, at first a crutch that you create to organize your next draft, becomes the whole world. It is a confusion of realization with reality. However, your good sense about what is important, which existed previous to the discovery of the architectonic, saves you, so you know what must be included even if it does not fit.

Kant, in *The Critique of Practical Reason*, says that the similarity in the structure of the architectonic of the *Critiques* is "an accord that occasions surprise and astonishment" (p. 106) and that confirms the correctness of the architectonic. See Beck, pp. 16–17, for some evidence for how un-surprising the accord should be. Proust (quoted in Weightman) said, "Writing is easy for me. But to patch things together, to set all the bones, that's more than I can face. For some time I have realised that I leave out the best pieces, because I would have to fit this detail to that one, and so on . . . ." An architectonic works because we leave out lots of material, and it encourages us to flesh out other parts.

It may be helpful to think of the argument as transcendental: to show the conditions necessary for advice to be possible among persons. We want a conceptual structure that permits us to talk about the phenomena in advice-giving. The words I use represent both ideal and technical concepts and ordinary usages.

The argument itself is dialectical and therapeutic. I set forth some particular aspects of advice and then elaborate on them. The form of elaboration is not arbitrary. The major dialectical and conceptual tension is between a picture of advice that incorporates persons and one that leaves them out. Some important requirements for advice-giving are lost when we leave out persons, and we find that this characterizes the ordinary ("alienated") situation we find ourselves in, and it accounts for the existence of the dilemmas in that situation. Advice is an ideal concept whose breakdown, in the sense of an articulation and a failure, reveals the phenomena. Therapeutically, the work we do on the dilemmas is a product of our forgetting certain aspects of advice. The patch-up jobs we invent to do that work are often quite limited and ultimately wrong.

The themes of breakdown and lostness are not accidental. They are a product of a fetishism (not unlike Marx's commodity fetishism). Advice, the actual relationship, is inverted, and the formal and fetishized advice, stripped of the complex of social relations characteristic of persons, is treated as necessary and more real. No single argument or disproof will reveal the fetishistic illusion, for it is highly articulated, subtle, and well-defended; only a series of forays, each of which indicates weaknesses in the fetish, and that it is a fetish, could possibly work. One may at no cost concede the partial truth of the fetishized or un-personal view of advice. The problem is not its partialness, per se, but its limitations and its claims to being necessary. (These observations were suggested to me in reading some of the unpublished work of Terence Turner.)

Another way of appreciating the strategic problem in this kind of argument is to compare it to the situation of a man who finds himself at the top of a mountain (at least he believes he is there) watching others climbing up a well-trodden, well-developed path that has yet to yield a way to the summit. The others feel that only limits of skill and endurance stand in their way, and in time they will make it. The man, looking at them from above (at least to his mind), can see a large crevasse that they will not be able to scale. But how is he to make them see that ahead of time? There are no easily available aerial photographs. If he tries to offer one, it will never be as detailed as ground-based photos. They can counter-argue that he may believe he is on their peak, but actually he is on another. The best the man can do is to offer a fairly detailed aerial view that indicates why the others might be wrong, and an examination of their local maps indicating internal contradictions and discontinuities in them.

The argument is a series of voyages from the ideal to its breakdown. There should be lots of scenery, yet it will be obvious that there are few conventional examples, cases, or stories. We are kept in the railway carriage and told about the structure of the scenery. Our examples are arguments that describe how we use our knowledge, such as in advice. My argument is about these arguments.

As for examples in transcendental arguments, Kant defends his lack of them, although he has some marvelous ones. See, especially, *The Critique of Pure Reason* (pp. Axviii–xix, A134, B372), where they are said to be ". . . necessary only from a popular point of view; . . . often interfere with our grasp of the whole; . . . sharpening of the judgment . . . [but] correctness and precision of intellectual insight, on the other hand, they more usually somewhat impair. . . . Examples [are] proofs that what the concept of reason commands is in a certain degree practicable."

*The Architectonic Structure*
Authors outline their arguments and chart the relationships of its constituent parts (whether dynasties or concepts) to aid their writing of a text. Tables of contents demonstrate sequential and topical order, but often not the conceptual relationships.

The chart gives the structure of the sections "Advice," "Roles and Advisors," and "The Conditions for Advice." The sections "Problems," "Stories," and "Understanding" and "Agreement" parallel concerns about professionals, planners, and experts respectively. These sections depend on the tension between advice with and without persons.

I do not claim that all my categorizations fit equally well, that certain other rearrangements might not be just as good, that the three-foldness I use is special or important (rather than convenient and adequate), or that I have rigidly followed my own system. I did use this architectonic structure to organize the discussion and the placement of various elaborations, and the naturalness of what goes where depends on it.

One also might make a list of defining sentences for the various interrelated concepts:

Persons understand their World by telling Stories.

Persons in a Community act in Public in Advice as Persons.

Persons affect Persons.

Persons claim Problems, which are claims on Situations and claims on Persons, by telling Stories in Advice to Persons.

Persons take Roles defined in Stories.

Persons tell Stories in Advice to Persons; the Stories are ways of understanding a Situation.

Persons in a Situation ordinarily give and receive Advice about the Extra-Ordinary and perhaps Monstrous recognized by Persons.

## ADVICE

[1] The description of persons in a community comes from Sellars, pp. 39–40 in particular. See also Aune, Strawson, Polanyi, Macmurray, 1957, 1961, and Simon, 1969. Rorty and Noonan emphasize the importance of wholeness and the interrelationship of the properties of persons. One way of capturing this is to speak of subject and object as being "moments" of the same person, depending on the situational aspect that the person is viewed from. Another way is to speak in terms of "treating persons as persons" in a community, which is distinguished from a Kantian universality. See Edel. Silverstein points out that the ability to know which hypothetical cases are relevant and "like me," and which others we can ignore, which shifts in role in which circumstances are appropriate, depends on "treating persons as persons." One must have a concept of a well-conducted person (for example, from C. S. Peirce or Santayana) to make a community. Note, as well, that person is derived from *persona*, for role or mask in a drama. See Buckley.

Whether plants, specifically trees, should be treated as persons has become a lively issue. I believe they should not, but see Stone for a

The Architectonic Structure for "Advice"

| Constitutive quality of advice | Based on | which Presupposes | Based on our | Reflecting the |
|---|---|---|---|---|
| Relationship of persons | Trust and personhood in a community, | Primariness of our experiences together, | Selves, | Psychological. |
| Basis in the world | Reasonableness and rationality, | Reliability of ordinary life, | Knowledge, | Scientific. |
| Understanding | Publicness, | What we do is sensible, | Affect, | Political. |
| The quality breaks down and results in the role of | Elaborated on in the discussion of | The quality is related to the feeling basis for advice, its conditions | Which permits us to | Which makes advice |
| Professional | Problems. | Empathy (drama) | Claim | Possible. |
| Planner | Stories. | Education and development in society | Grow and change | Viable. |
| Expert | Understanding and agreement. | Eros and mutuality | Care | Necessary. |

defense. Marx, e.g. p. 111, was most eloquent and trenchant in his discussion of the rights of trees versus those of persons. He is suspicious of the fetishistic character of such rights.

Monstrous is used to convey both out-of-the-ordinary and what a person would not do. A monster is also a sign, an omen. See Plato, *Theaetetus*, 163d6, 163e13, 203d6, where τερας (as in teratology, for sign, out of the ordinary) and δεινον (dinosaur, for fearful) are used. Δεινον is derived from α' δυνατον for "not possible." Also Vico, § 410, speaks of monsters (*mostri*) in terms of formalism gone awry. Lakatos, 1963, notes that "monster-barring rules" are needed in scientific investigations. See Stern, p. 75.

See Pitkin, 1972, for a discussion of the political and the moral. The political signifies the self-conscious we, the problem of knowing who we are, and how that is based in conflict and interest. The public character of our lives permits this knowledge and gives us our potential for affecting each other's claims. Arendt, 1958, section 7, offers a powerful definition of public, and discusses the importance of stories for the public life.

[2] Advice is both an activity and a concept. The definition of advice comes from Barnhart and Gove. The mediating character of advice is elucidated by Seeley, 1970. The bibliography of Kaufman and Friedmann was helpful.

Merton, 1949, p. 163, points out that "although all applied social science research involves advice (recommendations for policy), not all advice on social policy is based on research." Advice may be based on empiricism, standardized therapies, and specific researches. Our problem is to understand how these diverse sources can be sensible bases for advice.

I use *ordinary* to capture the expectable, regular, predictable although not necessarily predicted, character of life, which includes to some extent its disruptions and its possibility for being extraordinary. Lostness is defined by the ordinary situation and your knowledge of it, and how you act when you do not know what to do. You are in a situation defined by your self (cf. Heidegger, p. 346, "The Situation is the 'there' which is disclosed in resoluteness . . .") and you react *to* it as if it is separated off from you.

[2.1] Schurmann's discussion of the red versus expert issue in the People's Republic of China (pp. 507, 517) is suggestive of the problem encountered when persons become separated from advice. The "red" or party cadre is concerned about human goals and organization, while the "expert" is an educated Western-technology professional.

I follow the discussion of truth in Arendt (1968). Truth is constitutive of human life, and it depends on our capacity to live a decent, moral, well-conducted life. The "few sufficiently rich" ways reflect these constraints on what could be true and how we could go on together. Persons can usually figure out each other, so Quine's radical translation problems may be an artifact of his logical formalizations. Outside of formalization people can violate the rules in order to investigate peculiar cases, and so get around.

Friedmann's *Retracking America*, pp. 177–183, and "Public Interest," p. 7, suggest that dialogue provides for the otherness of each person, the authenticity of acts, the acceptance of conflict, total communication, shared interest, reciprocity, and a real time relationship. See Schaar, 1973, on patriotism as opposed to nationalism, and Stern, p. 80, on dialogue as opposed to coercion.

Lewis uses coordination games as a foundation to study why conventions might be stable. He shows how reasonable mutual expectations converge to what we would call a convention. An opposite view of human life is offered in Goffman's work, where the tenuousness of life's sense-fulness becomes definitive of life. On countertransference, see Halmos.

[2.2, 2.3] See Heidegger, p. 385, Wittgenstein, § 155, and Stern, pp. 79 ff., on experience and understanding. I am not so much concerned about a Kantian distinction of thought and knowledge, nor, so much, in the conflict that Hobbes exemplifies (see Wolin, 1970) between theory and a counselor's knowledge from experience.

[3.1] Halmos, pp. 156–164, analyzes the ideology of the counseling professions to show how contradictions and the overt denial of counter-transference become productive of caring practice.

## ROLES AND ADVISORS

[4] The discussion of authority follows Schaar, 1970, pp. 312–315.

The argument about claims is fundamental to epistemology. I follow Cavell, 1961, pp. 294–303, and 1969, pp. 311–313, especially in using "certainty" and "exhaustive," as well as Zaner, pp. 36 ff., and Polyani, pp. 300 ff. What we consider evidence for a claim will depend on whether evidence need be self-evident. For Cavell, a claim is rational when it has a context in which it could make sense, where a complex of meanings or related claims can also be made. Outside of such a context, outside of advice, claims cannot be made. (See Clarke for more on this problem of context.) More strongly, claims occur in a community, and the process of claiming involves other persons for whom we care (in the most general sense). Claims also focus attention on what is important and thereby set up a context, as Zaner argues. Claims may be on individual or corporate persons, or on persons who are part of the corporate body.

For Cavell doubt is a claim on others. (For Popper doubt is formal and logical.) Skepticism is an existential activity. Doubt is a mode of authenticity, and claiming and counterclaiming are ways of being authentic.

In *Personal Knowledge* (pp. 63-65, 300 ff., and 327-328), Polanyi has many parallels with Heidegger and with what I do here. But his model is the questing individual scientist, intellectually committed to his claims. Polanyi's conceptual problem is to generate a community. Advice, on the other hand, is performed not individually but with others, commitments in advice are professional rather than intellectual, and it is shared rather than tacit. For Polanyi, problems are something that we are committed to rather than a means by which we go on in life. His discussion of "accredited facts" (p. 304) is much like my discussion of claims.

[5-7] On professions and experts, I have drawn upon Moore, Wilensky, 1964, Archibald, Benveniste, Znaniecki, Benveniste and Ilchman, Kelly, Cairncross, and Gorham. The review by Martin is helpful. See also Kissinger and Merton, 1968. Gerver and Bensman speak of claims with respect to experts. On planners, see Friedmann, 1966, Kaplan, 1958, Webber, 1965, 1968, Deutsch, Meyerson and Banfield, and Miller, Galanter, and Pribram.

[6] Seeley's analysis of planning, 1962, 1970, is a synthesis of a cybernetic and a psychoanalytic model of planning: planning interposes impulse and action, it is a representation of the ego. Systems models (cybernetic or ecological, for example) are barren of predictive power without some dynamic theory about interactions. Linearity is usually assumed, but it would be nice to know if such assumptions made sense in terms of how people do learn. See, for example, Michael.

I am using a different cut than the usual comprehensive versus incremental one for planning. Cf. Clarke, p. 756, on contexts, where the philosophic is described as that place where we are least dependent on context. See Deutsch and Michael on cybernetic models. Michael's thesis is that certain psychological features of persons are needed to make long-range planning work.

Webber, 1965, p. 296, argues that scientific activity provides a model for planning. "His [the planner's] special character mirrors the special character of science. To a degree far less common in other interest groups, he has learned to doubt; to question his beliefs, his data, and his findings; to submit his conclusions to critical evaluation by his peers; to tolerate uncertainty and ambiguity; to bear the frustrations of not knowing, and of knowing he does not know; and, by far the most important, to adopt the empirical test for validity." He goes on to argue that planners, in their systematic accounting for the effects of actions, "may help to eliminate the most negative consequences of partisanship and of ignorance." See also Braybrooke and Lindblom's model of "disjointed incrementalism."

[7] The literature on expert advisors is venerable. Experts have functioned as tutors and educators and expert knowledge has included knowledge of the right goals. The argument (cf. Wolin on Hobbes) is often between experts on technical versus contextual and theoretical questions. Much of the more recent literature centers on burcaucratic expertise and leadership. See Goldhamer.

Pitkin, 1967, ch. 10, argues for a view of representation in terms of substantive acting for others. She points out (p. 212) that we have representation when there are no experts, seemingly in direct opposition to my argument. But her use of expert is closer to specialist in an area of knowledge. See also ch. 1, p. 25, on Hobbes, who saw an intimate connection between persona, persons, and representatives.

When massive ideological changes occur in a short period of time, experts may be redesignated. See Schurmann on China's shift from "red" experts to "expert" experts.

[8] A similar set of contradictions concerning obligation is to be found in Walzer, who, in order to resolve them, argues that "responsibility is to someone else and it is always learned with someone else" (p. 22). See Freidson and Benveniste on professionalism and expertise, and Merton and Kissinger on insiders and outsiders. Pirsig describes how technicians need not act robot-like. See Rosenthal on when clients are not objectified.

The quote from Plato is from the *Seventh Letter*, pp. 1579–1580; from Machiavelli, the *Discourses*, bk. 3, ch. 35, as quoted in Gorham. See also Hobbes's "On Counsel" (in bk. II, ch. 25, of *The Leviathan*), where counselors are sources of experience and are conceived in terms of memory and recall.

PROBLEMS

[9] "Social economic problems do not exist everywhere that an economic event plays a role as cause or effect—since problems arise only where the significance of those factors is problematical and can be precisely determined only through the application of methods of social economics." (Weber, p. 66.)

Problem solving as a technicized form of life is described by Rieff,

1972, p. 58, as anti-creedal. The possibility of transgressive and inter-dictory behavior disappears when all we do is just solve problems. The denial of this possibility becomes the denial of culture. See also Wolin and Schaar, pp. 87–88.

[10] I use Rittel and Webber for much of this paraphrase. Their reso-lution of the dilemmas (see Rittel, 1972, or Churchman, 1971) is in terms of a formal theory of argumentation or dialectic. See also Fried-mann, *Retracking*, 1973, on transactive models.

See Ackoff and Sasien for an example of the operations research model. The quotation is from Newell, pp. 367–369. More recent work in artificial intelligence is concerned with semantic and contextual factors.

Simon, 1973, argues that problems are always ill-structured, until we have well-structured them. He sees noticing/evoking and decom-position as the vital problem-solving strategies. See Dreyfus, 1972, for a description of problems not unlike the one discussed here under ad-vice. I follow his use of certain ideas from phenomenology, whose va-lidity is independent of his critique of artificial intelligence research. Another useful model is provided by Schutz's well-informed citizen.

PERSONS TELLING STORIES

[11] I use the notion of a story to emphasize certain characteristics of claims: their narrative and strategic quality, that they are educative, that they require a sense of what ordinary and reasonable persons would do. Stories can be true and extend our vision of reality. They are also texts and reports. Stories have audiences and readers. Conven-tional scientific explanations are stories in these senses.

Plato in the *Laws* and the *Phaedrus* distinguished stories (as myths) from knowledge, and storytelling from the dialectic. Here I am trying to capture the knowledge-based and dialectic character of stories as claims. It may also be the case that, as Hofstadter, 1974, p. 12, says, "Truth now, as for Fichte and Schelling, must be expressed in the form of a story or history. . . . Hegel was therefore compelled to think his systematic philosophy in the form of an epical myth or heroic novel."

Arendt, 1958, Churchman, 1971, Danto, Hexter, chs. 5 and 6, Ryle, p. 6, Vickers, Ward, Watkins, and Winquist, among others, talk specif-ically of stories; M. Black uses the concept of metaphor.

Stories have didactic and civic functions that are as useful in eval-uating them as are their formal and rhetorical properties. These are rather intimately related. The formal analyses are meaningless by themselves, and theories of stories in terms of filtration of information and knowledge utilization are likely to be just as barren.

Gombrich, p. 89, characterizes connoisseurship in a manner consonant with how we might evaluate stories: "for concepts, like pictures, cannot be true or false. They can only be more or less useful for the formation of descriptions. The words of a language, like pictorial formulas, pick out from the flux of events a few signposts which allow us to give direction to our fellow speakers in that game of 'Twenty Questions' in which we are engaged." Note that we are allowed to have, and usually must have, a strategic pattern in our questioning, as well as hypothetical right answers in mind, if we are likely to get any place in Twenty Questions.

Although I talk about professions, it is the professional's planning role of telling stories that concerns me in this section. There is a comparatively rich literature on the professions, on how exclusive and exclusionary their stories are, and on how they become isolated. See Wilensky, 1964, 1967, and for a review, Moore. Marshall, p. 152, indicates how the shift from leisure to labor and freedom to service has made the contemporary professions so very different from those of the past. Dr. Lydgate, in George Eliot's *Middlemarch*, which is set circa 1830, just begins to confront the scientific basis for medicine.

The statement about professions, ideologies, and technologies is as much derived from an essay by Warren as from the insights of Mannheim. See also Rose, especially pp. 18–26, for a similar argument. See also Freidson, ch. 15, also p. 330, and Reiff, 1971, p. 39. Freidson, p. 39, put it well: "expertise is not mere knowledge. It is the practice of knowledge, organized socially and serving as the focus for the practitioner's commitment. The worker develops around his work an ideology and, with the best of intentions, an 'imperialism' that stresses the technical superiority of his work and his capacity to perform it."

Foucault's épistèmes are related to modes of explanation that establish significance and relevance. An interesting theory of the evolution of style and fashion is to be found in Kubler. See also Simon, 1970. The argument about power and professions reflects one between K. Mannheim and G. Lukacs. A summary is provided in Lichtheim, 1970, pp. 34–43. The quote on blindness is from Scott, pp. 269, 274.

How do we arrive at common complaints? From a political perspective, we may look for an answer in terms of power and legitimacy, or how interest groups and issues become effective. From a sociological viewpoint, we ask how social movements develop and arise from social life and make their way into the political arena. Dahrendorf has explored this question (in his terms, from "quasi-groups" to "conflict groups"), and presents his answer in terms of the degrees of a group's self-awareness of "objective" conditions. Ideologies can perform this function. Smelser has given an alternative description in terms of external factors and how they affect a movement's history.

[12] As noted earlier, C. S. Peirce emphasized the importance of conduct, civic sense, and human personhood in a community, if science is to be a regulated activity. Merton's, 1973, characterization of science in terms of universalism, communalism, disinterestedness, and organized skepticism is helpful. It captures the qualities of a community needed for science—but also indicates why persons, in the largest sense, need not be present in science ordinarily. Science is a public (knowledge) activity, as Ziman describes. This is not inconsistent with Polanyi's description of its personal qualities.

On the rise of science, see Sellars on the manifest and original images of the world. Elkana speaks of "images of science" that determine what is considered scientific at a particular time; these images are directly related to the goings on of persons in a community. See also Lakatos (in Lakatos and Musgrave) on "scientific research programmes," which have affinities to science as telling (special) stories.

## UNDERSTANDING WITH OTHERS

[13] I use *dramatic* to epitomize the interactive quality of advice. Advice seems to require the technical characteristics of drama (for example, act, agency, agent, scene, and purpose, to follow Burke, 1968), and sometimes we even dissimulate in advice. See Pitkin, 1972, pp. 149 ff., for my use of the concept of the moral here.

Gouldner, pp. 268–272, on understanding, views dialectic and face-to-face communication as primary. The definitions of understanding and knowledge come from Barnhart.

[14] Kant's nomothetic formalism can make sense only if persons embody the golden rule. If we are willing to have a sufficiently rich concept of person, as Kant was, then our laws can be simple, general, and universal, both relevant to and fulfilling the nomothetic ideal.

The definition of intuition comes from Westcott, p. 40. See also Kaplan, 1958, 1964. Cases function here in a manner similar to the way they function in the law. Cairncross expounds on the importance of such expert advisors. Miller, 1971, points out that the boundaries of competence may be appreciated in wisdom, but the wise may not have the necessary expert knowledge. See also Palmer on Gadamer, where wisdom is defined as a "non-objectified accumulation of understanding," p. 195. Freidson, pp. 347–348, indicates the limits of wisdom, in terms of its dogmatic character, and the particular class origins and biases of a wise man. See Blum and Polanyi on the intuitive character of theories and tacit knowledge. An orderly world need not imply a formal one. Schutz, for example, has used the fact that we do have a common set of conceptualizations of the world as the basis for his non-formal philosophy of social science.

[15] See Chomsky, Harman, and Steinberg and Jakobovits. Likeness tests are discussed by Clowes. See Pitkin, 1972, pp. 199–200. Neisser provides an elegant description of learning in terms of articulating schemas.

Papert defines the superhuman human fallacy of demanding that a machine that purports to simulate human behavior begin as a *tabula rasa* or be capable of feats we do not expect of human beings. The theoretical critique of artificial intelligence in the second half of Dreyfus, 1972, is the source for some of this discussion.

On applying science, see Zetterberg, as well as Merton, 1949, and Rosenthal.

COMING TO AGREEMENT

[16] Kissinger, among others, warns of the dangers of many opinions coming to agreement.

The organizational consequences of conflict, and how beliefs are distributed in an organization, will depend on the structure of the organization and the kinds of tasks it performs. Well-defined tasks tend to be performed in much more rigid hierarchical structures than those that are looser and more cross-cutting. For example, innovative scientific research is highly dependent on individual initiative, and a less hierarchical structure seems best for it. See LaPorte, 1971. Many other activities, such as assembling automobiles, may also be best done in less structured groups. Structure is also determined by how well defined and known is the technical knowledge needed to perform a task. If it is less sure, as it often is in advice, personal commitment may be important, and structures will reflect that. The models I discuss here seem less applicable to Japanese society (see Nakane) than to a Western society. In Japan, hierarchy is balanced by mutuality, resulting in somewhat different flows of information and authority.

[17] Schelling, pp. 5 ff., has an extensive discussion of bargaining, and is the source of the quote. Persons who can make commitments are required if there is to be bargaining; bets and bettors are insufficient. The Appendix to Castaneda describes story creation.

[18] Helmer and Rescher describe Delphi methods. Various other kinds of town meeting formats that use sophisticated telecommunications methods seem to be developing. Raiffa covers what I discuss on decision analysis.

Another way of pooling opinions is a perceptron, a weighted sum of the opinions of a set of experts. No interaction is permitted between them. At any time the weighting factors given to each expert are fixed, although we can create a scheme whereby the perceptron could change its weighting factors depending on past experience. If we assume that the persons have fairly well-defined ways of operating and are not particularly complex, then the capability of a perceptron is remarkably limited. The ability of a perceptron to successfully analyze collective claims about new situations, except in some very special cases, will involve the perceptron's having an expert for each situation. The information characterizing these special case judges, and their weighting coefficients, may be greater than the information needed to describe the situation. If we are to combine our judges in a particularly simple way, and if we assume that the judges are not particularly complex, then our ability to combine judgments remains meager.

The perceptron's limits are proved by Minsky and Papert. Goffman, 1967, describes the real "action." Actually, Goffman's conception of action is very personal; my usage in the text is quite narrow.

[19] Buckley distinguishes economic (un-personal) and dramaturgic models. I use *dramatic* rather than *dramaturgic* in the text. See Simon, 1969, for more on design.

[20] Technologies cannot control monstrosity, but, Goode argues, they can offer protection from the inept. Janis explores the variety of pathologies of "group think." Prophylactics will work, but if an evolutionary and Darwinian process operates, resistant strains may arise.

It is tempting to try to be fairly systematic in characterizing the value of stories for understanding situations. In trying to set up artificial belief systems within a machine, Colby and Smith developed ways to measure the credibility of a proposition. They are based on the proposition's foundation in other statements that are believed (in the sense that it could be deduced from them), and its consistency with other believed statements (in the sense that they could be deduced from it). But if the story is not formally expressed this can only be a suggestion for what to look for, and the resulting theories of criticism would be much less regimented than the formal logical ones. There are some recent developments in "non-monotonic" logics that allow for a greater variety of modes of deduction, more in accord with what we do in actual life.

Wilensky, 1967, describes some of the modes of truth finding. Heuristics described by Newell are: generate and test, matching, hill-climbing, and heuristic search. Lakatos and Musgrave reviews the arguments about truth finding in science, in which Popper is "opposed" to Kuhn and Feyerabend. Lakatos's "scientific research programmes" are quite congenial to storytelling and advice. Merton, 1973, shows how the various social norms of science function to make science possible.

Objectivity has a history, but it also has a palpable absolute reality for us. I am exploring a mystification, a real illusion.

THE CONDITIONS FOR ADVICE

[22] Wispe, p. 441, defines empathy as "the self-conscious effort to share and accurately comprehend the presumed consciousness of another person, including his thoughts, feelings, perceptions, and muscular tensions, as well as their causes." Shevrin argues that empathy is a form of experience, not knowledge.

We can and must empathize because we are persons and not the other way around. See Heidegger, pp. 161–162, where he makes roughly this point in an argument against Scheler's notion of empathy.

Sympathy is the basis for utilitarianism, but it is also needed for understanding others under a Kantian golden rule.

[23] Quine has tried to use purely behavioristic notions to describe how our claims on another could make sense, without a concept of person or empathy. But if we are to be capable of appreciating which are the natural kinds of objects, we have to be persons, I believe. Quine argues explicitly against this point. His "persons," because they are formally regimented, cannot ask the breadth of questions, including self-referential ones, that we ordinarily do to clarify things. The indeterminacy he argues for seems artifactual of that limitation.

On sexual intercourse, see Nagel and Solomon. As for love and sexuality, O'Hara, p. xiii, is perhaps to the point: "As for measure and other technical apparatus [in writing poetry], that's just common sense: if you're going to buy a pair of pants you want them to be tight enough so everyone will want to go to bed with you. There's nothing metaphysical about it. Unless, of course, you flatter yourself into thinking that what you're experiencing is 'yearning.'"

See Meehl, 1954, 1977, on empathy, predictors, and intelligence in clinical judgment.

[24] I follow Lifton's distinction between thought reform and psychotherapy.

Maslow, 1969, describes the fear that inhibits a more personal science. The description of planners is from Meyerson and Dyckman, using Parsons's definition of a profession; see also Freidson.

[25] Our ship of life does not sink because most of life is ordinary and our expectations are reliable, not because of formalism. See Quine on Neurath.

## Criticism, Conversion, and Confession

On BART see Webber and Zwerling. My discussion of evaluation comes from the literature on criticism, but its major theoretical thrust is derived from Kant. Eitner is useful on quality, while the discussions of Indonesian historiography in Soedjatmoko show how magic works in history. John Freccero's lectures were crucial in helping me appreciate Hegel in terms of his "Before and After" model. I have also been helped by Peter Marris's work on grief and loss as a model of social change. See also Hirschman, Hansot, and Popper. Nietzsche haunts my discussion in this and the next essay. Heidegger and Kierkegaard supply most of what I want to say about commitment and confession. Taylor is useful on decisionmaking, and Freud fills in the psychology of anxiety. The anthropological work of V. Turner (and his discussion of Czikszentmihalyi in Moore and Myerhoff), and conversations with T. Turner, showed me how I might see these philosophical descriptions more concretely. Stace shows how mystical experience has a structure similar to conversion and confession.

An initial version of this essay was given as a lecture at MIT in 1977.

## Planning in Time

Hegel, Kant, Nietzsche, Heidegger, and Kierkegaard are my main sources. Strong's study of Nietzsche very much influences my description of genealogy. See Klerman on the soul.

## What We Are Up To

See Arendt, 1958, 1968, 1978, Bataille, Bickel, Burke, 1969, Frye, Gadamer, Habermas, 1970, Hegel, 1967, 1974, Heidegger, Kant, 1952, Neisser, Quine, Sacks (especially), Sarles, Sellars, Trilling, V. Turner, Unger.

## What Planners Do

[1] "During the period of delay [in planning] there occurs a complex process of 'consideration'—which, significantly, etymologically means taking count of the stars as they supply to impulse its astrological context. They do this supposedly by way of interpreting origin and loosely indicating outcome. This is the period in which to consult the astrologer, internal or external, before impulse issues irredeemably in action.

"The figure of the astrologer ought to be carried forward into the modern meaning and practice (neglecting, for the moment, the modern return to the ancient uses literally), with proper respect for the proper practice. The object could hardly be more rational and religious simultaneously, while the means, in all humility, were clearly involved with all high human uncertainty and risk. The object at once religious and rational, was to subordinate impulse through judgment (and even consultation with others' judgment) *to a simultaneous assessment of the state of the whole universe* (as declared by the stars in their complex relationships), *and, simultaneously, one's own special role in that universe*, not as capriciously or willfully chosen, but as itself declared by the consideration, the chorus of the stars speaking or singing together, at the moment of one's birth. Uncertainty and risk was known to enter by way of misreading, misinterpreting, failure in faithfulness, ambiguity, wish-thinking, fraud—all the liabilities to which imperfect man is heir and of which he is cultivator." (Seeley, 1970, pp. 3–4.)

[2] "One who advises a sick man, living in a way to injure his health, must first effect a reform in his way of living, must he not? And if the patient consents to such a reform, then he may admonish him on other points? If, however, the patient refuses, in my opinion it would be the act of a real man and a good physician to keep clear of advising such a man—the act of a poltroon and a quack on the other hand to advise him further on those terms." (Plato, 1961, p. 1579.)

[3] Reviewing our earlier discussion: There is an obvious and total, ordinary, everyday world. It is the way things are, "practical," "literal," "immethodical," "accessible," and "available." (Geertz.) Yet vulnerable. For we may lose our connection with it, losing who we are. Our talk-about has no more about. In anxiety, for that is what this is, if we stay with it, there is the possibility of calming down, of seeing it all as a unity. Such ecstasy is of course extraordinarily frightening, not as experienced, but as anticipated, since we might not emerge from it. Yet we seem to, chastened, graced, stigmatized. Being and returning to the ordinary.

Persons, who could become monsters, are here educable concrete reasonable men in a community, as Luther's regenerate reason regulates society by means of the word, without presuming on grace.

"Anxiety has an unmistakable relation to *expectation*; it is anxiety *about* [*vor*] something. It has a quality of *indefiniteness and lack of object*." (Freud, 1961, pp. 164–165.)

Mistakes are not just subject to clean replacement. They may be forgiven, but are always remembered. To err may be divine.

[5] "But when a man awakes to the possibility of a search and when such a man passes a Jew in the street for the first time, he is like Robinson Crusoe seeing the footprint on the beach. . . .

"The search is what anyone would undertake if he were not sunk in the everydayness of his own life. This morning, for example, I felt as if I had come to myself on a strange island. And what does such a castaway do? Why, he pokes around the neighborhood and he doesn't miss a trick. . . .

"As for my search, I have not the inclination to say much on the subject. For one thing, I have not the authority, as the great Danish philosopher declared, to speak of such matters in any way other than the edifying. For another thing, it is not open to me even to be edifying, since the time is later than his, much too late to edify or do much of anything except plant a foot in the right place as the opportunity presents itself—if indeed asskicking is properly distinguished from edification. . . .

"There is only one thing I can do: listen to people, see how they stick themselves into the world, hand them along a ways in their dark journey and be handed along, and for good and selfish reasons. It only remains to decide whether this vocation is best pursued in a service station or . . . .

"A repetition is the re-enactment of past experience toward the end of isolating the time segment which has lapsed in order that it, the lapsed time, can be savored of itself and without the usual adulteration of events that clog time like peanuts in brittle. . . .

"A rotation I define as the experiencing of the new beyond the expectation of the experiencing of the new. For example, taking one's first trip to Taxco would not be a rotation, or no more than a very ordinary rotation; but getting lost on the way and discovering a hidden valley would be. . . .

"The malaise is the pain of loss. The world is lost to you, the world and the people in it, and there remains only you and the world and you are no more able to be in the world than Banquo's ghost." (Percy, 1967, pp. 89, 13, 237, 233, 79–80, 144, 120.)

# Bibliography

Ackoff, R. L., and M. W. Sasien. *Fundamentals of Operations Research*. New York: Wiley, 1968. Ch. 2.

Allison, G. T. "Conceptual Models and the Cuban Missile Crisis." *American Political Science Review* 63 (September 1969): 689.

Archibald, K. "Three Views of the Expert's Role in Policymaking." *Policy Sciences* 1 (1970): 73–86.

Arendt, H. *The Human Condition*. Chicago: University of Chicago Press, 1958.

———. "Truth and Politics." In Arendt, *Between Past and Future*, pp. 227–264. New York: Viking, 1968.

———. *The Life of the Mind. Volume One: Thinking*. New York: Harcourt Brace Jovanovich, 1978.

Aune, B. *Knowledge, Mind and Nature*. New York: Random House, 1970.

Barnhart, C. L. *The American College Dictionary*. New York: Random House, 1960.

Bataille, G. *Death and Sensuality*. New York: Arno, 1977.

Bateson, G. *Steps to an Ecology of Mind*. New York: Ballantine, 1975.

Beck, L. W. *Commentary on Kant's Critique of Practical Reason*. Chicago: University of Chicago Press, 1960.

Benveniste, G. *The Politics of Expertise*. Berkeley, Cal.: Glendessary, 1972.

Benveniste, G., and W. F. Ilchman, eds. *Agents of Change: Professionals in Developing Countries*. New York: Praeger, 1969.

Berger, P. L., and T. Luckmann. *The Social Construction of Reality*. Garden City, N.Y.: Doubleday, 1966.

Bernstein, R. J. *Praxis and Action*. Philadelphia: University of Pennsylvania Press, 1971.

Bickel, A. *The Morality of Consent*. New Haven, Conn.: Yale University Press, 1975.

Black, M. *Models and Metaphors*. Ithaca, N.Y.: Cornell University Press, 1962. Chs. 3, 13.

Blum, A. F. "Theorizing." In J. D. Douglas, ed., *Understanding Everyday Life*. Chicago: Aldine, 1970.

Braybrooke, D., and C. Lindblom. *A Strategy of Decision*. Glencoe, Ill.: Free Press, 1963.

Buchler, J. *The Main of Light*. New York: Oxford University Press, 1974.

Buckley, W. *Sociology and Modern Systems Theory*. Englewood Cliffs, N.J.: Prentice-Hall, 1967.

Burke, K. "Interaction: Dramatism." In D. Sills, ed., *International Encyclopedia of the Social Sciences*, vol. 7, pp. 445–452. New York: Macmillan, 1968.

———. *A Rhetoric of Motives*. Berkeley, Cal.: University of California Press, 1969.

Cairncross, A. K. "On Being an Economic Advisor." In Cairncross, *Factors in Economic Development*. London: G. Allen and Unwin, 1962.

Castaneda, C. *The Teachings of Don Juan: A Yaqui Way of Knowledge*. New York: Ballantine, 1968.

Cavell, S. "The Claim to Rationality." Harvard University: Ph.D. diss., 1961–1962. Revised as *The Claim to Reason*. New York: Oxford University Press, 1979.

———. *Must We Mean What We Say*. New York: Scribner's, 1969.

Chomsky, N. *Language and Mind*. New York: Harcourt, Brace and World, 1968.

Churchman, C. W. "The Role of *Weltanschauung* in Problem Solving and Inquiry." In R. B. Banerji and M. D. Mesarovic, eds., *Theoretical Approaches to Non-Numerical Problem Solving*. New York: Springer-Verlag, 1970.

———. *The Design of Inquiring Systems*. New York: Basic Books, 1971.

Clarke, T. "The Legacy of Skepticism." *Journal of Philosophy* 69 (1972): 754–769.

Clowes, M. B. "On Seeing Things." *Artificial Intelligence* 2 (Spring 1971): 79.

Colby, K. M., and D. C. Smith. "Dialogues between Humans and an Artificial Belief System." In D. E. Walker and L. M. Norton, eds., *Proceedings of the International Joint Conference on Artificial Intelligence*, p. 319. Washington, D.C., May 7–9, 1969.

Dahrendorf, R. *Class and Class Conflict in Industrial Society*. Stanford, Cal.: Stanford University Press, 1959.

Danto, A. C. *Analytical Philosophy of History*. Cambridge: Cambridge University Press, 1965. Chs. 8, 10, 11.

Davidson, D. "Speaking and Thinking." Lectures at the University of Minnesota, 1975.

Deutsch, K. *The Nerves of Government*. Glencoe, Ill.: Free Press, 1963.

Dreyfus, H. L. "Why Computers Must Have Bodies in Order to Be Intelligent." *Review of Metaphysics* 21 (1967): 13.

———. *What Computers Can't Do: A Critique of Artificial Reason.* New York: Harper and Row, 1972.

Dyckman, J. W. "What Makes Planners Plan." *Journal of the American Institute of Planners* 27 (May 1961): 164–167.

Edel, A. "Review of R. S. Downie and Elizabeth Telfer: *Respect for Persons*, and R. S. Downie: *Roles and Values.*" *Journal of Philosophy* 70 (February 22, 1973): 101–106.

Eitner, L. "Art History and the Sense of Quality." *Art International* 19 (May 1975): 75–80.

Elkana, Y. *The Discovery of the Conservation of Energy.* London: Hutchinson, 1974.

Feyerabend, P. "Problems of Empiricism." In R. Colodny, ed., *Beyond the Edge of Certainty.* Pittsburgh, Penn.: University of Pittsburgh Press, 1965.

Foucault, M. *The Order of Things.* New York: Pantheon, 1970.

Freccero, J. Lectures at University of Minnesota, January 1976.

Freidson, E. *Profession of Medicine.* New York: Dodd, Mead, 1970.

Freud, S. "Inhibitions, Symptoms and Anxiety." In Freud, *Standard Edition,* vol. 20, pp. 164–165. London: Hogarth, 1961.

Friedmann, J. "Planning as Vocation, Parts I and II." *PLAN* 6, no. 3 (1966): 99, and 7, no. 1 (1966): 6.

———. "A Conceptual Model for the Analysis of Planning Behavior." *Administrative Science Quarterly* 12 (1967): 227.

———. "Notes on Societal Action." *Journal of the American Institute of Planners* 35 (September 1969): 311.

———. "The Public Interest and Community Participation: Toward a Reconstruction of Public Philosophy." *Journal of the American Institute of Planners* 39 (January 1973): 2–7.

———. *Retracking America.* New York: Anchor, 1973.

Frye, N. *Anatomy of Criticism.* Princeton, N.J.: Princeton University Press, 1957.

Fuller, R. C., and R. R. Myers. "The Natural History of a Social Problem." *American Sociological Review* 6 (June 1941): 320.

Gadamer, H. G. *Truth and Method.* New York: Seabury, 1975.

Garfinkel, H. *Studies in Ethnomethodology.* Englewood Cliffs, N.J.: Prentice-Hall, 1967.

Geertz, C. "Common Sense as a Cultural System." *Antioch Review* 33 (March 1975): 5–26.

Gerrish, B. A. "Martin Luther." In P. Edwards, ed., *Encyclopedia of Philosophy,* vol. 5, pp. 109–113. New York: Macmillan, 1967.

Gerver, I., and J. Bensman. "Toward a Sociology of Expertness." *Social Forces* 32 (March 1954): 226–235.

Gluckman, M. "The Reasonable Man in Barotse Law." In Gluckman, *Order and Rebellion in Tribal Africa*. Glencoe, Ill.: Free Press, 1963.

Goffman, E. "Where the Action Is." In Goffman, *Interaction Ritual*. Chicago: Aldine, 1967.

———. *Strategic Interaction*. Philadelphia: University of Pennsylvania Press, 1969.

———. *Persons in Relation*. New York: Harper and Row, 1972.

Goldhamer, H. *The Adviser*. New York: Elsevier, 1978.

Gombrich, E. H. *Art and Illusion*. Princeton, N.J.: Bollingen, 1960.

Goode, W. J. "The Protection of the Inept." *American Sociological Review* 32 (February 1967): 5–19.

Gorham, W. "Getting into the Action." *Policy Sciences* 1 (1970): 169–176.

Gouldner, A. *Enter Plato*. New York: Basic Books, 1965.

Gove, P. B. *Webster's Third New International Dictionary*. Springfield, Mass.: G. and C. Merriam, 1966.

Habermas, J. "Knowledge and Interest." *Inquiry* 9 (1966): 285.

———. *Toward a Rational Society*. Boston: Beacon Press, 1970.

Halmos, P. *The Faith of Counsellors*. New York: Schocken, 1970.

Hansot, E. *Perfection and Progress*. Cambridge, Mass.: MIT Press, 1974.

Harman, G. H. "Psychological Aspects of the Theory of Syntax." *Journal of Philosophy* 64 (February 2, 1967): 75.

Hegel, G. W. F. *The Phenomenology of Mind*. Tr. J. B. Baillie. New York: Harper Torchbooks, 1967.

———. *Lectures on the History of Philosophy*. Tr. E. S. Haldane and F. S. Simpson. New York: Humanities, 1896, 1974. See especially the Introduction.

Heidegger, M. *Being and Time*. Tr. J. Macquarrie and E. Robinson. New York: Harper and Row, 1962.

Helmer, O., and N. Rescher. *On the Epistemology of the Inexact Sciences*. Santa Monica, Cal.: Rand, 1970.

Hexter, J. H. *The History Primer*. New York: Basic Books, 1971.

Hirschman, A. O. *The Passions and the Interests*. Princeton, N.J.: Princeton University Press, 1977.

Hobbes, T. "On Counsel." In Hobbes, *The Leviathan*. Indianapolis: Bobbs, Merrill, 1958.

Hofstadter, A. *Agony and Epitaph*. New York: Braziller, 1970.

———. "Ownness and Identity: Rethinking Hegel." Manuscript, February 1974.

Hughes, H. S. *Consciousness and Society.* New York: Knopf, 1958.

Janis, I. L. *Victims of Groupthink.* Boston: Houghton Mifflin, 1973.

Kant, I. *Critique of Judgment.* Oxford: Clarendon, 1952.

———. *Critique of Practical Reason.* Tr. L. W. Beck. Indianapolis: Bobbs-Merrill, 1956.

———. *Critique of Pure Reason.* Tr. N. K. Smith. London: Macmillan, 1963.

Kaplan, A. "On the Strategy of Social Planning." Report submitted to the Social Planning Group, Planning Board of Puerto Rico, September 10, 1958. Mimeographed.

———. *The Conduct of Inquiry.* San Francisco: Chandler, 1964. Pp. 259–262.

Kaufman, S., and J. Friedmann. Bibliography for the course "Theory and Art of Advice." Los Angeles: UCLA, School of Architecture and Urban Planning, 1970. Mimeographed.

Kelly, G. A. "The Expert as Historical Actor." In W. G. Bennis, K. Benne, and R. Chin, eds., *The Planning of Change,* p. 14. New York: Holt, Rinehart, and Winston, 1969.

Kierkegaard, S. *Fear and Trembling.* Princeton, N.J.: Princeton University Press, 1954.

Kissinger, H. A. "The Policymaker and the Intellectual." *The Reporter,* March 5, 1959, pp. 30–35.

Kleinmuntz, B., ed. *Problem Solving: Research, Method, and Theory.* New York: John Wiley, 1966.

Klerman, G. L. "Behavior Control and the Limits of Reform." *Hastings Center Report* 5 (August 1975): 40–45.

Kordig, C. R. *The Justification of Scientific Change.* Dordrecht, Netherlands: D. Reidel, 1971.

———. "Theory Ladenness of Observation." *Review of Metaphysics* 24 (March 1971): 448.

Krieger, M. H. "Some New Directions for Planning Theories." *Journal of the American Institute of Planners* 40 (May 1974): 156–163.

———. "The Critique of Poor Reason: Using Literature to Teach Analysts." *Policy Analysis* 5 (Fall 1979): 505–520.

Kubler, G. *The Shape of Time.* New Haven, Conn.: Yale University Press, 1962.

Kuhn, T. S. *The Structure of Scientific Revolutions.* 2nd ed. Chicago: University of Chicago Press, 1970.

Laing, R. D. *The Politics of Experience.* New York: Ballantine, 1967.

Lakatos, I. "Proofs and Refutations." *British Journal for the Philosophy of Science* 14 (1963–1964): 1–25, 120–139, 221–245, 296–342.

Lakatos, I., and Musgrave, A., eds. *Criticism and the Growth of Knowledge.* Cambridge: Cambridge University Press, 1970.

LaPorte, T. R. *Organizational Response to Complexity: Research and Development as Organized Inquiry and Action.* University of California, Berkeley: Institute of Urban and Regional Development, January 1971.

Lemert, E. M. "Is There a Natural History of Social Problems?" *American Sociological Review* 16 (April 1951): 217.

———. "Social Problems." In D. Sills, ed., *International Encyclopedia of the Social Sciences.* New York: Macmillan, 1968.

Lewis, D. K. *Convention.* Cambridge, Mass.: Harvard University Press, 1969.

Lichtheim, G. *The Concept of Ideology and Other Essays.* New York: Vintage, 1967.

———. *Lukacs.* London: Fontana, 1970.

Lifton, Robert Jay. *Thought Reform and the Psychology of Totalism.* New York: W. W. Norton, 1961.

Lord, A. *Singer of Tales.* New York: Atheneum, 1965.

Macmurray, J. *The Self as Agent.* London: Faber and Faber, 1957.

———. *Persons in Relation.* London: Faber and Faber, 1961.

Mannheim, K. *Ideology and Utopia.* New York: Harcourt Brace, 1936.

Marris, P. *Loss and Change.* New York: Doubleday, 1975.

Marshall, T. H. "The Recent History of Professionalism in Relation to Social Structure and Social Policy." In Marshall, *Sociology at the Cross-Roads and Other Essays.* London: Heineman, 1963.

Martin, B. L. "Experts in Policy Processes: A Contemporary Perspective." *Polity* 4 (Winter 1973): 149–173.

Marx, K. "Debatten über das Holzdiebstahlsgesetz." In *Marx-Engels Werke,* vol. 1, pp. 109–147. Berlin: Dietz Verlag, 1961.

Maslow, A. *The Psychology of Science.* Chicago: Regnery, 1969.

Meehl, P. E. *Clinical vs. Statistical Prediction.* Minneapolis: University of Minnesota Press, 1954.

———. *Psychodiagnosis.* New York: Norton, 1977.

Merleau-Ponty, M. *Phenomenology of Perception.* Tr. Colin Smith. London: Routledge and Kegan Paul, 1962.

Merton, R. K. "The Role of Applied Social Science in the Formation of Policy." *Philosophy of Science* 16 (July 1949): 161–181.

———. "Role of the Intellectual in Public Bureaucracy." In Merton, *Social Theory and Social Structure,* pp. 261–278. New York: Free Press, 1968.

———. *The Sociology of Science.* Chicago: University of Chicago Press, 1973.

Meyerson, M., and Banfield, E. *Politics, Planning and the Public Interest.* Glencoe, Ill.: Free Press, 1964.

Michael, D. N. *On Learning to Plan and Planning to Learn.* San Francisco: Jossey-Bass, 1973.

Miller, G. A., E. Galanter, and K. Pribram. *Plans and the Structure of Behavior.* New York: Holt, 1960.

Miller, H. "Specialists." *Listener* 86 (September 2, 1971): 308.

Minsky, M. "Form and Content in Computer Science." *Journal of the Association for Computing Machinery* 17 (April 1970): 197.

Minsky, M., and S. Papert. *Perceptrons.* Cambridge, Mass.: MIT Press, 1969.

Moore, S. F., and Myerhoff, B. G., eds. *Secular Ritual.* Amsterdam: van Gorcum, Assen, 1977.

Moore, W. *The Professions: Roles and Rules.* New York: Russell Sage, 1970.

Nagel, T. "Sexual Perversion." *Journal of Philosophy* 66 (January 16, 1969): 5.

Nakane, C. *Japanese Society.* Berkeley and Los Angeles: University of California Press, 1970.

Neisser, U. *Cognition and Reality.* San Francisco: W. H. Freeman, 1976.

Newell, A. "Heuristic Programming: Ill-Structured Problems." In J. Aronfsky, ed., *Progress in Operations Research III*, p. 361. New York: J. Wiley, 1969.

Newell, A., and H. Simon. *Human Problem Solving.* Englewood Cliffs, N.J.: Prentice-Hall, 1972.

Nietzsche, F. "Ecce Homo." In Nietzsche, *On the Genealogy of Morals*, p. 295. New York: Vintage, 1969.

———. "Thus Spoke Zarathustra." In W. Kaufman, tr. and ed., *Viking Portable Nietzsche.* New York: Viking, 1968.

Noonan, J. T., Jr. *Persons and Masks of the Law.* New York: Farrar, Straus, and Giroux, 1976.

O'Hara, F. *The Selected Poems of Frank O'Hara.* Ed. D. Allen. New York: Vintage, 1974.

Palmer, R. E. *Hermeneutics.* Evanston, Ill.: Northwestern University Press, 1969.

Papert, S. *The Artificial Intelligence of Hubert L. Dreyfus.* Artificial Intelligence Memo no. 154. Cambridge, Mass.: MIT Project MAC, January 1968.

Percy, W. *The Moviegoer.* New York: Noonday, 1967.

Pirsig, R. M. *Zen and the Art of Motorcycle Maintenance: An Inquiry into Values.* New York: Morrow, 1974.

Pitkin, H. F. *The Concept of Representation.* Berkeley and Los Angeles: University of California Press, 1967.

———. *Wittgenstein and Justice.* Berkeley and Los Angeles: University of California Press, 1972.

Plato. *The Collected Dialogues of Plato.* Ed. E. Hamilton and H. Cairns. New York: Pantheon, 1961.

Polanyi, M. *Personal Knowledge.* New York: Harper Torchbooks, 1964.

Popper, K. *The Open Society.* Princeton, N.J.: Princeton University Press, 1966.

Quine, W. V. O. *Word and Object.* Cambridge, Mass.: MIT Press, 1960.

Raiffa, H. *Decision Analysis.* Reading, Mass.: Addison Wesley, 1968.

Rawls, J. *A Theory of Justice.* Cambridge, Mass.: Harvard University Press, 1971.

Reiff, R. "The Danger of the Techni-Pro: Democratizing the Human Services Professions." *Social Policy* 2 (May–June 1971): 62.

Reiner, T. A. *The Place of the Ideal Community in Urban Planning.* Philadelphia: University of Pennsylvania Press, 1963.

Rieff, P. *The Triumph of the Therapeutic.* New York: Harper and Row, 1968.

———. "Fellow Teachers." *Salmagundi* 20 (Summer–Fall 1972): 5–85.

Rittel, H. W. J. "On the Planning Crisis: Systems Analysis of the 'First and Second Generation.'" *Bedriftsøkonomen* 8 (1972): 390–396.

———. "Son of Rittelthink." *The DMG 5th Anniversary Report.* Berkeley, Cal.: Design Methods Group, University of California, January 1972.

Rittel, H. W. J., and M. M. Webber. "Dilemmas in a General Theory of Planning." *Policy Sciences* 4 (1973): 155–169.

Rorty, A. O. "Persons, Policies, and Bodies." *International Philosophical Quarterly* 8 (March 1973): 63–80.

Rose, S. M. *Ideology and Urban Planning: The Muddle of Model Cities.* Stonybrook, N.Y.: SUNY, [1971?]. Mimeographed.

Rosenstock-Huessy, E. *The Driving Power of Western Civilization: The Christian Revolution in the Middle Ages.* Boston: Beacon, 1950. P. 104.

Rosenthal, D. E. *Lawyer and Client: Who's in Charge?* New York: Russell Sage, 1974.

Ryle, G. *Dilemmas.* Cambridge: Cambridge University Press, 1954.

Sacks, O. *Awakenings.* New York: Vintage, 1976.

Santayana, G. *The Genteel Tradition.* Ed. D. L. Wilson. Cambridge, Mass.: Harvard University Press, 1967. P. 184.

Sarles, H. *After Metaphysics.* Lisse, Netherlands: Peter de Ridder Press, 1977.

Schaar, J. "Legitimacy in the Modern State." In P. Green and S. Levinson, eds., *Power and Community.* New York: Vintage, 1970.

——. "The Case for Patriotism." *New American Review* 17 (May 1973): 59–99.

Schelling, T. C. *The Strategy of Conflict.* New York: Oxford University Press, 1963.

Schumpeter, J. *Capitalism, Socialism, and Democracy.* New York: Harper and Row, 1950.

Schurmann, F. *Ideology and Organization in Communist China.* 2nd ed. Berkeley and Los Angeles: University of California Press, 1971.

Schutz, A. "The Well-Informed Citizen: An Essay on the Social Distribution of Knowledge." In Schutz, *Collected Papers,* vol. 2. The Hague: Martinus Nijhoff, 1964.

Scott, R. A. "The Construction of Conceptions of Stigma by Professional Experts." In J. D. Douglas, ed., *Deviance and Respectability: The Social Construction of Meanings,* p. 255. New York: Basic Books, 1970.

Seeley, J. R. "What Is Planning? Definition and Strategy." *Journal of the American Institute of Planners* 28 (1962): 91.

——. "Crestwood Heights: Intellectual and Libidinal Dimensions of Research." In A. J. Vidich and M. R. Stein, eds., *Reflections on Community Studies.* New York: Wiley, 1964.

——. "Thirty-Nine Articles: Toward a Theory of Social Theory." In K. Wolff and B. Moore, Jr., eds., *The Critical Spirit.* Boston: Beacon Press, 1967.

——. "Unplanned Thoughts on Planning." March 5, 1970. Mimeographed.

Sellars, W. *Science, Perception and Reality.* London: Routledge and Kegan Paul, 1963.

Shevrin, H. "Forms of Feeling: The Role of Ideologs in Empathy and Dream Imagery." Topeka, Kans.: Meninger Foundation, December 29, 1971.

Silverstein, H. S. "Universality and Treating Persons as Persons." *Journal of Philosophy* 17 (February 14, 1974): 57–71.

Simon, H. *The Sciences of the Artificial.* Cambridge, Mass.: MIT Press, 1969.

Simon, H. A. "Style in Design." In J. Archea and C. Eastman, eds., *edra two, Proceedings of the 2nd Annual Environmental Design*

*Research Association Conference,* p. 1. Pittsburgh, Penn.: Carnegie Mellon University, 1970.

———. "The Structure of Ill-Structured Problems." *Artificial Intelligence* 4 (1973): 181–201.

Simon, H. A., and L. Siklossy. *Representation and Meaning.* Englewood Cliffs, N.J.: Prentice-Hall, 1972.

Smelser, N. *Theory of Collective Behavior.* Glencoe, Ill.: Free Press, 1962.

Soedjatmoko et al., eds. *Introduction to Indonesian Historiography.* Ithaca, N.Y.: Cornell University Press, 1965.

Solomon, R. C. "Sexual Paradigms." *Journal of Philosophy* 71 (June 13, 1974): 336–345.

Stace, W. T. *Mysticism and Philosophy.* Philadelphia: Lippincott, 1960.

Steinberg, D. D., and L. A. Jakobovits, eds. *Semantics.* Cambridge: Cambridge University Press, 1971.

Stern, L. "Freedom, Blame, and Moral Community." *Journal of Philosophy* 71 (February 14, 1974): 72–84.

Stone, C. *Should Trees Have Standing? Legal Rights for Natural Objects.* Los Altos, Cal.: Kaufmann, 1974.

Strawson, P. F. *Individuals.* New York: Anchor, 1963.

Strong, T. B. *Friedrich Nietzsche and the Politics of Transfiguration.* Berkeley, Cal.: University of California Press, 1976.

Taylor, C. "Responsibility for Self." In A. Rorty, ed., *The Identities of Persons.* Berkeley, Cal.: University of California Press, 1976.

Trilling, L. *Sincerity and Authenticity.* Cambridge, Mass.: Harvard University Press, 1972.

Turner, V. *The Ritual Process.* Chicago: Aldine, 1969.

———. "Variations on a Theme of Liminality." In S. F. Moore and B. G. Myerhoff, eds., *Secular Ritual,* pp. 36–52. Amsterdam: van Gorcum, Assen, 1977.

Unger, R. M. *Knowledge and Politics.* New York: Basic Books, 1975.

Vickers, G. *The Art of Judgment.* New York: Basic Books, 1965.

Vico, G. *The New Science.* Tr. T. G. Bergin and M. H. Fisch. Ithaca, N.Y.: Cornell University Press, 1948.

Walzer, M. *Obligations.* Cambridge, Mass.: Harvard University Press, 1970.

Ward, B. *What's Wrong with Economics?* New York: Basic Books, 1972.

Warren, R. L. "The Sociology of Knowledge and the Problems of the Inner Cities." *Social Science Quarterly* 52 (December 1971): 469–491.

Watkins, J. "Imperfect Rationality." In R. Borger and F. Cioffi, eds.,

*Explanation in the Behavioral Sciences.* Cambridge: Cambridge University Press, 1972.

Webber, M. M. "The Roles of Intelligence Systems in Urban-Systems Planning." *Journal of the American Institute of Planners* 31 (November 1965): 289.

———. "Planning in an Environment of Change, Part I: Beyond the Industrial Age." *Town Planning Review,* October 1968, p. 179.

———. "The BART Experience: What Have We Learned?" *The Public Interest* no. 45, Fall 1976, pp. 79–108.

Weber, M. *The Methodology of Social Science.* Tr. E. A. Shils and H. A. Finch. Glencoe, Ill.: Free Press, 1949.

Weightman, J. "Threading the Maze." *The Observer,* May 19, 1974, p. 38.

Westcott, M. R. *Toward a Contemporary Psychology of Intuition.* New York: Holt, Rinehart, and Winston, 1968.

Wilensky, H. "The Professionalization of Everyone?" *American Journal of Sociology* 70 (September 1964): 137.

———. *Organizational Intelligence.* New York: Basic Books, 1967.

Winquist, C. E. "The Act of Storytelling and the Self's Homecoming." *Journal of the American Academy of Religion* 42 (1974): 101–113.

Wispe, L. G. "Sympathy and Empathy." In D. Sills, ed., *International Encyclopedia of the Social Sciences,* vol. 15, pp. 441–447. New York: Macmillan, 1968.

Wittgenstein, L. *Philosophical Investigations.* Tr. G. E. M. Anscombe. 3d ed. New York: Macmillan, 1958.

Wolin, S. S. "Political Theory as a Vocation." *American Political Science Review* 63 (December 1969): 1062.

———. *Hobbes and the Epic Tradition of Political Theory.* Los Angeles: Clark Library, University of California at Los Angeles, 1970.

Wolin, S. S., and J. H. Schaar. *The Berkeley Rebellion and Beyond.* New York: Random House, 1970.

Zaner, R. M. *The Way of Phenomenology.* New York: Pegasus, 1970.

Zetterberg, H. L. *Social Theory and Social Practice.* New York: Bedminster, 1962.

Ziman, J. *Public Knowledge.* Cambridge: Cambridge University Press, 1968.

Znaniecki, F. *The Social Role of the Man of Knowledge.* New York: Octagon Books, 1965.

Zwerling, S. *Mass Transit and the Politics of Technology: A Study of BART and the San Francisco Bay Area.* New York: Praeger, 1974.

# ✌৪ Index